LUTHER RICE: Believer in Tomorrow

LUTHER RICE
Believer in Tomorrow

Evelyn Wingo Thompson

BROADMAN PRESS
Nashville, Tennessee

4272-25
ISBN: 0-8054-7225-8

Reprinted in 1982 to commemorate the 200th
anniversary of the birth of Luther Rice on
March 25, 1783

Dewey Decimal Classification: B
Subject Headings: RICE, LUTHER//BAPTISTS—HISTORY
Library of Congress Catalog Card Number: 67-10034
Printed in the United States of America

Contents

1. What Manner of Man • 1
2. The World That Was Northborough • 4
3. The Inward Quest • 19
4. Leicester and Williams • 29
5. Andover • 42
6. Rebecca and Decision • 49
7. Ordination • 57
8. Voyage Out • 60
9. India and Change • 70
10. Return Home • 78
11. Convention • 84
12. Enlistment and Expansion • 100
13. Education—An Enterprise for Eternity • 113
14. Rice and Judson • 122
15. Baptist Circuit Rider • 138
16. Years of Trouble • 152
17. Dismissal • 174
18. The Shadowed Years • 182
19. The Last Journey • 196
20. Afterwards • 201
    Notes • 204
    Acknowledgments • 225
    Bibliography • 227
    Index • 230

1. What Manner of Man

Luther Rice was something of an enigma to others, even to himself. Once, queried about his unremitting toil for the denomination which had spurned him, he replied, "Just say the Lord saw fit to raise such a one as Luther Rice."

His conversion was the pivot about which all his life turned. Aspects of it, even to the fear of thunder, may be seen in the conversions of Luther, Bunyan, Milton, and fellow-countryman Brainerd; and with our present-day armchair psychoanalysing, it is easy to attribute such a conversion to human experiences or even to neurosis. But for Rice, the breaking in of the divine was the one reality in a transient world which increasingly buffeted and tossed his soul.

Reared in a church marked by a hearse-like atmosphere—confining to the ebullient Rice boys except for its music—Luther had an amazing quality of joy in his own religion.

His aptitude for happiness and anecdote brought criticism, for in his day frivolity was equated with levity and as such was a deadly sin for the Christian. Ill-nature and sulkiness were alien to his being. A resiliency of spirit kept him going when others would have wallowed in bitterness and self-pity.

Equally at home sharing the "hog-and-hominy" fare of a backwoods cabin or in the drawing rooms of Charlestown, Rice was adaptable and flexible, caring for the society of other men but not for creature comforts. An apple bought from a huckster, a piece of jerked meat and a cup of tea, clothes that served the purpose—these amply satisfied his tastes.

Power of persuasion was his greatest gift. Poised whether addressing Congress or a brush arbor meeting on the banks of the Nolin in Kentucky, he could sway a large audience or, in private conversation, capture a man in his own enthusiasm for a cause.

He preached like an angel, Alexis Caswell reminisced, and he prayed like a publican, recalled Henry Keeling, who was not alone in remembering Rice's humility in prayer.

As a money-raiser he had the shrewdness of a trueborn Yankee, yet in his personal relationships there was a naivety and openness which exposed him to the taunts of men like Henry Holcombe. And he was singularly unsuccessful with the women he loved.

Never fazed by the difficult, he made mistakes, in company with all men who *do* things; like all pioneers he could never be a member of the "wait-and-see" crowd.

Critics enumerated his faults. Personal criticisms centered around his hearty laugh, indiscriminate tea-drinking, and "wind-ing" his horses. The women in Chowan Association of North Carolina, having heard the monstrous tales of his tea consumption, counted the cups to find he had downed sixteen! It is a fact that he did not spare his horse and sometimes drove one beyond endurance. Feeling his own comfort and life were expendable, he naturally felt so about his mount. And though we may smile at a society where one man owned the life of another yet censored a person for mal-treating a horse, nevertheless it is apparent that Rice occasionally pushed his steed unmercifully.

He awakened an eternal quality in young men and evinced no jealousy when they superseded him in rank and influence. Welch, Wayland, Peck, McCoy—these are a few of those for whom the denomination is indebted to Rice.

He was a kind of catalyst for Baptists, accelerating and bringing to a head, movements which had been fomenting for many years. More than any other contemporary in his denomination, he viewed Baptists as a national group and attempted to bring unanimity and cooperation to their plans.

He became a Baptist because of a change in position on baptism where two centuries before, those making the transition from Con-gregationalist to Baptist did so on the basis of differing church policy, particularly the separation of church and state. Rice, Judson, Peck—all gifts to Baptists from the Congregationalists, as was Roger Williams in the seventeenth century—each came to the Baptists because of a change in feeling about the validity of infant baptism. This explains, at least in part, why Rice petitioned Congress to assist Columbian College in its financial troubles, and why he had no misgivings about the Indian schools being financed by the govern-ment.

2

He was castigated for not returning to India by those bound by inertia or cynicism never to leave their own firesides. Obviously Rice possessed no consuming desire to rejoin Judson, or if so, it was displaced by an equally consuming desire to "hold the ropes" at home.

He talked too much, spread his talents too thinly, and briefly, during the unfortunate episode at Washington, assumed a martyr tone. With his overly optimistic nature, he was not apt to foresee failure and he could not resign his cause to defeat even when the odds became overwhelming. Some termed this his "excessive hopefulness."

Since the evaluation of any life is in the eye of the beholder, his contemporaries gave varying judgments of Rice. His enemies called him a failure. Even some of his friends agreed. The accusation of misused money (hurled by those who accomplished his dismissal) was slow to die. Those who beheld Columbian College as a disastrous undertaking felt justified in their stand when it floundered.

The failure of his dream for a great national Baptist university was inherent in the plan of organization, or lack of it, which Baptists adopted. A long and tortuous process brought Baptists to the stage where they could sublimate local interest and need to that of the larger, national group. A century and a half later the process was not perfected. It was his successors, not he, who relinquished the college, and Baptists were to rue the day.

If Baptists had patron saints, Rice would be the one for state secretaries, for he was the first in the general sense of the word, visiting the associations to distribute the published reports of the Board and receive their associational reports, taking a census of the spiritual conditions in each region, encouraging the called ministers, and always laboring indefatigably to seek out and train more competent ministers.

Some, mostly southerners, looked kindly upon Rice and what he did for them, and within their ranks his plan of organization found its nearest fruition. He became esteemed as one of the great pioneers among American Baptists, a man frustrated in many of his dreams, but withal, a "frustrated saint."

2. The World That Was Northborough

The country was full of Rices. Ever since Edmund and Tamazine had landed at Boston Harbor in 1638, Rices had been settling the towns and countrysides of New England. In those days, when early death was commonplace, it was told that eight of Edmund's eleven children lived to be more than ninety. Prolific and robust, Rice height and longevity soon became legendary. They were a strong breed, fitted by physique and temperament to combat the wilderness and, when necessary, the Indians.[1]

In the second generation they married into many of the Old Bay State's foremost families. There was Abigail Rice who married a Smith and passed her name down in the fourth descent to a famous first lady, Abigail Smith Adams. There was another daughter, Mary, who married Thomas Brigham of Marlborough and became the great-grandmother of Elias Howe and Brigham Young.[2] This generation branched out from the homesites of Sudbury and Marlborough, spreading its bravery and hardihood to pioneering new townships.

No less than 427 Rices fought in the Revolution. One of these was a minuteman from Northborough. Amos Rice marched on Lexington that memorable April 19 as sergeant under the command of fellow townsman Captain Samuel Wood. His company of minutemen was gathering by the Assabet River to hear a patriotic address by Pastor Peter Whitney when the rider on a white horse came with the cry, "The regulars are out; they've marched on Lexington!" There was only time to rush home, fetch powder and packs, and bid a hasty farewell to families. Reassembling in the yard of their captain, they heard the pastor invoke God's blessing and were off to the rhythm of Joseph Sever's drum and Ebenezer Hudson's fife. Of the fifty-four men in Northborough's company, eight were Rices.[3]

After that first day's pursuit of the British back to Boston, many of the farmer-soldiers did not feel obliged to stay. General Artemas

4

Ward, a Shrewsbury neighbor, and commander until Washington superseded him, was plagued by his regiment's tendency to slip away home to personal responsibilities: spring planting, the tending of the livestock, the ordering of domestic affairs. But persistence being a salient trait of the Rice family, Amos stayed through the siege and fought in the Battle of Bunker Hill. Though many of the men served briefly or intermittently, Amos was on Northborough's quota for the duration.

Still, he was at home during lulls in the campaigns and especially after the fighting moved southward. Following the Siege of Boston, his Northborough company returned home for a respite.[4]

These were busy years for Amos and he conducted himself well. He was a member of the Committee of Correspondence, a group of the most able men of each community who planned the local course of action against the British. Commanding a company of soldiers in camp and under fire called for qualities of leadership which farming had never elicited. The cause of patriotism provided an acceptable outlet for his yearning to do more than farm. He rather liked the hustle and stress of a march, the tenseness before battle, the camaraderie of camplife. His executive talent was needed and used as the committee sat in the village inn and plotted "dark treason mixed with rum."

Entering the Revolution as a sergeant, by 1776 he was a second lieutenant in Colonel Job Cushing's regiment. In '78 he was stationed in Rhode Island, an officer in Colonel Nathaniel Wade's regiment.[5] In 1780, he was one of eight again under contract for a three-year term for which Northborough voted "to pay and clothe them at their own expense," and to give them "40 shillings each a month, in hard money." At war's end, Amos was a captain and in his home town he was known as Captain Rice ever afterwards.

Life had moved along on the farm. When Amos went off to war in 1775, wife Sarah was left with the care of five small children— sons Amos, Jr., Asaph, and Curtis, and two daughters, Sarah and Elizabeth, all under eight years of age. Every second year another child came; in '76 it was a boy, John, and in '78 another son, Jacob.[6] These war years also brought family sorrow, for baby Jacob died at the close of his crucial second summer, and five-year-old Elizabeth succumbed to one of the childhood epidemics so costly to colonial households.

Financially, Amos was more fortunate than most veterans who

were paid in depreciated currency. He was not in debt and the farm had prospered. There were seven growing children, ranging from a toddler born in 1781 and named Jacob (after the Jacob who had died, as was customary then) to sixteen-year-old Amos, Jr., big enough to carry a man's share of the work on the farm skirting the village.

Northborough lay in the valley of the Assabet River between the low hills of Marlborough on the east and those of Shrewsbury and Boylston on the west. By the Post Road it was thirty-six miles from Boston Statehouse. This road followed an early path made through the shady forests by the Indians and called the Connecticut Path.[7] Often called the Great Post Road, it was one of the most highly traveled roads in New England, twisting its way from Boston to New York. Levi Pease was talking of providing regular stage-coach service along it.

During the winter of 1783 the *Massachusetts Gazette* was eagerly scanned for news of the peace conference in Paris. The commissioners were still negotiating and every arriving vessel was sought anxiously for news. The February 20 *Gazette* had a small item: "We hear that the December packet arrived in New York harbour, on Wednesday last week from England and it is reported that she brings advice that the parliament and Great Britain has acknowledged the independence of the states."[8] Still an air of uncertainty held.

On March 25 the men waiting for their meal at Samuel Allen's grist mill likely discussed this news about the peace conference, postwar inflation, the lack of a market for farm produce, the scarcity of cash, and Pease's prospects for his stagecoach line. As the talk turned to local gossip, someone was certain to tell that Captain Amos Rice had another son, for this baby's birth coincided with the nation's. The Treaty with England was signed September 3.

The new baby was attended by Sarah's half-sister, Elizabeth Bennet, who had recently married a Rice cousin and was living nearby.[9] Sarah's older spinster-sister, Catherine, soon arrived from Boylston to take charge as she had at the birth of each previous child. Devout and strongminded, this Catherine was to have a decided influence in the baby's life. As she dressed him in the dark calico dresses she could not have foreseen how much he was to be "after her own heart." When he was six weeks old, he was taken in the white christening gown to Sunday service in the square white church and baptized by Pastor Peter Whitney.[10] Following the Puritan

6

custom, biblical names had been selected for the older children, but the new baby was named Luther for his Uncle Luther Rice, husband of Elizabeth, and a fellow-veteran of Amos since minuteman days.

On the first Sunday in October, 1783, in Northampton, England, Dr. John Ryland wrote in his diary, "This day Baptized a poor young shoe-maker." His name was William Carey, who even then was reading borrowed copies of *Captain Cook's Voyages* which revealed to him "God's sigh in the heart of the world," leading him to begin a movement that would touch the laughing babe in a Northborough cradle.

It had been seventeen years since Amos brought his bride to the farm home of his father Jacob. Cold Harbor Meadow had been in the Rice family since the 1660s, when the family lived in Marlborough. They had used the Northborough land only for grazing cattle in summer, calling it the "cow lands." Amos had built a substantial house on a corner of the 330-acre farm, on a gentle rise facing the village a half-mile away and approached by a lane from the Post Road. It was a two-story frame with a massive chimney and a pitched roof that sloped in the back to one-story with the usual lean-to kitchen. There were sheds, barn, and woods in the background and a well with its sweep near the back door.[11]

The five older brothers and sister Sarah, eleven when Luther was born, welcomed this ninth child and last son in the family. He was a happy child, large for his age, healthy as his forebears, soon walking and talking—a constant care to be kept from the open fires, the barnyard, or the path of a passing teamster. He was full of energy like his brothers but this energy was not frowned upon in his home. Someone was always there to smile when he overturned the churn or reached for the burning candles. So he grew and early showed that friendly, self-contained poise which was remarked upon during all his adult life. His world of home was a good place; the people in it loved him and he looked with friendly blue eyes upon all those who came into it.

When he was two and had been promoted to a trundle bed, sister Hannah was born and occupied the family cradle. Now the farmhouse was bulging with eight children. Work was the order of every day. Each child was assigned a part of the chores and farmwork. Shirking was not tolerated; an idle mind was "the devil's workshop."

7

The tasks were endless: woodchopping and hauling, bringing water from the well in heavy wooden buckets, tending gardens and cattle, haying in the heat of July's sun, harvesting in the autumn, and making cider, candles, and soap. The home was self-sufficient and in winter, a mere boy could be called on to help with carding the wool, hackling flax, spinning, or turning the meat as it roasted.

In the long winter evenings, activity centered around the enormous fireplace filled with blazing logs, the warming pan, cranes, pot-hooks, and trivets adorning it. When Asaph brought out his bass viol and Amos, Jr. and Jacob joined him on the flute and violin, this musical family noticed young Luther tilting his head and listening intently. They surmised that another musician would soon join the ensemble. Soon he participated in the family fuguing sessions as the brothers chased each other up and down the tunes. Sometimes they composed their own songs and music. On a rainy day many years later, Luther recorded that he had spent the day helping brother Amos "make a piece of music."

There were games, too—hull-gull and checkers played with kernels of corn. There was eating—apples from the shining pewter bowl, chestnuts roasting in the ashes, cider from the earthenware pitcher.

The farm was a good place for a boy to grow up. A few yards back of the house Cold Harbor Brook, flowing from the high ground of Shrewsbury, ran near the barn and meandered on to join the Assabet. This stream was an enchanting place for Luther, John, and Jacob to explore—wading and fishing, scouring its banks for berries in summer and nuts in the fall, skating, and trapping muskrats in the winters. In the front yard there were lilacs by the door in the spring, and the roadbank was ideal for winter sledding.

These six brothers were like boys at any age, ingenious at devising fun. There was stool ball, mumble-the-peg, wrestling, sleighing, and snow fights on the way from school. The usual intersibling rivalry found Luther pitted with Asaph and John to counter the wiles of Amos, Curtis, and Jacob. Luther could gain recognition by fighting or by being amiable; and since for the youngest, fighting was always on unequal terms, he chose amiability and it became a behavior pattern for life.

From the front window he could see across the meadows to the white village church and at night, to the flickering lights of other houses. Soon his world expanded beyond his home and farm to the village and surrounding country.

8

First there were the trips down the dusty road to Grandfather Jacob's small house with its great stone chimneys. Grandfather could keep a boy from play with his marvelous tales, the kind that sent a shiver to the very marrow of his bones, making him crouch nearer the fire as evening came on. He would tell about the time in 1704 when seven Indians suddenly rushed down a woody hillside in Marlborough and seized five young Rice cousins who were in a flax field. The Indians killed and scalped the youngest and took the other four captive, carrying them to Canada. One, Asher, was redeemed by his father four years later; the others grew up in Canada, two of them marrying Indians and becoming members of the tribe. Timothy became a chief among them and once visited Marlborough, saw his old home and the people of his childhood, but could not be persuaded to remain. He was still living in Canada when Luther heard the story.[12] Grandfather told these happenings so vividly that Luther felt he was one of the boys in the hayfield. The flickering shadows of the fire danced on the wall not unlike stealthy Indians.

Or Grandfather could dip into the family annals and tell of the solitary hand-to-hand encounter of Thomas Rice who, in 1705, wheeled on Graylock, his Indian captor, delivered him a fatal head blow and, unperturbed, returned to his hayfield to finish the morning's scything. Sometimes Grandfather reminisced of early days when pioneer life was hazardous, or of the exciting prerevolutionary days when Worcester County was a seedbed of patriotism. There was the time in 1773, five months before the Boston Tea Party, when a peddler was reported to be at a tavern in nearby Shrewsbury with a bag containing about thirty pounds of tea, and a number of "lightfaced Indians" hurried from the Great Swamp at Northborough, seized the tea, and burned it in the Post Road before the tavern.[13] Luther reckoned his father may have been one of the "lightfaced Indians."

Other favorite stories were of father Amos in the dugouts on Breed's Hill; the nights when the indefatigable Paul Revere rode through with news of the plans of Hancock and Adams; the snowy day in 1775 when British soldier spies were rudely hastened along the Post Road toward Boston; and the time in 1776 when all the local oxen were commandeered to drag the Ticonderoga cannon to Boston.

The clatter of wooden wheels or the sound of the driver's horn on approaching Ball's Tavern signaled a race to the Great Road to see the passing stagecoach. Luther delighted in seeing the stage go rattling by, its driver up front, the passengers bumping inside the unsprung carriage. This stage gave access to the world beyond Northborough, and most of the important personalities of his day passed along this road: Benjamin Franklin, the Adamses, the Hancocks, and when Luther was six, President Washington himself.

The President's coming was a red-letter day for the whole town and for days the chief topic of conversation in the farmhouse. On Friday, October 23, 1789, hours before the President's passing, Luther and his family joined the hundreds lining the Great Road in the village. How proud they were to see Father riding at the front of the procession in blue officer's coat with red facings, brass buttons gleaming, his best horse finely groomed. On "sandy Hill, the first hill after crossing Stirrup brook, in Northborough just beyond the house of William Bartlett, Captain Rice's company of horse, well mounted and uniformed, were waiting to escort him to Marlborough."[14]

Next came Tobias Lear, the President's secretary, on a white steed; two aides astride dapple-gray horses; and then the President's carriage. It was drawn by big bays mounted by Negro boys, with the coachman on his high seat at the fore end of the carriage. All eyes sought the occupants of the coach and mothers' arms were tugged as children wanted to know which person was the "father of the country." Inside the coach sat Major Jonathan Jackson, U.S. marshall and aide to the President, and "His Grace," General Washington, smiling and raising his hand in salute to these people who had come from miles around. Some, especially the children, were disappointed that Washington wore a plain brown suit, which made him appear the least elegant person in the entourage. Amos Rice's mounted company escorted the President to Williams' tavern in Marlborough. There the party dined amid an assemblage of officers from nearby towns who had served under Washington only fourteen years before.

Back home relatives dined with the Rices. The Goddards, Graves, Fays, Howes, and Rices from adjoining areas shared the generous fare spread for this special occasion on the long table in the kitchen. To the usual pork and beef, rye and wheat bread, newly harvested vegetables and the ever-present cider, there would be roast duck and chickens, and pound cake, cranberry tarts, mince, apple and pumpkin pies. To Luther, relegated to a second table with a flock of cousins in the low-age brackets, this feast was an anti-climax.

That night the events of the day were recounted, as they would be many times. Amos told how every shutter at the yellow mansion of General Artemas Ward in Shrewsbury was closed and no sign of life was evident, even though the procession went within a few feet of the front door. The General still bore a grudge against this man who not only superseded him as commander at Boston but demoted him, he felt, to a lesser command.

That same autumn Luther walked down the lane, crossed the Great Road and turned into the plains road to the South School where he was assigned a backless bench facing Nahum Fay, his teacher. Mr. Fay, a first cousin of Luther's,[15] taught in the local schools for forty years, giving only a short term at each school since there were four districts to be taught. All pupils sat together in the eighteen-foot square room, bare and boxlike with its small windows and crude desks. Its coldness was somewhat relieved in winter by the warmth of blazing logs in a fireplace. Luther studied from the horn book, the *New England Primer,* Noah Webster's *Speller,* the *Psalter,* and the Bible. The pupils learned by rote with lessons droned aloud, creating the hum that pervaded every classroom of the time. Luther practiced his writing on a slate with a stylus made of sharpened goose quills. Arithmetic texts were only beginning to come into use but the Rices owned one,[16] probably Nicholas Pike's *New and Complete System of Arithmetic* published in 1788. Luther went from sums to long division and "vulgar" fractions.

It was not thought expedient to make learning attractive, and the rigor of school life weeded out many pupils. Lessons were "said" back to the teacher, line for line, a good memory being the better part of success. Luther was one of those not daunted by this harshness, liking school, eager to pursue his studies, noted for his geniality. His mother added the catechism, prayers, and Scriptures to his courses of study. He was constantly urged to "improve your opportunities" or "improve your time." John Davis, future governor of Massachusetts and United States senator, sat in the same schoolroom. So did Warren Fay, son of the teacher and one of Luther's special chums, who later attended Harvard and became a minister.

Luther came from a family of readers. In 1790 a group of "about thirty gentlemen . . . united, and established a social library containing one hundred volumes."[17] Two of these men were his older brothers, Amos and Asaph. The books were heavy fare for the mind of a young boy, mostly theological treatises or histories of New England. As late as 1839 the only novel appearing on the shelves was *The Vicar of Wakefield*.[18] Luther was studious, though, and borrowed frequently from this library, absorbing the foreboding theology along with the sense of history.

Schoolmaster Nahum Fay was an important figure in the town and held many town offices. The minister, however, was the topmost man of the town, learned and voluble, a leader not only in religious matters but civic and social as well. The Rev. Mr. Whitney reared a family of ten children in the large, white manse he built near the meeting-house, whence they marched in soldier-like precision to the church twice each Sunday. Mr. Whitney wore a white wig, curled and coiffured, and a long black gown. He preached long sermons. Some thought him not a strict Calvinist and when he altered the church covenant, the Balls and Livermores objected and a permanent rift developed between them and the minister. Luther's mother seems to have been among those who were dissatisfied with the pastor's theology, and it was from the area in the township where these families lived that the evangelical branch of the Congregational Church was later to draw its members.

Whitney was both opinionated and composed. As he conducted his forenoon services for Fast Day on Wednesday, April 26, 1780, this equanimity was tested when a note was passed to the pulpit. "Your house is on fire," he read. By the time he had calmly finished the service, the house had burned to the ground.

The services were often tedious, the winter coldness of the meeting-house being matched only by the coldness of the theology. Any secular thought was to be squelched on the Lord's Day. Deacon Isaac Davis uttered the prevailing adult attitude when, en route to church, a grandson exclaimed at the sight of a squirrel. "Squirrels," admonished the deacon, "are not to be mentioned on this day."[19] The theological yardstick by which they were to measure themselves was hard and unbending. No slightest festivity entered the church's calendar. Christmas was carefully *not* observed, no such "popish recognition of a doubtful date" to be countenanced.

The Rices joined in the singing and as each boy matured, he became a member of the choir. Asaph accompanied on his bass viol, the congregation not acquiring an organ—that "devil's bagpipe" —for many more years.

12

When the church was erected, Grandfather Jacob had been the tenth highest taxpayer at the meeting and had chosen "the pew Ground behind the Men's Seats next to the west alley."[20] This pew the family still occupied, though there were so many boys that some had to sit in the gallery or on the steps, where the slightest misdemeanor exposed them to the tithing man's rap.

Mr. Whitney frequently exchanged pulpits with the Shrewsbury minister, Dr. Joseph Summer. Dr. Summer held to colonial dress—three-cornered hat, silver knee and shoe buckles, white stockings, and ruffled shirt. Six feet four inches tall with flowing white wig, he was a man of much "presence," so much so that one wee girl informed a startled parent, "Mother, I have just seen God ride by on horseback."[21] Dr. Summer was a strict Calvinist, but he was generous toward those who differed. He was a peacemaker and diplomat.

Other regular guests were Rev. Reuben Puffer, popular pulpiteer of Berlin, "well furnished" in mind and manner, and Dr. Nathaniel Thayer of Lancaster. In his latter years, Mr. Whitney exchanged pulpits so frequently that he preached at home only one Sunday in every three or four, thus giving variety to the parishioners during his forty-eight-year pastorate.

These preaching men were the hero material from which the village boys fashioned their ideals. All of them influenced young Luther, but if there was one he attempted to emulate in manner and conduct, perhaps it was Dr. Summer.

Ranking below the minister but something of a local personage was the town doctor. Northborough was fortunate in having a resident physician, Dr. Stephen Ball, whose family served the town and surrounding area for three successive generations.

When someone was ill, a member of the family would ride for the doctor and return with Dr. Ball, whose saddle bags or two-wheeled gig so reeked of drugs that his passage, even on the darkest night, could be detected. Whatever the ailment, the medication was likely to be the same: bleeding, emetics, calomel and jalap, and concoctions of herbs—cooling herbs to abate fevers and heating herbs to prevent chills.[22]

All his life Luther had a phobia about bloodletting, perhaps stemming from times in childhood when he witnessed its inefficacy, maybe at the death of brother Curtis or Grandfather Jacob.

Dr. Ball kept a school for fledgling physicians, and when he died in the '90s his quiet but genial son succeeded him as the town doctor. The second Dr. Ball rode in a clattering yellow gig drawn by a "Parmenter mare." Medicine was much the same as in his father's time except that the younger doctor dispensed optimism along with his drugs. In his belief that a healthy mental state abetted recovery, he was a man out of his time. He came by this conviction early in life when he dined in the home of a patient who, being a practical jokester, told him the meat they were eating was horseflesh. Dr. Ball became very ill until he was assured that the meat was beef. Thereafter he always included strong words of encouragement along with his doses of medicine.

The innkeepers were also men of prestige and character, and Northborough had two popular inns on the Post Road—the Martyn or Munroe's in the center of town, and Jonas Ball's a mile along on the Post Road toward Shrewsbury. Both were centers of politics and conviviality, as well as stagecoach activity.

Eccentric characters always loom up conspicuously in small towns, and included in this category in Northborough were the remnants of the Nipmuck Indians, the original inhabitants of the area, selling their brooms and baskets. Sarah Boston, one of the last of the Hassanamiscoes of Grafton and of gigantic stature, dressed in homespun blankets and skirts of many colors. She bore a congenital resentment against white people and no one, not even strong men, risked her irascibility. She had been known to lie down in the middle of the road and defy a teamster to drive over her, then leap at him viciously if he spoke roughly to her. She read fortunes in tea leaves and was good help in soapmaking or at haying time on the farm.

But Sarah was no favorite with the children as was another Indian, Bets Hendricks, who played her violin for their dancing. Bets lived with Simon Giger (though seldom peaceably) over toward Shrewsbury.[23]

Another local "character" (more welcomed by children than their parents) was Tom Cook, of Robin Hood propensities. A well-featured man, tall, blue-eyed, and quick-witted, he was the sort of person parents would not wish their children to emulate. But his pockets were always overflowing with toys and suckets and he was happy to regale boys with prejudiced versions of his adventures. He called himself the "leveller," but his adult acquaintances preferred "thief," or the more generous or less victimized, "the honest thief."

14

Cook's daring and skill were remarkable even for his ancient profession. He would slip into the kitchen of a well-to-do farmer and snitch the pudding from the pot, carry it to a poorer neighbor and place it, undetected, in *his* pot. A favorite ruse was to steal an object from a farmhouse, perhaps the best feather bed, tie it in an unsavory bundle, knock at the front door of the same house, inquire of the unwary mistress if he could leave the pack and, receiving a curt "no," proceed with a salved conscience to bestow it as a gift on some elderly person needing such a plump featherbed.

Or he would take a bag of meal from the wagon of a teamster, swagger ahead, and give it away before the owner's eyes. Under hot pursuit he would take off his shoes, tie them backwards on his feet, and walk away in the snow. His searchers would look for hours, seeing from whence he had come, but unable to tell where he had gone. His cleverness and daring were matched only by his courage. Once when apprehended and sentenced by the judge to be hanged "by the neck until you are dead, dead, dead," he cooly replied, "I shall not be there that day, day, day." And sure enough, he wasn't.[24]

These local eccentrics must have been a source of amazement to young Luther and as he encountered them on the highway or, as sometimes happened, in his own dooryard, he must have wondered at their lives, such a contrast to his own family's.

The most important people in Luther's boyhood were members of his family. His was a family world and any identity he had as a youth was within the context of this large clan. There were cousins by the dozen. When the first Federal census was taken in 1790, there were about six hundred residents in the town and ten of the one hundred families were Rices, far outnumbering the ancient Brigham family, the Fays, and the Goddards who were all Rice kinsmen of varying degrees. The ten in the Amos Rice family were matched by the ten of the Seth Rice household on an adjoining farm.

There was much visiting back and forth—to Uncle John Rice's in Shrewsbury, to his mother's people (the Bennets and the Graves) in Boylston, to wealthy Uncle James Goddard's at Berlin. Along the Berlin Road lived the Asaph Rices, whose ebullient children burned down the barn to get rid of the rats. It did the job, bringing them a kind of local fame.

William Houghton records:

How strange, indeed, that Asaph Rice
So pestered was with rats and mice,
His children thought 'twould be no harm
To clear them out, to burn the barn
When from the church the parents came,
The barn was gone, the rats the same
Ne'er troubled more was Asaph Rice
In that old barn with rats and mice.[25]

Occasionally the postman tacked a letter on the inn wall from Uncle Jacob in New Hampshire. This elder brother of his father's settled as minister in Henniker soon after leaving Harvard. The town was a land grant to Worcester County veterans of the expedition against Quebec in 1690. Grandfather Jacob owned some of this land. For several years after he was installed, Uncle Jacob lived on this land and pastored the church, sometimes receiving the stated salary, oftener not. A severe attack of measles left his health impaired and prevented his preaching regularly. His mild theology did not please some of the parishioners and his state of health gave them cause to force his resignation. He resigned but since the town was in arrears with his pay and could not obtain another minister quickly, he continued to preach for them when he was able. They invited candidates to preach from time to time, and extended a call to them, Mr. Rice presiding at each of these meetings. The salary offered being low and Henniker an isolated place, none accepted. Some years passed in this fashion, Uncle Jacob living on the land which his father had willed him and preaching for the congregation when they could secure no one else. Finally, in 1802, after he had served the church for thirty-five years, paid and unpaid, wanted and unwanted, another minister was obtained. Four years later Uncle Jacob went to Brownfield, Maine, and served there as minister until his death.[26]

There was a strong religious strain in the Rice family heritage. The first settler, Edmund, had been a deacon and each generation had contributed its devout men along with its pioneers and soldiers, but this uncle was the nearest kinsman who was a minister. His tenacity to duty, his humble willingness to serve even after being rejected, reveals an especial kind of valor, gall, or courage of the spirit which could not have been lost on the boy Luther. Perhaps this was family mettle—this persevering in duty once duty was clear, regardless of personal preferment.

Within the home there were family changes. Postwar times were not always easy. Cheap, plentiful money gave way to a time when cash became scarce and many debts were incurred. The most unjust burden fell upon returning soldiers who received certificates in lieu of pay, these certificates convertible only for a fraction on the dollar. There was ferment among the farmers, for the market for crops had been curtailed by cutting off exports to Jamaica; and this ferment became open in Shay's Rebellion in the late '80s.

In consequence, many New England sons looked to other areas as wagon after wagon went into the valleys to the West, along the Great Lakes, or to the Province of Maine.

When Luther was ten, his brother Amos married Lucinda Brigham. After their second child was born in 1795, they moved to East Andover, Maine, where some of the proprietors of Henniker lands had gained rights of substitution.[27]

Asaph married the daughter of Abraham Wood, a man skilled in music and brother to Amos' old minuteman captain. The couple settled in Grandfather Jacob's old home. By the turn of the century Asaph was well on his way to becoming a prosperous merchant and realtor, wealthy enough to ply his eccentricities, always signing his name in capitals, ASAPH RICE, when he headed petitions on political issues.[28] He served in many town offices and espoused Jeffersonian tenets. He was an extrovert, known as a good speaker, one of the town's best musicians, and a man who did his own thinking. Luther adored Asaph and Asaph encouraged him to be a free thinker, to study what was new, and to assert initiative in new areas.

To sister Sarah, the mother's namesake and the elder daughter in the home, a boy baby was born in 1792 and named Pliny Billings. Sarah was then nineteen and unmarried. What effect in terms of shame and sorrow this had on other members of the family, including Luther who was only nine years old at the time, cannot be assessed. A few weeks later Sarah faced her neighbors in the church to the extent of public confession and the child was baptized, October 28, 1792. Sarah remained a spinster, became a seamstress, and lived to be eighty-eight. Once in her old age she petitioned, along with other single ladies, that the church set aside a pew for their use.[29]

In the late 1700s brother Jacob went to Boston, the trading and social hub of New England life. He was employed in mercantile business, acquired a store, and lived there unmarried all his life.

His liberal thinking—that "state of mind that was Boston"—concerned Luther in later years.

Luther's mother was a woman of initiative, not highly educated but a person who "improved her opportunities," possessing a "vigorous and clear mind," "in many respects, an extraordinary woman."[30]

Luther's first biographer made much of his father's drinking. In this Amos Rice followed the accepted pattern of the day. Intemperance became such a problem in Northborough, as in other towns, that a temperance society and the town council—Asaph being a member—took measures of restraint. But this came twenty years later and when Luther was a lad, rum was part of the daily diet, as were sweetened cider and beer. Drinking accompanied all community affairs, even the raising of a church building. Flip, made of beer, egg, the swish of a red-hot loggerhead, and a dash of rum or whiskey, was the tavern fare. Even the ministers on their rounds were served toddy.

Amos was a prosperous farmer, as were many in Northborough and, like others, he had a small family business to improve idle hours, rainy days, and winter months. Whatever the business was, Luther worked at it too, equipped with a leather apron. Considering the stand of hardwoods that grew on Amos' acreage, it appears likely that some form of cooperage was Amos' "trade," and that he made buckets, tubs, and butter churns in the "shop" that flanked his house on the east side.

Amos helped each son financially. As a veteran, a town officer, and a large landowner, he appeared a man of importance in the eyes of his sons. In probate records he was always titled "Gentleman."

One of the few definite acts of Luther's boyhood comes to light from these last years of the century. Asaph recalled the episode: "At the age of sixteen, in company with another youth, without consulting his parents or friends he entered into a contract to visit the state of Georgia, to assist in obtaining timber for ship-building. He was absent on this expedition for six or seven months. Painful apprehensions were indulged that he would be thrown into vicious society, and acquire habits which might involve him in ruin. On his return, however, the following spring, to the great joy of his family, no perceptible change in his morals had been effected."[31]

Like his brothers, Luther sought self-expression, thought of going "down East" to Maine, and was beset by many forces, the pull of contradictions. His childhood, though happy, was not all lightness and promise. Many of his acts were viewed as "bad" by his elders and he was to be plagued by unconscious fears all his life.

The dark, doubtful events of a small town made a boy look within himself. There was poor Sarah. There was death—his grandfather when he was six, his brother Curtis when he was twelve. Even when quite young, those nearest him noticed that "he united with the sprightliness and sociability of his disposition, a singular dignity of manners"[32] and was "the subject of serious impressions.[33]

The scenes and people of Luther's boyhood were typical New England and late Puritan merging into a broader and larger world which was to renounce much in the old theology to seek new frontiers, physically and intellectually. As the old century closed, there was a conscious launching out into new lands and ideas. Luther was to be in the vanguard among the pioneers.

3. The Inward Quest

There had been much snow this January, 1802. Yesterday had brought more and today the skies were leaden. Now a few flakes were falling in the early twilight. Returning from the village, Luther mounted the rise toward the house and, stopping at the hedgerow, breathed a deep sigh as he looked at the white fields stretching away on either side. He wished he shared the scene's quiet peacefulness.

Walking on, he saw his father and John going toward the barn to do the evening chores. He quickened his pace. Perhaps he could find his mother alone and speak with her. He had to talk to someone.

As he neared the door, he could hear the thack-thack of the loom and, entering, he saw her weaving by the hearth in the semilight cast from the fireplace. Looking up at this youngest son, a smile of pride flitted across Sarah's face. He was a good boy, a fine looking son. Lately, the neighbors often remarked, "You have another

19

six-footer. Luther is as tall as Asaph; he's a Rice all right." He *was* tall at eighteen, stalwart and energetic. He looked like the Rices and had the self-assured, competent air of the Graves. Jestful, he was thought overly gay and confident by some. None suspected the almost intolerable anxiety behind his blithe gaze. None except Sarah. She sensed that her youngest son was troubled and now, as he entered, she arose and lighted a candle to augment the glow from the fire.

Luther had been wanting this time alone with his mother, and now he confided his increasingly troubled state of mind. He yearned to be a Christian but though he prayed and attended church regularly, he only became more disturbed. Sarah Rice listened sympathetically but she did not know what to say to alleviate his confusion, so she urged him to call on the pastor.

A few days later Luther described to Mr. Whitney, as best he could, how great a sinner he felt himself to be and how he had struggled to have peace with God. Neither prayer, nor meditation, nor vows to reform seemed to assuage his inner turmoil. The minister did not understand the intensity of these guilt feelings. He thought Luther was over-dramatizing his plight and advised him to present himself for membership in the church in the manner of the Half-way Covenanters, the "I've done my part, God, now you do yours" commitment.

Sunday, March 14, 1802, eleven days before his nineteenth birthday, Luther was admitted to the church and entry was duly made in the parish registry, the clerk noting his age,[1] since membership usually came after a person was twenty-one.

To his dismay the promised peace did not come, and he felt worse than before. The old uneasiness returned with greater intensity. Feelings of deepest guilt rolled over him. Often in the coming months he found himself wholly engrossed in assessing this sickness of soul. He knew he was in a morass of confusion and began recording the drama of his inner life.[2]

Diary keeping was almost an avocation in his day, and his first entry was made on February 25, 1803:

I intend, from this time, if God permit, to keep something of a diary; not only to set down my own remarks, but also to record the dispensation of Providence towards me.

I will begin with relating a circumstance which happened last night. I sat up till late, reading a book, the title, if I mistake not, *Religious*

Courtship, my Mother sitting up to hear it, my father also sitting in another room. When I left off reading it, my Mother left the room; I then took the Bible, and after reading a chapter, laid it away and sat down. After sitting there a while thinking of my wretched condition, I took again the Bible, meaning to read that chapter which contains the account of St. Paul's conversion, and pray that I also might be convicted and converted. After having read the chapter, I laid away the Bible, and kneeling down, prayed, that the same light which shone round Paul might also shine round my heart, and that I might be struck down and convicted.[3]

In his Bunyanesque pilgrimage toward redeeming grace, Luther was completely possessed by the mounting storm. He alternated between despair and hopeful expectancy. On Wednesday, the ninth of March, after finishing John Newton's *Life,* he wrote, "Oh, I must form this hard conclusion, that I am possessed of that carnality of mind which is enmity against God . . . I am unable to help myself in the least and can only cry, 'Oh, wretched man that I am, who shall deliver me from the body of this death!' " Seven days later he was writing, ". . . alas, I cannot determine after all whether the Lord's graciousness has visited my heart, or not."[4]

Even his hope seemed a presumption upon God. In this, Rice was a child of his time, a product of inbred Puritanism. Man was unspeakably depraved, either elected by God before birth or doomed. Grace was wholly unmerited and never a thing to be grasped. Waiting in contrition the sinner could only pray that an all-wise Father would deign to save him.

Conversion had not yet been reduced to its barest essentials by the revivalists. Heirs of Edwards' theology, such as young Luther was, ran the risk of being awakened but not enlightened. Enlightenment was more than acceptance on the part of man; it was also redemption by a Creator who intervened in history and in the personal life of man. And though its coming was instantaneous, it resulted from specific steps taken by the sinner, profound repentance and a marked change in life being prerequisites. After man had done his part he could only wait upon God (witness the Half-way Covenanters). If he were of the elect, eventually he would experience an intuitive awareness that God was working within his heart.

During those months of subjective probing, Luther tried to analyze his own heart and its condition. His keen conscience about his guilt led him to lacerate his own soul in attempts at true penitence.

21

The self-castigation often approached morbidity. He vowed to sit up all night and petition for salvation; he resolved to drive under every desire of his body, to fast, to refrain from any levity or frivolity. There raged a perpetual battle between the spirit and the flesh.

In his search, his reading seemed to help him more than the long sermons of Pastor Whitney. "Yesterday, I went to meeting. Mr. Whitney delivered a sermon in the forenoon from Luke 22:2 . . . In the afternoon, Proverbs 14:32. I will only say that I was too drowsy and Satan too much busied my thoughts to gain much by the discourse. I read an elegant election sermon delivered May the 25th, 1763 . . . I also read several of Newton's excellent letters."[5] This entry is followed by a résumé of his reading. Time and again he painstakingly recorded the gist of his day's reading and applied the contents to his own spiritual dilemma.

During the spring of 1802 Luther continued to read the *Life* and *Letters* of Newton. John Newton had led a profligate sailor's life before his conversion at twenty-three. He had been greatly influenced by those "Great Awakening" preachers, Wesley and Whitefield. His writings were widely read in the New England church of Luther's day. Northborough, though not far from Boston, had not been infiltrated with the French infidelity so rampant following the Revolution, nor yet with the Unitarian tenets which had decimated so many of the Boston churches.

Already Luther was thinking that if God ever saved him he would become a minister, and this meant more education. "This evening my father has told me that I may go to the seminary."[6] He was referring to a private school built on public land in Northborough in 1780, his father being one of the original stockholders. It was located across the road from the meetinghouse, at the fork of Boylston Road and Pleasant Street, a short distance from the Rice home. Luther attended here two years. The enrolment was small and the school closed after his second year. His attendance was irregular due to his helping his father and brother Asaph. "This week I have been to school about half of each day, the other half cared for the cattle."[7] And again: "This week I have been to school except Monday which day I mended a sleigh tongue; the other days I have taken care of the cattle in the morning which prevented my going to school in season."[8]

But his primary yearning was for exemplary conduct and any

22

lapse in piety was much regretted. On March 1, 1803, Aunt Rebecca Fay, his father's sister, age seventy-four and long the widow of Paul Fay, was visiting. She was a "great snuff taker though she governs it with difficulty."[9] He lent her 12½ cents to buy snuff but afterwards it bothered him "because I was grieved to see her so bewitched by such a habit." That same day "while foddering the cattle in the twilight I seemed to be fearlessly thoughtful."

Often he recorded his studies alongside his misdeeds: "I was foolishly angry with the calf this morning for not drinking its milk. This evening I finished reading *Religious Courtship*."[10] After reading this book he resolved "if ever I marry, to marry none but a religious woman."

To the families of Northborough the coming of spring brought work in the fields, and Luther was caught up in the rhythm of seedtime and harvest. As he witnessed the laws of planting and reaping, the unrest was only accentuated in his heart. Since "as a man soweth, he shall reap," surely justice required that he pay for his sin. Sometimes he felt his guilt to be so great that he was irredeemable; he was in a treadmill and all his effort made the self-involvement more cloying.

"I labor under a complication of disorders summed up in the word *Sin* . . . and when I seem to have made some proficiency a slight turn in my spirits throws me back and I have to begin all over again. There is an inseparable connection between cause and effect."[11]

In April he worked for four days with a neighbor, Mr. Jonathan Hastings. "Alas our conversation has been upon low subjects. I still sigh and mourn when I have time for reflection."[12]

From his summer's earnings as a field laborer he bought Richard Baxter's *Saints Rest* and *Call to the Unconverted*, Mrs. Bowers' *Devout Exercises of the Heart*, Mather's *Cathechism of Children* and *Call to a Devout and Holy Life*, and Hallow's *Letters to his Daughters*. He was so impressed with the *Call to the Unconverted* that on his next trip to Worcester to market the butter he bought a copy for his Aunt Bennet and a few weeks later another copy for his brother Amos in East Andover.

Luther was having another struggle which was to continue all his life, this one with his naturally ebullient personality. Bred into his Puritan concept of piety was the feeling that frivolity was a sin and leisure was to be abhorred. He was quick-witted, sociable, loved to talk and laugh; but always afterward, remorse would set in. "I have this day been to training but alas! I have not come home with a good conscience! I stayed too long and I became too noisy and joined too much in the spirit of the worldly. Oh, when shall I become more wise." There would be company to sit until bedtime; he would be caught up in the fun and then would feel "vain and exceedingly foolish and trifling in my conduct and conversation."[13]

Winter came early in 1803, snow blanketing the fields in early November. Periods of hope began to intersperse the gloom, signs heralding his new birth had he the faith to believe them. And occasionally he did: " . . . notwithstanding the sad state of my mind there is something within which seems to witness that God does intend to deliver me."[14]

December 1 was a cold day and the Massachusetts legislative authorities had declared it Thanksgiving Day. There were services, but as Mr. Whitney turned over the hour glass to begin the second half of his exhortation, Luther found it difficult to sustain his attention. That night he had a severe siege of remorse and guilt. He felt that divine wrath was more than he could bear. It never seemed to occur to him that, in envisioning God as capricious or vindictive, he was assigning to him attributes which were really Satan's. He wrote, "If He strike me to hell in his wrath, into whosoever hands this may come they may take warning and fly for refuge to lay hold upon the hope set before thee."[15]

As he went to the barn in the early twilight of December 17, he began to pray: "I even thought I felt the Holy Spirit at work upon my heart . . . this was not far from sun setting . . . I conclude I must be still unconverted though I hope from this and other circumstances that I will not long remain so."[16] Each evening while at the barn, "I have made it my practice after having fed the cattle in the twilight to pray before coming to the house."[17] Sometimes he brought the milk to the house, ate in the warmth of the big, colonial kitchen, then walked "back to the barn and wearied myself in attempting to meditate and pray."

In January of 1804 he began to rise during the night and spend time in prayer. Often he would slip out of bed in the bitter cold and kneel on the frigid floor of his upstairs bedroom to pray until daybreak. Surely, he thought, if he "spent" himself in prayer and contrition, God would heed and hear.

On the nineteenth of this new year he went again to Whitney's big white house on the Berlin Road. "I did fully disclose myself to him. I received little or no satisfaction from him except that I may yet benefit from a book which he lent me, *Directions for Getting and Keeping Spiritual Peace and Comfort,* by the excellent Mr. Baxter."[18]

In these months Luther "sometimes had a longing to inform some minister of my condition." On January 16 his brother John and he donned their snowshoes and walked across the crusty white fields to Westborough to consult Rev. John Robinson, pastor of the church there and a relative of the Rices through marriage. Robinson was a strict Calvinist; he told Luther to disregard his own feelings, act upon the Scriptures, and leave the rest to the Lord.[19]

Luther became concerned for those around him. "Souls perishing all around me," he wrote. "I must either be more bold in setting myself against every appearance of evil and endeavoring to do good to the souls of others or perish with them."[20]

Each evening this January he went to the village singing school. Some of these schools were conducted by itinerant instructors or the schoolteacher, but probably Abraham Wood led this one. Wood was well versed in vocal music and had written a book of "Divine Songs set to Music in Three and Four Parts." The meetinghouse choir was taught to read music and sing psalms, and the singing school was also a favorite gathering place for the young people. Luther was delighted that he was chosen as "second singer" for the choir. He and his brothers and sisters, each with his own candle (likely a "turnip" candle), bundled into the sleigh and rode the mile to the village. Sometimes they walked, harmonizing favorite hymns to dispel any eerie feelings as they passed "ghost hill."

Luther often rode over to Berlin to attend singing school, or to other towns within riding distance. Neighbors often accompanied them and on the cold, starry night of January 4, "I came from the singing school in company with one whom I can't but think is a poor ignorant unconverted person, it was almost all the way impressed upon my mind to speak to him respecting eternity! . . . yet I did not and now it troubles me."[21]

Five days later he was writing, "I hope I do not stand entirely still; but whether I move towards safety or towards destruction I cannot tell."[22] Still grappling with his aggressively friendly nature, he found it more difficult since he was charmed by one of the girls also attending the singing school. "Perhaps I should suffer less in going to the singing school if I did not see Miss——there; I do not esteem her, she is not at all such a character as I approve, and yet I love her, or rather, have a passionate propensity towards her."[23]

Each New Year's Day and each birthday was a time of resolution and commitment for Luther and on this March 25, he became twenty-one. "No longer under my parents I hope to be entirely at the disposal of God."[24]

On March 30, John, "the dearest of brothers," left home to go to East Andover, Maine, where their oldest brother, Amos, was doing well on the newly opened land. Since Jacob's leaving for Boston, John had shared Luther's room, his bed, and his secret longings and plans, going with him to visit neighboring ministers, listening as he talked out his doubts in the dark of the night. So Luther keenly felt his leaving. As John took each member of the family by the hand and bade them farewell, Luther was provoked with himself that he could not show his feeling toward this brother whom he was never to see again.[25]

Perhaps because Luther had reached his majority, Amos gave him a contract for this summer's work. Except for the days when he went to training or muster, or, as the twenty-second of June, "worked out my highway tax being $1.22," he cared for his father's cattle, worked in the fields or shop. When his father did not need him, he tended brother Asaph's cattle.

As the hot, sultry days came bringing winds, lightning, and sudden summer squalls, Luther was filled with foreboding. Feeling unready to meet his Maker, the dark clouds rolling and the claps of thunder made him fearful and trembling. "How shall I endure the summer. Oh, that I were sure of an interest in Christ . . . then why should I fear."[26] At the sound of a storm in the night he would awaken in a heavy sweat. It seemed that God's judgment was in the storm and he could not withstand it.

Another minister whom he came to admire was Mr. Samuel Austin of the First Congregational Church in Worcester. Warren Fay, Luther's cousin, was studying under Dr. Austin, and Luther began to visit the minister, seeking guidance. "The more I see of that man, the better I like him," he wrote. Mr. Austin, Hopkinsian in his theology, advised him to further educate himself, and this Luther resolved to do.

In the autumn of the year, his father surprised him by giving him a deed to forty acres of land and adding thirty dollars for the summer's labor, a generous return.[27] Perhaps the father was trying, in his way, to help Luther find himself.

It was in 1805 that he began to feel comfort in regard to his salvation and to make plans toward more education. The nearest academy which he could attend was at Leicester. On March 25, in his annual birthday self-evaluation, he recorded, "This day through the wonderful long suffering and forbearance of God I arrived at the age of 22 . . . how little has been done as ought to have been done in the past . . . how much precious time has been lost . . . today I have felt a longing to sit under the ministry of powerful preachers of the gospel."[28]

But his father's open scorn and daily rain of ridicule made it difficult to believe God had forgiven him. If his own father could not accept him, how could the Heavenly Father?

Amos Rice was a church member though he had never been a deeply devout person. He was happy for Luther to be religious, but when he became obsessed with spiritual matters, Amos was unable to understand. Age may have been a factor in some lack of rapport between the father and son; Amos was forty-one when Luther was born. Now over sixty, perhaps he expected this youngest of his six sons to stay on the farm and care for him in his old age. It was what a man had a right to expect; had he not done as much for his own father, Jacob? To that end he had given Luther the tract of land and his own horse, hoping it would awaken an interest in farming. Two of his sons had gone to Maine, one to Boston, one had died, Sarah had presented a family scandal— Amos had experienced his share of family worries. This son, who had been so amiable and tractable as a child, was diffident about his farm labors, always poring over books and writing, dashing off to "conferences," as he called his prayer meetings. Luther was something of an enigma to Amos.

When he was drinking, Amos would tell Luther what he really thought about his zeal for the holy life. Luther accepted his father's taunts and buffoonery as a parent-honoring child brought up in the best New England tradition—with good grace. In his persistent search for God, only a few times did his father's trying ways creep into the pourings into his diary. Once he ventured, "Happy the condition of those children whose own holy parents can tell them by their own experience what they must do to be saved!"[29] And elsewhere: "Oh, my poor father, he is ranting about the conference. Poor man, but how shall I write it . . . he is in liquor. Oh, Lord, thou hast all hearts in thy sovereign hands . . . have mercy upon my poor father and make him a monument of thy boundless grace."[30] Another time he attended a prayer meeting which was very beneficial, he felt, "but what shall I answer for myself for since I came home I have talked saucily to my father. Oh, Lord, lay not this sin to my charge in that great day."[31]

Perhaps Amos Rice sensed the over-anxiety as Luther grappled with his problem, and used ridicule to bring him to reality. If this were true, he employed the wrong tactic, for all his life Luther was to evince "uncommon obstinacy" when opposed.

And he desired God. To know him had become the consuming passion of his life. He would pit his family, his standing in the eyes of the community, even life itself upon the outcome of this quest: "None but an omnipotent can prevent me."[32]

Saturday, September 14, 1805, the thought came, "Whether I would be willing to give Deity a blank and let Him fill up my future destiny as He should please!" Many times before this day he had tried to make his surrender complete but always the self-maligning doubts, the old wrestlings, returned to plague him. This day the thought persisted and over and over he said to himself, "I *would* give God a blank to fill for me." After supper he went to his room and "I did then on my bended knee give of myself to the Eternal Jehovah, soul and body, for time and eternity to be dealt with as He should see fit."[33]

After worship the next day he reaffirmed his commitment in his diary, closing with a prayer, "Most merciful Creator . . . I beseech thee, that I may never retract the solemn surrender I have this day made of myself to thee . . . O, Lord, if thou espiest any flaw, *any secret reserve,* I beg of thee to discover it to me and help me to do it aright for thy dear Son's sake. Luther Rice."[34]

The terrible anguish of the past three years burst forth into release. The next morning he went to the barn to feed the cattle, singing in his beautiful baritone voice:

> Come sound his praise abroad
> And hymns of glory sing
> Jehovah is the sovereign God
> And universal King!

It was no easy salvation nor casual commitment. In his prolonged travail there was no unilateral concept of God, no "buddy-buddy" feeling, and there never would be. Always, God was to be high and lifted up. He had stooped to save and it was cause to marvel for a lifetime. Luther's favorite text, and one he would preach again and again, was "What is man, that thou art mindful of him?" (Psalm 8:4).

These years provide the clue to his life, for the deep paradox of his faith was "though I am nothing, through Christ I can do all things." If the "though I am nothing" was not often discerned, it was nevertheless there, the undersong of his life, for over and over through the years he would write at the end of a wearying day, "Oh, miserable worm that I am." Others, seeing only the superlative self-confidence, the "I can do all things," often misjudged wherein it lay. Had God not saved him? Then he could afford to be an incorrigible optimist. Whatever God wanted Luther Rice to do, he could do, and nothing else really mattered. God had broken through the fabric of the old self, through the fallible, the sin, the darkness, and it was "more and more unto the perfect day."

4. Leicester and Williams

On the frosty morning of November 15, 1805, Luther arose before day and, saddling his horse by the light of a horn lantern, mounted and rode down the lane to the Great Post Road. Turning westward, he jogged past the sleeping farmhouses, by the sprawling yellow mansion of General Ward, and on to the hilltop town of Shrewsbury with its white steepled church. As the hoofbeats sounded on the frozen ground, he had time to think about the decisions he had made since that day two months before when tranquility had come to his disturbed life.

The agony of his prolonged penitence was over and never returned. "My feelings often vary, and vary much, but not my hope."[1]

Still, he had problems. The most pressing was that he equip himself for college and to have funds for this, he purposed to "keep school" so that he might enter Leicester Academy.

Bearing letters of commendation from his teachers and minister, he reined in at one of the taverns—Farrar's, Howe's, or Pease's, for Shrewsbury was well supplied with them. He inquired for the school committee and applied for the position of schoolmaster. All day and for several days thereafter he went from town to town, in each place meeting with disappointment, arriving in one village "about one and a half or two hours after the committeeman had gone into another town in pursuit of one."[2] When he had given up hope of teaching, suddenly word came from Paxton, over beyond Worcester, that he could teach there. Perhaps Dr. Thayer, frequent guest minister in Luther's church, assisted in his securing this place.

Elated, Luther packed his clothes and books, the same from which he had been taught. Into his saddle bags he stuffed his flute and pitch pipe and a hymnbook or two, such as "The Singing Master's Assistant" (written by William Billings and known as "Billing's Best"). Luther was also to teach the village choir in the evenings.

Paxton was a mere village, its one country schoolhouse serving the families along the single street and those of the farms stretching across the hills. But it had had one notable schoolmaster, Eli Whitney, who taught there in the eighties, tutoring the choir in the evenings as Luther did.

He boarded in one of the farmhouses, sampling the best cooking, arising early, riding to the school on the horse his father had given him, building the fires and teaching his pupils much as he had been taught. At night he would return to conduct the singing school, "lining the hymns" on Sunday, and saving enough for a few weeks in school. It was a pattern often repeated by young men seeking higher education.

The winter session was short and he was back at his father's home by the middle of February,[3] staying a few weeks before leaving again for school, this time as a pupil at Leicester Academy, five miles beyond Worcester.

Leicester, a town similar to Northborough, with less than a thousand residents, enjoyed the reputation of being the most beautiful town in Worcester County. One hundred and fifty houses dotted the slopes and fair valleys, presided over by the stately mansion of Colonel William Henshaw atop Mount Pleasant to the west.[4]

The academy sat on the hill site where, during the Revolution, one Aaron Lopez had operated a store. During the hostilities Lopez had moved inland from the Portuguese Jewish colony at Newport, Rhode Island, and "kept store" on a scale previously unknown in the area. Wintry Saturday afternoons, hundreds of sleighs drew up on the hillside and in summer, wagons lined the roads leading to the store. Lopez was drowned when thrown from his gig into a brook in 1782, and two residents bought the store and converted it into an academy "for the purpose of promoting piety and learning."[5]

In Luther's day, the academy consisted of the original barracks-like building, oblong and two-storied, with classrooms on either end, the middle section a large room used for exhibitions and dining. It was cold and drafty, the wind whistling around its chimneys, sending gusts through its cracks, and rattling windows during inclement weather.[6]

The academy was coeducational. The girls were from local families or boarded in the homes of the townsmen. The male students were not so lucky; they lived above the classrooms at one end of the ramshackle building, the faculty at the other end in scarcely more comfortable quarters. Board was seven shillings a week including room rent and meals in the commons.

Northborough long had sent students to Leicester. Stephen Ball, Jr., had been a preceptor there in the '90s and John Davis and Luther's cousin, William Goddard, both younger than Luther, were already students there when he entered. Dr. Joseph Summer of Shrewsbury, chairman of the board of trustees, attended the noted annual exhibition days in May and the graduation "exercises," lending his six-foot-four "benign countenance and noble presence with flowing white wig" to the processionals.

Luther was examined and accepted as an advanced second-year student. The academy gave a good foundation in Latin and English grammar with a smattering of Greek. Penmanship was a serious subject and Luther's script was changed from a rather square, legible hand to the florid, excessively cursive style which was the embellished trademark of the educated in his day.

One of the school's most famous teachers, Ebenezer Adams, was the principal preceptor and taught Latin. He was a Dartmouth gradu-

31

ate and would return there shortly for a long and distinguished career. He possessed a "strong intellect," and was remembered as an "able and accurate instructor, credited with making good scholars." He also served as Justice of the Peace and postmaster of the town, and along with the other preceptors could be seen "walking the commons and streets with cocked hats and silver knee buckles . . . hair queued with ribbons, hanging half way down their necks."[7] Luther's other teachers were William J. Whipple and Luther Willson, both almost as young as he.

By the end of May, he was back home again. "For 10 weeks preceding the last I have been at school. I hope I have made some progress in literature. I have enjoyed, through the mercy of God, a good measure of health. I have lived in the midst of religious acquaintances and friends from whom I have received many tokens of friendly esteem and respect."[8]

The summer of 1806 was filled with work for his father and prayer meetings held in various places, often in the home of his pious Aunt "Katy" Graves, eight miles away.

With the zeal of the new convert, Luther began to reexamine some of the tenets of his faith. The signing of the half-way covenant seemed a worthless act, in some instances actually hindering the new birth. Having experienced its powerlessness to help, he tried to prevent others from making the same error. When a Mr. Bibbs and his wife presented themselves to the church for admittance to the half-way covenant, he visited them and "endeavored to convince him of the absurdity of the practice."

The low spiritual state to which he felt his church had fallen alarmed him. Since there were no prayer meetings in the community he continued to enlist friends to meet for prayer and devotional talks. The vacant seminary schoolhouse was engaged for the purpose, but neighbors suddenly opposed this innovation, seemingly with the backing of authority.[9]

Authority in spiritual matters was the person of Mr. Whitney, now elderly, and obviously not one to welcome Luther's ventures into his arena. He had guarded his prerogatives during all the thirty-five years of his Northborough residence and had a proprietary feeling about all things religious. He had not understood Luther's burden of sin, and now he definitely lacked sympathy with the criticism of his flock's spiritual temperature. Who did this upstart of a self-appointed assistant think he was? Mr. Whitney was aware of his rights—he had proved that in his tussles with neighboring ministers—and he did not mind squelching anyone who infringed.

The schoolhouse was forbidden for the prayer meetings. Neighbors and relatives withdrew the offer of their homes. This opposition did not deter Luther. He found ready support from his older brother Asaph.[10] In looks and temperament this brother and Luther had a close affinity. Though he did not participate in Luther's conferences, his home was opened to the group. This period cemented their brotherliness, for from this time, between these brothers fifteen years apart in age, there developed a beautiful and binding friendship. For the rest of his life, Luther poured out his innermost thoughts and hopes to this elder brother and Asaph, in turn, aided him in all his undertakings. He financed some of Luther's college and seminary work and followed his career with loving concern.

Luther's witness so touched Asaph that years later, to Luther's first biographer, he wrote: "This opposition he met with was principally from professors of religion. His naturally good temper secured for him the friendship of the early companions, for though he was serious, he was not morose; though religious, he was not austere. He maintained such consistency of conduct, that like the princes and governors of old, they could find no fault with him, except it was in relation to his God. Although his father rarely spoke peaceably to him; he bore all with such meekness of manner, and kindness of language as fully to demonstrate that he had imbibed another spirit. His conduct in and out of the family was uniform."[11]

The summer brought sadness, for in late August the family received word that Luther's brother John lay critically ill in East Andover. Luther's father hastened away and returned September 2 with the news "that brother John is dead. No more," wrote Luther, "shall I enjoy in this world the peaceful society of a brother to me most dear."[12] Luther remembered the morning two years before when John grasped each member of the family by the hand, and painfully recalled his own inability to express affection for his brother. But he was comforted in knowing that John was a believer and in "the consoling hope that he is gone to rest." The family was stunned when, the following December, a message came telling of the death in Belfast of Amos, Jr., the eldest brother and the first to try his fortune in Maine Province. He had gone to Belfast in the late autumn, fell ill of a fever and died before any of the family could be summoned.[13]

Arriving back at Leicester in the autumn, Luther found the old building replaced, and his principal also. The new structure was a simple, cheaply built academy, more commodious than the old,[14] and Rev. Zephaniah Swift Moore, town minister, was serving as interim headmaster. Dr. Moore was to go on to Williams later and then to the presidency of Amherst.

Luther's remaining year at Leicester went swiftly. He taught again at Paxton, but his thoughts already were turning toward college. He decided to attend Williams, in the Berkshire Mountains.

His confidante and cousin, Warren Fay, was studying at Harvard, the usual choice for men in his area. It was Uncle Jacob's alma mater. For some reason, Luther chose the more distant Williams. It may have been the low tuition but, more likely, it was Williams' spiritual climate. No doubt Luther had heard of the revivalistic and evangelical zeal which had permeated Williams during the preceding years, and his advisor, Dr. Samuel Austin, was beginning to view Harvard with alarm.

Asaph offered to purchase the forty acres of land which his father had given Luther in the fall of 1804, and would pay him $900 in instalments,[15] making it possible for him to stay at Williams until he was graduated.

Sometime during the spring and summer, he traveled to Williamstown, was examined for entrance and accepted as a sophomore.

Williamstown was an isolated community of two thousand souls, nestled in the Hoosac Valley, encircled by the Berkshires. Students experienced difficulty in arriving at the college, for from the south the stage went only to Pittsfield, and there was no service from the east. A classmate of Luther's, Justin Edwards, walked the forty miles from his Westhampton home each term. Mail was brought twice weekly by a courier who rode a horse over the Hoosac Mountain from Greenfield.

Luther arrived at a propitious time. Williams had not always been marked by high spirituality. In post-colonial times when the college was young, French skepticism and atheism had been rampant. In the six classes graduating from 1793 to 1799, only seven men professed Christianity.

The turn of the century brought a new era that had its beginning in another state. In 1799 a great revival swept Litchfield County, Connecticut. The pastor at Norfolk in that county, Rev. A. R. Robbins, was a trustee of Williams and influenced young men to enrol there. Soon these Norfolk and Torrington students entering

Williams deepened the religious spirit until in 1805-06, the college was in the midst of a revival.

In the spring of 1806, Samuel J. Mills, Jr., son of the Torrington minister, entered as a second-term freshman. Several of his father's parishioners who had preceded him to Williams were active in the revival movement led by a junior, Algernon S. Bailey. The freshmen were deeply impressed by the upper classmen's activity, but none more than Mills.

By the summer of 1806, the weekly prayer meetings held in students' rooms had grown until they began to meet twice a week and in two different places. On Wednesday afternoons they prayed under some willow trees south of West College, and on Saturday afternoons in a thick grove of maples in Sloane's Meadow, north of the college and about half way between it and the Hoosac River. Mills was already a leader of the group.

One hot, sultry Saturday, the overcast sky looked threatening and only five men appeared: three freshmen—Mills, James Richards, and Harvey Loomis, and two sophomores—Francis L. Robbins and Byram Green. Meeting in the grove, their conversation turned upon Asia, which they had been studying in Jedidiah Morse's geography textbook. They were fascinated by the East India Company's work in opening up that closed and unknown continent. As they discussed the immorality, ignorance, and misery of those unevangelized lands, Mills proposed sending the gospel to light the darkness. He became intense, enthusing, "We can do it, if we will!" Each agreed except Harvey Loomis, who felt a venture into such lands futile and dangerous; he suggested that a crusade was needed to precede the gospel's entry into Turk and Arab lands.

The dark clouds continued to roll, accompanied by thunder and lightning. Mills suggested that they seek shelter under a haystack in the meadow, continuing their discussion and prayer. Crouching under the rick's overhang, each except Loomis engaged in prayer, Mills praying last and in his exuberance petitioning the Lord to "strike down the arm, with the red artillery of heaven, that shall be raised against a herald of the cross."[16] Then they sang the last stanza of an Isaac Watts hymn:

> Let all the heathen writers join
> To form one perfect book;
> Great God, if once compared with thine
> How mean their writings look!

The group continued to meet in the grove until cold weather drove them inside. Then Byram Green's mother offered them the warmth of her big kitchen. She sat in another room with the door ajar, listening, and soon neighbors were invited to audit the young men's meetings.

When Luther reined in and dismounted at Williams in the fall of 1807, he could not have been too impressed with the physical aspect of the college. The plain buildings consisted of East College, the exclusive domain of the juniors and seniors, and West College, which held the recitation rooms and dormitory for the underclassmen. The rooms were bare, unpainted and unpapered with no carpets on the floors and furniture of the meagerest kind. Students fetched their own water from a spring at the foot of a hill south of East College. They also provided candles for their rooms and firewood for the open fires. Even the furniture in the classrooms was owned by the various classes and sold by them to their successors, this arrangement based on the theory that private property was more cared for than public. Meals were taken at town boardinghouses which charged nine or ten shillings per week.

Rev. Ebenezer Fitch was president; Professor Gamaliel S. Olds taught mathematics and natural philosophy; and along with two tutors, these comprised the entire faculty. The first year curriculum was mostly languages—English, Latin, and Greek. The second year added logic, rhetoric, and math.

One of Luther's first acquaintances was Samuel Mills, Jr., now an inconspicuous-appearing sophomore who spent more time talking to fellow students than studying. He was described by a contemporary as lacking the "strong physique which gave his father so much dignity. His physical appearance was rather against him. His skin was sallow, his eye not brilliant, his voice not clear, but he kept himself well and was studiously neat in his appearance."[17] He was mature also, twenty-three years old, with the spirit and magnetism of a great enthusiasm.

His enthusiasm was for missions, and Mills noticed Luther at once, marking him as a man to enlist. But he found Luther did not have to be wooed, for he plunged into the group's activities with zest and energy. Soon he was informing Asaph, "I have deliberately made up my mind to preach the gospel to the heathen, and I do not know but it may be Asia."[18]

At vacation times, Luther rode east with a classmate, William

Eaton, from Framingham. In his hometown there were the inevitable changes. Pease was straightening the picturesque, winding roads; the old, square church was being replaced with a beautiful new structure complete with steeple and a Paul Revere bell. Jacob was home from Boston, expounding his intellectualism and free thinking. During the time Luther was forging his hard-won faith, Jacob, an avid reader like the other Rice brothers, had imbibed the literature of French descent, with its ridicule of the nonintellectual and its atheisitic and caustic bent, until he viewed faith as the product of unthinking and mediocre minds.

Back at Williams, Luther could not dismiss Jacob from his thoughts. In an affectionate letter from "an anxious, longing heart," he entreated,

You are not requested to lay aside your reason but to exercise it. You are not desired to receive any proposition as truth upon the mere ipse dixit of another, but do yourself the justice candidly to weigh the evidence, and to yield to the decision which reason, unbiased, uncorrupted, necessarily forms in view of truth . . . Is it an apostacy from wisdom to treat eternal concerns as vastly more important and interesting than those of a temporal nature: Is it an aberration from true dignity or greatness, to pay a serious respect and reverence to the name and worship of the Almighty? Is it a breach of propriety or deviation from refinement, to revere and worship our Maker: Does it discover a more refined, or more exalted mind, to live without God in the world? To treat his holy name with irreverence, and his worship, with neglect.[19]

He begged Jacob to examine the lives of Sir Isaac Newton and Chief Justice Hale, and see "if their *weak* side is manifest by their attachment to Christianity, . . . You may, perhaps stifle the accusation of this internal monitor for a season; but, believe me, my brother, your triumph will be short, your peace of no considerable duration. Conscience will soon awake. She will have a hearing, 'Your leave unasked.' "[20]

In the prayer group there was elation because Gordon Hall, a senior and one of the most attractive men at Williams, had openly professed his faith and joined the group. Hall's dedication to the cause had been coveted for some time, for he was a brilliant and outstanding scholar, amiable and steady, a man both students and faculty felt destined for a notable career. Entering Williams in 1805, he was graduated in three years as valedictorian, with an offer of a tutorship. He declined this and went to live with Dr. Leonard Porter at Washington, Connecticut, to study theology and await divine leading.

In the fall of 1808 after Hall departed, Mills, Rice, and others in the prayer band envisioned a more formal organization for the promotion of missions, and in the northwest room of the first floor of East College a society was born. It was a mustard-seed beginning with only five men signing a pledge to effect a mission to the world's teeming millions in foreign lands.

The idea seems to have been Mills', and their alliance was patterned after the societies originating in European countries, perhaps the *Illuminata* furnishing a model in organization and policy. The *Illuminata* was a secret society of German origin which had crossed the Atlantic with the French Revolutionary soldiers and was atheistic in its thought, its members pledging to "serve, assist, and mutually support each other."[21] Their pact, pledging mutual help, impressed the missionary group since it was obvious that the heroic task they had set for themselves could be accomplished only in unity.

Mills attempted to draft the society's constitution but could not bring it off acceptably, so the slight, blond Richards, assisted by Ezra Fisk, wrote it.

The society was to be known as the Brethren, a name Mills chose, and its object was "to effect in the persons of its members a mission or missions, to the heathen."[22] Its pioneering lay in the phrase, *in the person of its members.* There had been earlier societies in America, some of them contributing to the foreign mission endeavors of the English, and some to missionary work among the Indians and in western areas of America. These prior societies sought to promote missions, to give, to pray and send; but the Brethren set itself the task of going, *in the person of its members,* to foreign lands.

Success lay in the quality of personnel rather than in the number of recruits, so safeguards were set regarding prospective enlistments. Before admitted, each man was screened by at least two members who weighed the candidate's character, situation, and ability to bear an assignment. If there were obvious flaws or hindrances to his serving, he was rejected. At first they felt no candidate who was engaged or planned to marry should be admitted. Each man must keep himself in readiness to go at any time the Brethren designated him, and each must abide the collective decision of the body and refrain from accepting any commitment which might hinder a ready departure to foreign lands. The group could dismiss a member, and each had to "solemnly promise to keep inviolably secret the existence"[23] of the society. Records were kept in code. Twenty years later, Ezra Fisk, cowriter of the constitution, stated that secrecy was invoked because of "fear of failure; public opinion, which could see in foreign missionary projects only overheated zeal and fanaticism and the modesty required of them lest they be thought rashly imprudent."[24]

Small wonder that only five signed in the beginning: Samuel J. Mills, Ezra Fisk, James Richards, John Seward, and Luther Rice. Mills and Richards were the only two from the famous haystack prayer meeting.

Meetings were held at noon in a student's room and on November 9, they passed a resolution, recorded in cipher, "that we will, every Sabbath morning at sunrise address the Throne of Grace in behalf of the object of this Society."[25] They read reports and letters of the London Missionary Society printed in the *Connecticut Evangelical Magazine* and *The Serampore Periodical Accounts*. They republished missionary sermons of Drs. E. D. Griffin and John Livingstone, and they chatted endlessly about the possibilities of a mission. Sometimes they spoke of "cutting a path through the moral wilderness of the west to the Pacific."[26] Some favored South America, Mills inclined toward Africa to which he felt the white race especially indebted, and, as noted by Rice's correspondence with his brother Asaph, Luther thought of the Orient.

Convinced they must have the prestige and backing of the fathers of the church, they listed ministers whose support and cooperation was desirable, the roll including Drs. Samuel Worcester of Salem, Jedidiah Morse of Charlestown, Joseph Emerson of Beverly, and Samuel Spring of Newburyport.

In late autumn of this same year, the sophomore class rebelled against the tutors and signed a petition asking President Fitch to remove them. This he refused. They persisted and caused such confusion and disharmony that all the instructors except the president resigned.[27] A vacation was announced to give the trustees time to secure another faculty, so Luther rode east to visit his parents.

Sister Hannah had married one of the neighbor's sons, Reuben Babcock, and moved away. Sarah and Amos were tall and unbent by more than sixty years, but now they were alone except for daughter Sally, having lost in death three of their grown sons—Curtis, Amos Jr., and John. Jacob was in Boston, Luther in the ministry. Remembering that the youngest son often stayed on the farm and cared for aged parents, even as Amos had done for Grandfather, Luther was disquieted by the thought.

In early 1809 Asaph wrote that their father was selling more of the farm. "Inscrutable are the ways of Providence," Luther replied. "Several years since, I formed a purpose to come into possession of that inheritance which father has now sold, and to take care of our parents in their declining years. To fulfill this office of filial duty, appeared to me on several accounts desirable."[28] He added that perhaps he betrayed great self-ignorance in implying that among the children he was best fitted to perform this task, his past conduct perhaps not being the best commentary on that intimation, but that it would have been a delight. By his father's rebuffs, and now the selling of most of the farm, the very ties which bound him to his home were severed.

Mills, about to be graduated, busied himself welding the ties of the Brethren, talking, working, and buttonholing potential members. He moved quietly but relentlessly and with such singlemindedness that his studies suffered to the extent that he was the poorest scholar in his classs. The other Torrington men, Harvey Loomis and Orange Lyman, received honors, but Mills ranked so low that the faculty did not allow him to participate in the graduating ceremonies. As the processional entered, he supposedly mumbled, "If God be for me, what matters the faculty is against me."

With Mills gone, the leadership mantle fell to Luther. Already he had become the group's orator, distinguished for his persuasivenesss. He and Mills were different in person but very alike in their restless energy and persistence, their ability to organize. Each possessed a flair for leading and the rare corollary of being able to work just as diligently when another was leading. Now Rice collected funds for the Brethren, supervised the on-campus work and corresponded with others.

Every post brought news from Mills at Yale. The year before Mills entered, Edwin Wells Dwight, a prayer group member, had transferred to Yale where he had met Obookiah, a Hawaiian waif brought back by a whaler. Obookiah was then living in the New Haven home of a Captain Birnam. The Yale students befriended this youth and one day Dwight found him dolefully weeping on the steps of the administration building. "I am weeping because I cannot go to school and learn," he replied to Dwight's query. Soon Dwight and other Yale students were teaching the seventeen-year-old.

Mills had hardly unpacked before he rushed to Dwight's room where he met Obookiah. Soon the lad was under Mills' tutelage and the Brethren at Williams were hearing that surely Obookiah was a sign that the time had come for sending the gospel to the Pacific.

The youth became ill and Mills took him home to the large white manse at Torrington where the Elder Mills and his devout wife cared for him, and he thrived and was a marvel to all. Gordon Hall, who stopped overnight at Mills' home and met the lad, was impressed with his aptitude and eagerness to learn and his desire to return to the Pacific isles with the gospel.

These happenings were conveyed to the Brethren and read with eagerness as they huddled around the hearth of a member's room at noontime. The fraternity was close knit; in writing to John Seward, Mills gave him perfect freedom to open his letters to Rice:

We can have no separate interest. I trust our bosoms will always open to the inspection of the *Brethren*. I should pursue a different line of conduct toward the world, and in their presence I should always appear with my wrapper on, girt close around me with a belt of wampum.[29]

Perhaps the group was having second thoughts on the marriage ban, for Mills confided:

I have not found many acquaintances in town amoung the fair. I know but three or four. These are eminently pious, and have much of that unaffected loveliness and simplicity of manner so truly captivating. Don't be alarmed. I am not yet caught in an evil net. But in truth our hearts need steeling to give up all hopes of domestic happiness, the one bliss (as says the poet) which has survived the fall. But let us remember what Mr. Horne says, 'That man is not fit for a missionary who sighs for the delights of a lady's lap'.[30]

The Berkshire Mountain Association licensed Luther to preach during his last year at Williams. In the spring of 1810, at the president's suggestion, he transferred to Andover for a semester's work, thus saving a half-year's time at each school. Mills and some of the other Brethren were already at Andover where they had been joined by like-minded students, anxiously awaiting Luther's arrival.[31] But he did not matriculate until the summer term.

5. Andover

The Andover grounds were still mushy from the thaw when Luther drove his horse and chaise up to the door of Phillips Hall in the late spring of 1810. The walks were not laid and the landscaping awaited student labor. The few buildings erected sat apart from Andover village on a hill, and though the land sloped it was poorly drained, especially the boggy huckleberry lot next to Phillips Hall through which students treaded a precarious path at this time of year.

The seminary was new, having been founded only in 1807 by the prominent Phillips family who earlier began the Andover and Exeter Academies. They were aided by men in the two leading schools of Congregationalist thought, the Hopkinsians or "consistent" Calvinists, and the regular group led by Professor Eliphalet Pearson, a strict Calvinist who had resigned his Harvard professorship in a huff over its ascending Unitarianism. Dr. Jedidiah Morse of Charlestown—minister, geographer, and editor of the *Panoplist*—assisted in uniting these forces to establish a school to train ministers and counteract the "radical" Harvard trend.[1]

Many of Luther's prep and college mentors were active in the new seminary, so it was inevitable that Luther chose Andover. President Fitch and Ebenezer Adams of Williams and Samuel Austin, his advisor since Northborough days, were each allied to the new endeavor. Most of Andover's founders were men who had evinced "enthusiasm for revivalistic and evangelistic religion"[2] and an intense interest in missions. Samuel Worcester of Salem, officer of the Massachusetts Missionary Society, was a director; and Moses Stuart, an evangelical minister of New Haven, became one of the first teachers.

There was nothing either elegant or generous about student life in Luther's day. Morning chapel was at seven in winter, six in summer; the persistent call of a bell broke the slumber of professor and student alike. When the bell was commissioned from Paul

42

Revere, Dr. Spring had remarked that it would awaken "sleepy, lazy professors, who love a morning bed."[3]

Emphasis was on "plain living and high thinking." Meals were served in the cold commons room back of Phillips Hall, accompanied by readings from equally cold theology. Student committees debated whether such luxuries as sugar and warm bread should be on the table. At times austerity took the form of substituting molasses for meat on the menu. But students retaliated by telling of the young Andoverian who became ill and had the doctor summoned; and following the medical practice of the day, the doctor resorted to bloodletting. Molasses was all that would flow from the student's veins.[4]

Some years later the faculty petitioned trustees for heat in the dining room, stating that "during the whole winter season the students are accustomed to take their meals in a room without fireplace or stove."[5] During Luther's last year, the faculty requested that a wood-house be built where students could cut firewood, since the basement in Phillips Hall was too low for them to stand upright to chop wood. They drew their own water, trimmed their lamps, built and kept fires in their rooms.

But there were pleasant diversions. A choir composed of those having "tolerable voices" (Luther qualifying) was begun while he was there. Nearby was the store of gentle Mark Newman, ex-principal of the nearby academy, a place the students could buy sundries, candles, a quire of paper, or even the makings of a suit.[6] Eastward, a little off the Salem turnpike, was Prospect Hill, a favorite retreat of the Brethren; here they often walked and thrashed out plans and ideas. From its summit on a clear day, they could see the farmland for miles around, the neat stone-fenced fields, the steeples of twenty-eight churches, and the white sails of ships at sea beyond Salem.

Since Andover was near Boston and other areas more settled than the lonely Berkshires in which Williams was located, there were pulpits nearby where the students could supply. Luther was soon filling one of these pulpits on a regular basis. The Brethren visited those whom they hoped to enlist in their cause as they preached in these churches on weekends.

Luther had hardly unpacked before he was enmeshed again in Brethren plans. Williams had sixteen students at Andover, more than any other college, and among them were Justin Edwards, the

43

best scholar in Luther's Williams class, and **Rufus Pomeroy,**
Francis L. Robbins, James Richards, Harvey Loomis, Ezra Fisk—
all Brethren.

Hall had quit studying under Dr. Porter at Washington, Connecticut, and both men had come to Andover, Hall as student and
Dr. Porter as professor. Mills had transferred from Yale and blind
Timothy Woodbridge, another Williams alumnus, roomed with Mills.
The Williams men set up a relay-reading team to assist Woodbridge
and he in turn threw his considerable influence into the Brethren
cause.[7]

Richards and Robbins had been at Andover since the previous
fall, and they had been joined by others who were interested in
establishing a mission. Among these were slight Samuel Newell from
Harvard, who had recently recovered from a serious illness; Samuel
Nott from Union; and a chestnut-haired Brown graduate, Adoniram
Judson, who had become the focus of the group, displacing Mills
as leader. These men had continued the talks and plans made at
Williams, though the Brethren records and organization were not
transferred to Andover until the first fall Luther was there. By that
time Judson, Nott, and Newell had graduated.

Luther found the members immersed in talking, writing, and visiting prospective supporters. They continued to discuss the best site;
some preferred the islands of the Pacific from which Obookiah
came, and this claim was strengthened by the boy's having lived
at Andover one semester and been tutored by the seminarians.[8]
Others favored the East, Rice among them, and Judson is credited
with first suggesting Burma as a specific country. Judson had read
a sermon, "Star of the East," by Dr. Claudius Buchanan, a minister
of the evangelical sector of the Anglican church, former chaplain
of the East India Company, and vice-provost of Fort Williams College
where Carey taught in Calcutta. Decisive, brilliant, with enormous
self-confidence, Judson pursued his choice with such vigor that it
soon became a unanimous one. To Burma they would go. The
Brethren were further intrigued by the somewhat distorted *Account
of an Embassy to the Kingdom of Ava* by Michael Symes, British
officer and ambassador to Burma, who vividly portrayed Burma
as the great literate and cultured country of the East.

Sometimes when the group met or walked in the grove behind
the seminary, they read from the *Serampore Circular* published by
the English Baptist mission in India. All evangelical Christendom

knew of the thrilling events surrounding its unique founders—Carey, Knight, Fuller, and Thomas.

The origin of their work was an oft-told story. Thomas, the East India surgeon, writing home and describing the spiritual destitution of the Hindus; the vignette of Carey, cobbler working at his bench while he studied the leather wallmap and prayed for men's souls around the world—these were familiar stories. And there was the meeting when Fuller read a letter from Thomas in India, and feelingly remarked, "There is a gold mine in India, but it seems almost as deep as the centre of the earth. Who will venture to explore it?"

"I will venture to go down," came Carey's prompt reply, "but remember that you must hold the ropes."[9]

This incident moved the young seminarians as it had others, and when American ships sailed to India, many carried offerings collected from American churches across denominational lines; and countless prayers were offered for India.

For Judson (and soon for the others too, for he was most persuasive), the Orient's teeming millions and ancient cultures represented the ultimate challenge, and they were the men to take it. But there were obstacles. No mission could be begun until support was enlisted; the group would begin with their teachers.

Professor Moses Stuart already shared their ardor, Mills and he having revealed their mutual interest while at Yale. A young man still in his twenties, Professor Stuart concurred with the volunteers in seeing the likelihood of a successful mission, whereas the older men foresaw problems, early deaths, closed doors. By nature a scholar, Professor Stuart was to become one of Andover's renowned biblical interpreters and writers. He was an insomniac and a perfectionist, but kindly and approachable. The students flocked to his home and not only found a sympathetic hearing, but also he assisted in planning their strategy.

Another professor who gave an ear to their ventures was Dr. Edwin Griffin, a man of elegant tastes and erratic performance, an immense man with an immense voice. "Sometimes," blind Timothy informed his brother, "his eloquence comes down like a mountain cataract; and sometimes his words are tender and subdued, and wing their way into your heart like a dissolving fluid. He is the most unequal man I ever met with."[10] Devastatingly critical in homiletics class, he had "warm social affections," and his interest in the Brethren schemes continued when he went from Andover to the pastorate of the Park Street Church in Boston.

Another teacher who consented to aid their cause was Dr. Leonard Porter, in whose home Gordon Hall had studied between his Williams and Andover days.

In June, 1810, shortly after Luther entered, Hall appeared before the Brethren at Andover to inquire whether or not he should accept the pastorate offered him by the church in Woodbury, Connecticut. They felt he should not commit himself to a pastorate, but his request for advice electrified the group into action.

The annual associational meeting was to convene in Bradford in a few days, so on the summer afternoon of June 27, 1810, the day before it began, the students arranged to present their plans to some of the delegates who were in Andover for prior meetings. Future Brethren plans, as well as the lives of the volunteers, would hinge upon the action of the church fathers toward their proposal.

On this warm June day, Drs. Worcester, Griffin, and Spring met with the Rev. Mr. Reynolds of Wilmington and Dr. Sanford of Reading in the front parlor of Professor Stuart's large, white house.

Serious and self-effacing Samuel Newell presented their case, chosen perhaps because he knew Professor Stuart from New Haven days but also because he was discreet and calm. Rice had been at Andover only one term and was not yet known to some of the men. Both Mills and Judson tended to overpress, Spring once remarking to Worcester in Judson's presence, "We had better send them out for this Judson will never let us rest."[11]

That night the group reassembled. As he walked toward the Stuarts', Jeremiah Evarts, a New Haven lawyer who had recently moved to Charlestown and was to succeed Morse as editor of the *Panoplist,* fell in with Rev. John Keep, a delegate to the association and a Yale classmate of Evarts', and they discussed the seminarians' proposal. Keep was surprised to find Evarts "entirely familiar with the subject which the young men had presented during the afternoon." Not only this, Evarts assured Keep that "the American churches should and would sustain them, and that an appeal to secure the necessary aid ought to be made without delay."[12]

At the Stuart home quite a discussion ensued. One delegate said it was a doubtful venture into the unknown. Another thought there were heathen enough to convert at home—the Indians in the hinterland, the unchurched on the frontier. All knew the extreme difficulty faced in gaining entrance, to say nothing of living conditions in East India Company territory. Mr. Sanborn voiced the most skepticism, but Dr. Worcester countered by eloquently expressing the points in favor of a mission, "grouping the prominent facts."[13] They caucused and then told the young men to draw up a memorial and present it to the Bradford meeting on Wednesday.

Most of Tuesday was spent in writing and editing this statement which Judson was to present. Six men—Judson, Nott, Mills, Newell, Rice, and Richards—signed their names. Checking with their advisor, Professor Stuart pronounced the memorial well-phrased but suggested six names were too many and would elicit apprehension from the association. Many delegates were unaware the movement even existed. Financing such a large number of men would be difficult, and the conservatives might be intimidated by the size of the group, reasoning that this sudden response resulted from hot-headed impetuosity and caught like fever, rather than from premeditated commitment. So the names of Rice and Richards, neither having completed seminary work, were dropped. This gesture was to place an undue burden on Luther in his presailing days, but at the time there was nothing to do but concur in the decision as to whose names should be omitted.

While dew still glistened on grass and flowers Wednesday morning, Drs. Spring and Worcester were on the road to Bradford. The meeting convened at 9 o'clock, but they did not ride in haste, for much had to be planned and decided relating to the proposal before the association met. As they jogged along in the chaise, Dr. Worcester proposed a name for the organization, "The American Board of Commissioners for Foreign Missions,"[14] and they discussed the members, its regulations, even the means of raising funds, so confident were they (at least Dr. Worcester) that the association would act favorably.

By the time they passed through Haverhill and crossed the three-arched bridge that spanned the Merrimac, most details were already decided.

The students, trudging on foot, riding horseback, or by chaise as Luther did, were anything but confident as they approached Bradford. Their elders acted so slowly, it seemed, and so much depended upon this meeting. As they entered the Bradford Academy where the first sessions were held, their thoughts were racing, feelings high.

It was a destiny-determining week, for more than their life work was to be decided during this two-day session. Here in Bradford homes where students and delegates were entertained during their stay, Judson and Newell met their future brides. (The previous rule that Brethren should not marry had been overridden, perhaps by Judson and other non-Williams members.)

As they convened in the church after the preliminary sessions at the academy, there was an air of expectancy, for word had spread that momentous events might occur. All eyes strained to see the group of young men from the Divinity College as they entered and sat near the front. Awe and a still hush prevailed as Adoniram walked to the rostrum and read:

The undersigned members of the Divinity College, respectfully request the attention of their reverend fathers, convened in the General Association at Bradford, to the following statement and inquiries: They beg leave to state their minds have long been impressed with the duty and importance of personally attempting a mission to the heathen; that the impressions on their minds have induced a serious, and, they trust, a prayerful consideration of the subject in its various attitudes, particularly in relation to the probable success and the difficulties attending such an attempt; and that, after examining all the information which they can obtain, they consider themselves as devoted to this work for life, wherever God, in His providence, shall open the way. They now offer the following inquiries on which they solicit the opinion and advice of this Association: Whether, with their present views and feelings, they ought to renounce the object of missions, as visionary or impracticable; if not, whether they ought to direct their attention to the Eastern or Western world; whether they may expect patronage and support from a missionary society in this country, or must commit themselves to the direction of a European society; and what preparatory measures they ought to take previous to actual engagement. The undersigned, feeling their youth and inexperience, look up to their fathers in the Church, and respectfully solicit their advice, direction, and prayers.[15]

Each of the four men gave a short testimony, telling of his sense of call as a foreign missionary. The association appointed a committee of Drs. Worcester, Spring, and Mr. Hale, secretary of the meeting, to consider the memorial and report its recommendation to the next day's session. Thus the outcome was assured, for Dr. Worcester could convince Dr. Spring and Mr. Hale would accede to the two divines. The committee report recommended,

That there be instituted, by this General Association, A Board of commissioners for Foreign Missions, for the purpose of devising ways and means, and adopting and prosecuting measures, for promoting the spread of the Gospel in foreign lands.[16]

The students may have had a sinking feeling within as they heard the vague intentions of the committee; they were admonished "humbly to wait the openings and guidance of Providence in respect to their great and excellent design."

So Luther continued in the seminary. In August of 1810, he rode back to Williamstown to receive his diploma, heard a baccalaureate sermon on Daniel 3:4 by President Fitch which "awakened my missionary feelings,"[17] delivered the poem "On Man" at the graduation, and returned east to Andover. Since most of the Brethren were now at Andover rather than Williams, the records were transferred there in the autumn of 1810 and it is likely that Luther carried them east in his saddle bag. At the first Brethren meeting at Andover in the fall, he was elected president.[18]

6. Rebecca and Decision

The Board of Commissioners met in Farmington, Connecticut, on the fifth of September, adopted a constitution, and elected officers. They sent a circular to the churches setting forth their purpose and asking members to awaken in missionary zeal, advising the candidates for appointment to continue their preparation and hold themselves in readiness.

That winter the Brethren at Andover decided they needed a larger society whose purpose was to promote missions, but whose membership would not necessarily be committed to go as missionaries as were Brethren members. On January 8 of the next year this was effected, its name being "The Society of Inquiry on the Subject of Missions." The preamble of the constitution stated that its purpose was to acquaint the members on the subject of missions.

Any student of the seminary who had been enrolled for three

months, was a believer, and had passed the scrutiny of the prudential committee could become a member. The object was "to inquire into the state of the heathen; the duty and importance of missionary labors; the best manner of conducting missions, and the most eligible places for their establishment; also to disseminate information relative to these subjects and to excite the attention of Christians to the importance and duty of missions."[1]

At society meetings, held every third Tuesday evening, members read papers on missionary themes and held discussions, the group gradually gathering a missionary library. Without eliciting suspicion or even revealing the existence of the Brethren to non-Brethren members, the society was controlled by them.[2] They kept members in office; the prudential committee, which passed on all new members, were all Brethren.

The year 1810 to 1811 at the seminary was a busy one for Luther. He began studying French and "Syriac" and although plagued by a cough and "pain in the chest and general languor,"[3] he persisted in his studies, rented his chaise to augment his income, and preached in neighboring pulpits where he was well-paid and popular. And he made a painful decision about the girl he loved.

He had long been interested in girls and several had persisted in his dreams. The village lass whose charm distracted him at singing school, and a "Miss A." whom he contrived trips to Worcester to see,[4] were two of these. His misgivings about the first and his hopes about the second were entrusted to his *Journal* but somehow nothing ever came of either romance.

He read Defoe on family and the courting of a wife and had definite ideas about the role of a minister's wife. She must be an "ornament of grace" in the manse, discreet, well-bred, and intelligent.

Sometime during his Williams days, he met the perfect mistress of the manse, or so he dreamed.

He had become good friends with William Eaton, a classmate from Framingham. William often used Luther's chaise and horse, and they must have ridden the 165 miles or so to Williamstown together. It was natural that Luther would visit the Eatons at Framingham.

The Eaton farmhouse was on the north edge of town and secluded, bounded on one side by a grove of soughing pines, on the other by rolling fields cut through by a tree-lined brook.[5] The father, Ebenezer, had fought at Bunker Hill as had Luther's, and later he ran an inn before becoming a prosperous farmer.

In the white frame home were four unusual and talented girls, and Luther was not the first young minister to come wooing. Joseph Emerson, fresh out of Harvard, taught the Framingham school before moving to Beverly as pastor in 1802. He had fallen in love with the family, Nancy in particular, and they with him. Emerson became the great molding influence in their spiritual and intellectual life. In 1803, he married Nancy and though she lived less than a year after marriage, he always considered the Eaton family his own. Two wives and twenty-five years later he lovingly addressed them as "Beloved Parents and Sisters."[6]

It was Rebecca, the second daughter and exactly his age, whom Luther loved.

Her mother was a religious woman, given to regular prayer and devotion. Her brother William was studying for the ministry, and the father, a self-taught man, was well read in history and fond of biblical prophecy, being a premillenialist.[7] He could discuss the second coming for hours and may well have done so with Luther.

But the father's greatest pride was his daughters. It was unusual for a father to prefer that his daughters be academically accomplished along with the usual skills of needle, shuttle, and cookery, but such a father was Ebenezer Eaton. Emerson, who corresponded with all the girls as well as Nancy after he became a pastor, once wrote Betsey, "You and your sisters are highly favored. Your father gives you time and opportunity to improve your minds and takes peculiar satisfaction in your progress."[8]

Rebecca tended to be a conformist and a perfectionist, one of those women who have the ability to organize and execute plans. She taught school as Luther did and was at Beverly and Salem during part of his time at Andover. She knew Judson's fiancée, Nancy [Ann] Hasseltine, whose sister, Rebecca Hasseltine, became Emerson's third wife in 1810.[9]

Luther must have seen something of his mother in Rebecca, for she had a strong personality, deep convictions, an intense social consciousness that was to manifest itself in helping fallen girls in the future, and she liked independence. The courtship was smiled upon by their friends. They noted that she was eminently qualified to be a minister's wife. With Luther's ability to speak, his good sense in business, and the similarity of their backgrounds, they seemed ideally matched. Sometime in late 1810 they became engaged.

The previous spring, Judson, chafing at the delays, had written

Dr. Bogue of the London Missionary Society asking whether they would accept and appoint "two or three young unmarried men, having received a liberal education wishing to serve the Saviour in a heathen land, and indeed susceptible of a passion for missions."[10] Some of the Brethren disagreed with Judson about appealing to England for aid,[11] but the following January when funds were still far from adequate to equip even one missionary, the prudential committee decided to send Judson to England to ascertain their sentiment on a joint mission.

Judson sailed in early January, returning in August after a hazardous trip. His ship was captured by the French and he and all other passengers taken prisoners. But he did reach London, from whence he brought news that the London Society would send the four missionaries but thought it impractical to share responsibility. If they were to do the financing, the appointees would be wholly under their watchcare, employed "by this society in India."[12]

While Judson was abroad, the widow of John Norris died, bequeathing thirty thousand dollars to the Board for missions. Though the money was tied up in litigation instituted by the family to break the will, the Board would eventually receive it and was no longer in the dire straits it had previously appeared to be.

During his last months at the seminary, Luther came to a painful knowledge concerning his engagement to Rebecca: she was unwilling to accompany him as a foreign missionary.

It is not known why she became engaged without realizing that Luther was committed, by virtue of his Brethren membership, to a missionary life. Perhaps she thought it was a passing fancy, that he would settle down to some prestigious pastorate where she would preside over the manse as the town's leading hostess and arbiter of its social scene. Luther was a superb speaker, a skilled musician, educated and amiable. Would not his talents grace any pulpit in the land? Why waste them on a heathen land?

Perhaps Luther proposed without revealing his Brethren ties and in so doing they were unaware of their differences about a mission. Her later life indicated that Rebecca desired a career of her own and would have found it difficult to sublimate her ambitions to those of a husband. During the next year they had earnest talks about their future, but he who changed the course of many a life in years to come could not convince her that the path of either duty or love lay in Burma.

His dilemma was compounded by the realization that he had unwittingly committed himself in honor to two divergent courses. His membership in the Brethren was a pledge to hold himself in readiness for appointment at any time he should be designated; he was to make no plans or promises which hindered his going. Yet how could a man honorably break his engagement to the woman he loved? Months passed with his trying to persuade her to go, but she remained adamant in her attitude.

At graduation time in 1811, Luther took an examination of dismission from the seminary and left in September without graduating.[13] But he stayed in the area, teaching and preaching at Exeter, and returned to Andover for the Brethren meetings, keeping in touch with the other men.

And he was present in Worcester, September 18, 1811, when the Board met and considered the correspondence with the London Society and what Judson had learned. Newell and the other candidates were present to hear Judson's report. There ensued a lengthy discussion in which, years later, it was reported that Judson in his pique about the delays, overstepped the bounds of discretion in speaking to his elders and received a "formal and solemn reprimand." The cautious members favored deferring appointment because of the possibility of war with England. However, the positive members carried the day, and it was voted to appoint Judson, Nott, Newell, and Gordon Hall "as missionaries to work in Asia, either in Burma or Surat, or possibly Prince of Wales Island or elsewhere, as in the view of the Prudential Committee anywhere Providence might open the door."[14]

There were some surprises in the list. Not one of the original haystack prayer meeting men was among them. The most surprising omission was Mills, whose name had been on the June, 1810, petition presented to the association at Bradford. He was now replaced by Hall. Richards and Robbins were still in school and the explanation for Mills was that his modesty deferred to the more academic Hall.[15] Also, it may have been that the Brethren thought Mills more suited to stimulate missionary interest at home and recruit others for appointment. Yet Mills' biographer was probably correct in stating that "*the* reason was that the Brethren did not select Mills to go out."[16]

And Luther was not on the list because he had not resolved his quandary about Rebecca, but that fall they mutually agreed to break their engagement, a decision which left Luther in anguish. He wrote Asaph: "Frequently, the conflict in my breast had been exceedingly distressing. My missionary brethren have always conversed as if I was going with them; and I have rarely been able to hold for a moment an opposite language. At times duty has seemed to be clear, and I have felt devoted to this cause. Those seasons have been always happy ones . . . I hope the season of hesitation, of doubt and perplexity, is now past."[17]

The other men were having no such difficulty.[18] That June day in 1810 when the group presented the memorial at Bradford, the Andover students had been entertained in the home of Deacon John Hasseltine, where Adoniram Judson met and fell in love with a daughter, Ann. She not only consented to go but became something of a matchmaker for Samuel Newell. Harriet Atwood, seventeen-year-old daughter of Widow Atwood of Haverhill, had been introduced to Newell by Mills, who was well-known in Bradford and Haverhill. Harriet was a lovely girl, frail, sensitive, and studious. Newell wondered about her health. Her father had recently died of tuberculosis, and other members of the family had succumbed to the same disease. But when he sought counsel from one of his elders, he was advised that a fine piece of china, though delicate and fragile, often outlasted a utilitarian piece. So he continued to court Harriet and though she hesitated, Ann encouraged her and eventually she consented.

Samuel Nott was engaged to Roxana Peck and she planned to accompany him, so it was only Luther's fiancée who declined. Perhaps Rebecca's maturity played a part in her decision, for Harriet was still in her teens and Ann Hasseltine was twenty-three, but Rebecca was twenty-seven. Any mature person realized that it was no lark on which they were embarking. It would be grueling, lonely, heartbreaking work. Prudence would stay at home and the Eatons were a prudent family. Rebecca's answer remained "no."

During the winter of 1811, Luther continued at Exeter, New Hampshire, though he kept informed on the progress of the Board toward launching the mission.

The four eager appointees pestered the committee to find passage, but sailings were increasingly infrequent as England began blockading major ports and halting American vessels on the high seas. So the months passed and Luther could postpone a definite decision a little longer, for he was still seeing Rebecca and did not feel the decision was irreversible. Hall and Newell went to Philadelphia to study in the new medical college there, and Judson made his headquarters at Andover, preaching, visiting Ann at Bradford, and chafing under the delay in securing passage.

Suddenly in January of 1812, Hall and Newell came from Philadelphia saying that Robert Ralston, longtime friend of missions, had arranged for sailings aboard the ship *Harmony,* Captain, Michael Brown. It was bound for Calcutta in mid-February. This news galvanized the prudential committee and the appointees into action. There was only $1,200 in hand, and the men had not even been ordained.

Even some of the prudential committee thought it impossible to equip the men and get them aboard the vessel. Dr. Spring said to Dr. Worcester, "Brother Worcester, I fear you are going too fast. I doubt if we shall have the means to pay the sum, which we must borrow."

"There is money enough in the churches!" cried Worcester.

"I know that, very well. But how can you get at it?"

"The Lord has the Key and before the missionaries shall have reached their field of labor, we shall have enough to pay their outfit, and to continue their support."

The Lord may have supplied the key but Dr. Worcester did the turning, for he moved with alacrity and zeal. He sent circulars into all the churches, dispatched the seminarians in twos to churches for miles around to collect funds, and solicited every individual who would listen. He was assisted by the Rev. Mr. Emerson, Rebecca's in-law, now married to Ann Hasseltine's sister, and by Drs. Morse and Griffin and the Andover professors.

There was much to be decided. In early January it was voted that they should ask the missionaries to go unmarried, but this action was almost immediately rescinded. February 6 was set as the latest date for the ordination which would enable the men to reach Philadelphia to embark on the *Harmony.* Then it was learned that the *Caraven,* a three-mast brig, under Captain Augustine Heard, was to sail from Salem about the same time and Pickering Dodge, the owner, would supply passage for the missionaries for $300 each. This alternate passage was accepted also, the Board feeling it would lessen the risk involved if the missionaries were on two ships rather than one.

The Salem *Gazette* for January 31 contained notice of the service:

55

"The public exercises are to be holden at the Tabernacle in this town to commence at 11 A.M. A collection will be made on this occasion in aid of the mission by which to embrace a very unexpected opportunity for conveying them to India is now fitting out with all possible dispatch."

Suddenly Luther wavered no longer, and the prudential committee was faced with another decision. He not only was going, but he wished to be sent with this group. The committee felt they could not commit the Board to underwrite his support and therefore could act only as individuals. Luther accepted their terms, knowing only members of the Board were responsible. They told him he must raise money for his own passage and salary until he could be officially appointed by the full Board. Of this decision and its stringent terms, he wrote,

This matter was adjusted only 11 days previously to the day of ordination. The prudential committee was not authorized to appoint a special missionary and it was owing entirely to an intenseness of feeling which could neither be restrained by myself nor resisted by the Committee that I was able to force my way through the almost insuperable difficulties of the case so as to go to India at that time. I had to provide by begging funds for my outfit, passage, etc., and all this in the space of nine days, for two of the eleven before ordination had been fixed upon. Three more were consumed in agonizing and successful, successful only because agonizing, efforts with the Prudential Committee, leaving only six days to provide the necessary funds. By the signal aid of providence this was effected.[19]

He went to Worcester where Dr. Austin's church contributed to his passage; Asaph gave him $56, and other friends and churches made up the needed amount.

The churches were responding magnanimously, many denominations contributing so that the committee could pay the salary of each missionary for one year in advance, plus outfitting them.

As in any new venture, there were dissenters and scoffers too. Rev. William Bentley of Salem, always caustic, noted that "Colonel Hathorne says the ordination is a farce to get possession of the Norris legacy," and added his own judgment of the missionaries: "We learn nothing favorable to their talents or experience."[20]

7. Ordination

All roads led to Salem, February 6. They came by chaise, gig, wagon, horseback, and sleigh, and those not having any conveyance, walking. Among the latter were many Andover students, for before sunrise they were pouring from Phillips Hall, the homes of Squire Farrar and Professor Porter, and other boarding places.

Even some of the academy students were allowed to walk the sixteen or seventeen miles there and back. Two teen-agers, Asa Cummings and William Goodell, made the trek and many years later, Goodell recalled the day: ". . . one of the coldest known that winter. It was exceedingly slippery, and we had to strain every nerve and exert every muscle to keep on our feet, while at the same time, we had to press forward with all the eagerness possible in order to arrive in time."[1]

Rice was there, cloaked with fatigue. The last nine days' toil, coupled with the persistent anxiety about Rebecca, rendered him almost numb.

The service began at eleven. A council consisting of Salem Tabernacle Church, the North Church of Newburyport, the Congregational of Charlestown, Dr. Griffin of Boston, and the Andover professors (excepting Dr. Stuart who was unable to attend) examined the men, their motives, Christian knowledge, and experience. This ecclesiastical council gave the candidates some instructions. They were requested to scrupulously abstain from all meddling with political concerns. Immediately upon reaching a field of labor, they were to organize as a mission and elect a secretary and treasurer. They were to form a church and attend to the ordinances, and "treat converts with charity and caution."[2]

The Tabernacle was packed "like rows of new pins in a paper," the people overlooking from the galleries, the aisles traced only by the ridges of those standing. The crowd was estimated at two thousand. Every eye was fixed on the front where Luther and the

57

four other men sat on a large settee as Dr. Griffin offered the opening prayer. There were hymns, probably "Farewell to the Missionaries,"[3] accompanied by Dr. David D. Mussey on the bass viol.

Dr. Woods preached the sermon, his subject "Motives for Missions," his text Psalm 67, a long sermon to which the candidates and audience were inured. "Whether you are duly qualified for the mission," he counseled, "does not, you are sensible, depend either on your opinion, or on ours; but on Christ's who searches the heart and tries the reins of the children of men, and will soon reveal the real character of every one before the assembled universe."[4] Further on he warned, "You are to expect much adversity, much opposition, many dark days when your hearts will swell with grief."[5] There was the sound of stifled weeping and the half-audible sighing of hearts touched at the sight of these five men, so gifted and capable, going out for a lifetime among the pagan. Awed by the solemnity "in that great assembly there was, at times, a stillness 'like the stillness of God, when He ariseth in silence to bless the world.' At times the whole great assembly seemed moved as the trees of the wood are moved by a mighty wind."[6] "We are seven," said Judson that day, "like the five loaves and two fishes blessed of our Lord wherewith to feed the multitudes."[7]

As the men knelt on the floor, Dr. Jedidiah Morse gave the ordaining prayer. The audience was almost overwhelmed with emotion as the five bowed their heads and five ministers stood, one behind each candidate.

There was Judson—brilliant, impulsive, persistent—a man who would suffer much and accomplish much as "the apostle to the Burmans." He had turned down the associate pastorate of the "biggest church in Boston," but Baptists would almost deify him in the years that lay ahead.

Gordon Hall, like Rice, unmarried, valedictorian at Williams as Judson was at Brown, the "beloved disciple" to student and professor alike, sat next. His selfless motto, "Duty is ours, consequences God's,"[8] typified his steadiness, the kind which would enable him to labor seven years in Bombay before baptizing his first convert. Of his appearance a friend remembered that he "stooped slightly when he walked and seemed meditative . . . dark intelligent and penetrating eye."[9] When offered an attractive pastorate his ready reply came, "No, I must not settle in any part of Christendom. Others will be left whose health or pre-engagement requires them to stay at home, but I can sleep on the ground, can endure hunger and hardship. God calls me to the heathen. Woe to me, if I preach not the gospel to the heathen."[10]

Slight, blond Newell knelt next. Serious, possessing "uncommon modesty," he would be the first to tread the valley of the shadow as he parted from Harriet within the year. Beside him was Nott, well-born, tall and wiry, whom ill-health would force home where he would outlive all the others.

And there was Rice, the tallest, the most athletic, energetic, gifted in speech and voice, a persuasive man but troubled in his thoughts this day as he wrote, "worn down with fatigue and agitation of mind, I did not realize it so impressively as was desirable in an event most sacred."[11]

Perhaps it was the sight of Nancy Judson and Harriet Atwood which wrought such mixed feelings in Luther, for the two girls had slipped from their seats in a front pew and knelt in the aisle as the men were kneeling for the ordaining prayer. The disturbing thoughts about Rebecca could not be dispelled. Was he too hasty in going out with the first group? Might she have consented had he waited longer? Why did all his decisions appear to be neither black nor white but a confusing shade of gray, as was this choice? Which was the right thing to do? If he could only be sure.

The spectators were moved at the sight of the two women as much as by the men, for was it not more sacrificial of a woman to leave the comforts of her native land for a pagan culture, customs, habits, and the lack of medicine, than for a man? Harriet, only eighteen, the "belle of Bradford," slender and pale, beautiful and gifted, a high color in her cheeks now, seemed so gentle. Were others than Newell wondering if she could survive the harshness of India? Did any foresee that she would be the first casualty among the ranks? To a friend she wrote, "Perhaps no sympathizing friend will stand near my dying bed,"[12] but from the ship she penned less mournful lines to her mother: "Do not be anxious for me. God will take care of me."[13]

Beside her knelt Nancy, vivacious and self-confident like her husband, but also capable of great devotion, single-mindedness to the task, and intensity of feeling and expression.

The prayer over, Dr. Spring gave the charge and Dr. Worcester extended the right hand of fellowship, saying the setting aside was "an act of our hearts."

At 3 o'clock the four-hour service was over. Friends and relatives began making tearful farewells. Asaph, who had ridden over from Northborough, grasped Luther by the hand and bade him farewell, thinking perhaps it was for the last time, and people began going home in the early twilight, across the crusty snow. The academy students found the homeward journey rough going; even the seminary students were exhausted. William Goodell went as far as his legs would propel him but the moment came when he willed them to move and they only sprottled in the snow. He would have frozen had not some seminary students happened along and carried him to a nearby house, where he remained until the next day. Nevertheless, his comment on the day was: 'I felt amply repaid by being so thoroughly inoculated with the missionary spirit, that a reinoculation has never been found necessary."[14]

Meanwhile a discussion between the Board members and the families of the ladies going out had brought the decision that the Newells, instead of proceeding to Philadelphia to take passage on the *Harmony* with the Notts, would stay and sail on the brig with the Judsons, since otherwise Ann Judson would be the only woman aboard. Other women would be going out in the *Harmony* and Roxanna Peck Nott would not be alone. This change in plans meant that Gordon Hall and Luther would have to go to Philadelphia, a disappointment to Luther for he and Judson were very close. Yet he never disliked the prospect of a trip, and the journey to New York and Philadelphia would be interesting. But first he had business to attend. In the evening he mounted his horse and took the road to Exeter, New Hampshire, a lonely and empty road that night.

8. Voyage Out

A great crowd assembled on the Philadelphia wharf, Tuesday, February 18, 1812, to see the missionaries embark. Sailings were familiar sights to Philadelphians, but there had never been another like this. The two young bachelors, Hall and Rice, had spoken in the churches, Hall already known by them from his months as a student in the new medical college. The newlyweds, Samuel and Roxanna Nott, fascinated the watchers. The sight of a young bride going abroad for life, which they assumed it would be, was astounding.

The *Harmony*[1] had dropped down to New Castle, so the group boarded a packet which carried them downstream to her. At New Castle, they transferred their food and possessions to the *Harmony* and found their accommmodations very pleasant. Going ashore, Rice preached from the text, "How shall we escape if we neglect so great salvation?" a favorite sermon of his through the years.

The next day the *Harmony* tacked down the Delaware to Port Penn but picking up no wind, returned to port. On Sunday "having reached the wharf the Captain and some others went on shore, company and drinking in the cabins this evening."[2]

The delay in their departure and that of the *Caraven*, which did not sail from Salem until the nineteenth gave the Board more time to collect funds, the indefatigable Dr. Worcester posting about the country seeking contributions until the very hour of sailing, and thereby fulfilling his prophecy to Dr. Spring that the money was in the churches and they could obtain it.

Within his cabin, Rice set his things aright and tried to straighten and sort his thoughts and feelings. The last few days had been hectic and provided little time or privacy to dwell on his own frustrations and the turmoil in his mind. The night following the ordination, he had ridden to Exeter where he bade farewell to the friends he had made while teaching there. The next day he returned to Andover, put up his things in great haste, took leave of the students, and accompanied by Justin Edwards, went to Boston and took the stage to New Haven. There he met Hall and they boarded a packet for New York where they were received kindly in the churches. On the thirteenth, after collecting in New York, Rice went to Philadelphia by stage in company with newly-wedded Roxana and Samuel, and "Mr. Johns a Baptist missionary for India." There they were entertained by Robert Ralston, spoke in the churches, and were favorably received by all denominations. They were "devoutly committed to the gracious care of the heart of the church." Rice was gratified that "the attention paid to the missionaries by the Philadelphians, the deep interest they appeared to take in its success excited emotions which language cannot express."[3]

When Rice, Hall, and the Notts reconnoitered the ship, they found thirty-nine souls aboard the sturdy little vessel, including the crew and the super-cargoes,[4] as those caring for the cargo were called. There were two French Catholics bound for Mauritius (then called Isle de France while it was under French rule), a Dr. Dugarreau, and two other groups of missionaries. These were Mr. and Mrs. Robert May and a Miss Green of the London Missionary Society, and the John Lawsons and Williams Johns of the English Baptist Society. Mr. Johns was the one who had been a fellow-passenger on the stage from New York to Philadelphia, and Rice found him a man he could neither forget nor dismiss. It was a strange series of events that listed these Baptist missionaries as passengers on the *Harmony*.

The powerful East India Company, offering more resistance to the gospel than did the pagans, had made it impossible for appointees to be sent directly to India. To circumvent the company's policies, societies had resorted to sending them via America.

These missionaries had arrived in Philadelphia late in 1810 and reembarked for India aboard a brig, the *Daphne,* which met with disaster at sea, limped back to port, and refitted. However, the missionaries thought her unseaworthy and refused to sail aboard her again.[5] Thus they were some months in the States, awaiting passage at a time when relations were strained between Britain and the United States and sailings were infrequent. Lawson supplied a church at Poughkeepsie and Johns preached in Rhode Island and Massachusetts, distinguishing himself by raising over $4,600 from Salem and Boston Baptists for the Serampore translations.[6]

It was the twenty-fourth before Rice finally recorded that they had left Port Penn: "With a strong wind go briskly down the river. Send back several letters by the pilot. Begin to be seasick. Get out to sea."[7]

The missionaries settled down to a regular routine of study, prayer meetings, singing, Sunday worship which the ministers alternately conducted, and for Rice, flute playing. Soon they began to discuss their doctrines and since the most obvious difference between Congregationalists and Baptists of the time involved infant or believer's baptism, naturally they discussed this area.

When Rice was growing up in Northborough there was a changing mood about Baptists. Congregationalism remained the state church of Massachusetts. Baptists still had the "taint of heresy" about them, but they had emerged from their days of hounding and harassment and were experiencing marked growth. There was no Baptist church in Northborough. As in many Massachusetts towns, Northborough had a few with Baptist leanings. Since the Separatists were growing in number, Rice certainly heard talk about them, and Baptist societies existed in nearby Upton, Shrewsbury, Berlin, and Boylston, all places he visited.

And he knew Captain Luther Goddard of the Baptist church in Shrewsbury, a clockmaker and minister who had itinerant preaching engagements in the area. Being an artisan like many of his fellow churchmen, Goddard would preach to a Baptist Society, gather the watches in need of repair, and return them when he appeared for his next preaching engagement.

In 1806, when Rice and his cousin Warren Fay began holding evangelistic prayer meetings, they first met in homes and then in the unused seminary building, until "opposition became so strong that the house was shut against their admission."[8] After that, Seth Grout invited them to his home. Town annals record that as the group "passed through the village on their way from the Seminary to Mr. Grout's they were ridiculed by persons who were assembled at the public house [Munroe's Tavern], apparently for that purpose."[9]

During the years of Rice's spiritual questing, he vainly sought help from Mr. Whitney. Turning to others, he found counsel in Seth Grout, one of the few Baptists living in Northborough.

Mr. Grout, a nailer from Maine, had come to Northborough a few years before and owned a carding shop on the Post Road in the center of town. At first he joined the local church, serving on the building committee along with Asaph Rice. But after a few years he withdrew to the Shrewsbury and Boylston Baptist Society and still later (about the time Rice sailed for India), the Baptist Church of Northborough was organized in his shop, derisively called the "Gospel Shop."[10]

The Balls, Fays, Warrens—the few families who supported the prayer meetings—all lived in the part of Northborough from which the members of the Baptist church were to come in the years that lay ahead.

Thus it was the Baptists, or those with Baptist bias, who encouraged Rice when he needed it most during his youth. Whatever he may have thought about their differing theology, he would have held kindly feelings toward these persons of Baptist persuasion.

He corresponded, according to his own account, with a Baptist friend, probably Mr. Grout, while at Williams College and questions were raised about the validity of infant baptism. Though this friend was not highly educated, Rice was disturbed by his logic. During this period his ledger book reveals that he was reading and selling books on baptism.

Once at Andover he was given the negative side in a debate on infant baptism. Thinking he could not muster a convincing case, he was surprised to find his assigned position not only defensible but disturbing. The professor felt it necessary to rise to the aid of his opponent. He planned to pursue the subject but never found the time until on the voyage out. Dr. Johns forced it upon him.

When they were less than three weeks at sea, both Rice and Johns began to make *Journal* entries about their discussions on baptism. Johns wrote, "In the evening Mr. Rice having introduced the subject, he and I had some conversation on Believers' baptism,"[11] and the same evening Rice noted, "Had some conversation with Brother Johns respecting word 'baptise.' I wish he would reason candidly and not rest conclusions upon his bare assertions."[12] John's *Journal* conveys the impressions he was wishing the same thing about Rice. Each was inclined to argue his point, and the debates were heated.

Dr. John's sea chest contained books on baptism. Rice borrowed some of these and he afterwards remembered, "Some remarks from the pen of Dr. Campbell, which had not before met my observation, were of a nature, that induced me to suspect sprinkling not to be a proper mode of baptising; . . . "[13] After reading this treatise on baptism and talking again with Dr. Johns, he wrote, "May the Lord guide us in the way of truth for his name's sake,"[14] and Johns mentioned the same talks: "This evening bro. Lawson, with myself, &c. and our paedobaptist brother Rice had a long conversation on our difference of sentiment. It continued to a late hour."[15]

In these discussions the two men followed the usual apologetics of their respective communions, Rice defending infant baptism by drawing parallels from the Old Testament circumcision of infants and Johns pursuing the New Testament meaning of the word "baptizo" and the practice of the early churches. Johns deplored Rice's reliance on "Israelitish traditions,"[16] and Rice lamented Johns' "dogmatism and want of candor."[17]

Rice was a poor sailor and his journal entries were a barometer of the weather. If the day was fair he would record, "winds favorable, still seasick," or if becalmed, "pleasant weather, somewhat better of seasickness." As the green seas washed over the deck and the undulating voyage seemed interminable, he knew its very success would bring more queasiness. Sailing was hazardous still, and whether due to ill winds or the inability of the captain and crew, they made poor speed and were consistently off course. As they hit gales and the sails were torn away, the wind whining in the rigging and the shuddering of the wooden ship were reminders as he tossed on his bunk that endless seas lay between him and the strange land ahead, the loneliness of a missioner's life. And Rebecca was teaching back in Beverly.

Occasionally they sighted another ship, but the situation with the English daily worsening, they were wary of other vessels. On the third of March they passed the *Powhattan* bound from Lisbon to New York and thought it might be the *Caraven,* but it was not; for the *Caraven,* though sailing about the same time, picked up more favorable winds, rounded the cape, and was far into the Indian Ocean before the *Harmony* neared Africa.

Veering off course they sighted the Isle of Sal on the twenty-seventh. Rice climbed the shrouds to get a better view of the land; they passed the *Brahmin* of Philadelphia bound for the Island of Mao.

Rice engaged in his perennial stocktaking on March 25, for he was twenty-nine. It had been a crucial and life-deciding year, "various and singular vicissitudes have I passed through the last year; particularly in regard to a connection with———and respecting missions."[18] His resolve to "have no secret reserve" had been tested, costing him the parting with Rebecca, whose name he could not, out of deference to her, record in his *Journal.* Yet still he prayed on this birthday, "O Lord, pardon me and my problem heart."[19]

One of his most persistent entries concerned the continuing conversations with Johns. Rice and Johns did not get along well, for Dr. Johns seemed contentious and had a kind of martyr complex. Even the saintly trio at Serampore were going to find it difficult to bear Johns, and the other missionaries grieved over his stumblings.

Dr. Johns had been medically trained at the expense of English Baptists; his colleague, Lawson, was an expert typesetter and artist. Lawson was to be allowed to stay in Serampore but the authorities, despite the dearth of physicians, were to shuttle Johns back to

England, for which he never forgave Carey. On board ship Dr. Johns mistreated his wife, or so the other passengers thought. They refused to attend services when he led and Rice, intrepid to a fault, decided that the other missionaries should talk with him about his behavior. Their talk resulted in Rice's vowing to be more sympathetic towards Johns and Johns's continuing in his old ways.

Rice's New England conscience was scandalized by the way the sailors profaned the Sabbath—"work going on upon deck for which I think the captain blameable."[20] The captain also vexed Rice by fishing during Sunday services.

Captain Brown may well have felt cramped with all the divines aboard. Dragging on sodden ropes, in salty seas, beset by hurricanes— it was not a life that bred gentility, and though Ann Judson effused over the Sunday School behavior of the *Caraven's* Captain Heard and crew, the *Harmony* crew used salty and "profane" language. Nevertheless, the captain, second mate, boatswain, and other crewmen often attended services. And Captain Brown was jolly and a good sport. On All Fool's Day, he rushed into the dining room during breakfast, excitedly telling the passengers about the fantastic and grotesque fish just pulled from the sea. Hastening on deck, they found it a consummate trick.

Nearing the equator they noticed that no shadows followed them on deck. Schools of porpoises, whales, an occasional waterspout, broke the day's monotony, and sometimes, as on April 4, there was "a very pleasant treat of a young shark for breakfast."[21] This same day they saw another ship to leeward, going in a southernly direction. Every sighted ship filled them with hope and apprehension, hope that it be the *Caraven* with their colleagues, apprehension lest it be an enemy ship. The captain ordered a gun to be fired, standards were hoisted, and it was seen to be flying under Spanish colors. They were anxious as mounted guns came in view, but the vessel sent two men over, and it was found to be a ship built at Portland, Maine, from Havana bound to Angola in Africa, "engaged in that most detestable traffic, the *slave trade*."[22]

Rice continued to be seasick and nearly all the passengers were ill at some time during the voyage, dysentery becoming a fellow passenger. Seasickness could not be left behind when the very success of the voyage depended on picking up the trade winds. The rhythmic sway and rock on days when the seas washed over the deck and rushed down into the cabin, the foul smell below made the rancid food, old gingerbread and tea biscuits no longer inviting. A small fire in the galley in the daytime—for preparation of an occasional fresh dish and for brewing tea and coffee—was the only heat.

Aboard the *Caraven,* which was nearing its destination, poor Harriet was having her troubles. She and Samuel, less enthusiastic and energetic than the Judsons, were in a smaller cabin. Eighteen years old, pregnant and sick, she wistfully longed for a "still room with a bowl of milk and a loaf of Indian bread."[23] On days when the "heavy seas . . . have repeatedly broken on deck and rushed with violence down into the cabin," she complained of "the weariness of excessive rocking" and the "intolerable smell after rain."[24]

Veering far off course and now in the southern hemisphere where it was winter, on May 2 the *Harmony* seemed to be approaching land, for they sighted albatross and cape birds.[25] But they neared not the cape but the Tristan da Cunha Islands, three small islands almost equidistant from South Africa and South America. Between two of these islands, which were the peaks of submerged mountains, treacherous and the graveyard of many ships, they almost foundered. When beaching on the rocky shores appeared imminent, Rice found himself objective and unafraid though the captain was "in a horrible rage on account of our situation," stamping and swearing "at a most shocking rate."[26] Mrs. Johns was badly bruised by "losing her balance and fetching away with the baby in her arms in the cabin," but they all survived the incident.

Johns continued to be a source of friction. Rice lamented,

Dr. Johns, I am sorry to have the occasion for this recount, has long since rendered himself offensive perhaps to most on board the *Harmony* by his improper temper and conduct. By improper I mean a haughty, imperious, dictatorial, peevish, cross, hateful disposition. By improper conduct, the treatment of his wife and other individuals also. By some improper remarks respecting Miss Green (from the London Missionary Society) he has lately involved himself in difficulty with one of the Supercargoes (the reason why he was threatened with being turned out of the cabin). And he has endeavored to draw us, Hall, Nott and myself, into his quarrel. This has occasioned various conversations with him in which we have severally expressed to him with considerable plainess the views we entertain of his conduct.[27]

The *Harmony* picked up the South Atlantic current and skirted the Cape of Good Hope on the fourteenth of May. They had been at sea eleven weeks, and on June 8 they put in at Port Louis.

It was a picturesque city marching right down into the sea, encircled by a sentinel of mountains. Nott, Hall, and Rice hastened ashore and met a sea captain from the States, who directed them to the markets where they purchased fresh fruits. That night they received a message from the local chaplain, Mr. Thompson, stating he "requests the favor of any missionaries who had arrived in the American Ship, to call upon him at his room in Government House, whenever they may be at leisure."[28]

Mr. Thompson, company chaplain in Madras and temporarily in Mauritius for his health, discouraged them about establishing a mission in the East and strongly advised against settling in India or any other place "within the limits of the Company's dominions."

"There are missionaries enough at Calcutta," he insisted. "Sir Barlow, the governor of the Presidency of Madras, positively forbids all preaching, and even other circulating of Bibles." He also added, "The internal conditions put the country of Burmah out of the question as a missionary field at present."[29]

Thompson "strongly recommended Ceylon to our attention. Observed that it had many nominal Christians . . . the people seem prepared and wish, to receive the gospel . . . the Bible is already printed in the Tamil language of the Coast and might easily be accommodated to that of Ceylon."[30] He also suggested Madagascar.

From these conversations the trio began to see that their most virulent opposition would not be from the Indians, nor the pestilence, disease, and physical hardships of the life they had chosen, but from the powerful East India Company about which they had heard and whose awful jurisdiction they were about to enter. This company had recently "declared that they had hoped the age was become too enlightened for attempts to make proselytes: . . . that the conversion of fifty or a hundred thousand natives of any degree of character would be the most serious disaster that could happen, and they thanked God that it was impracticable."[31]

The company was unwilling to hazard its commercial enterprise on the effect of the gospel; the Serampore groups were scathingly labeled "a nest of consecrated cobblers" and "Methodist tub preachers and apostates from the anvil and loom."[32] Even the Anglican church lent its support in maintaining the status quo. The rebuffs the American group received were an old story to the English Baptists, for they had sought and found refuge for their mission only in the Danish settlement of Serampore.

Nearly a month was spent at Port Louis, Hall, Nott, and Rice talking to every sea captain arriving from an Indian port or any other country they might enter. Bombay, Burma, Ceylon—all were canvassed. They called on another company chaplain, the Rev. Mr. Shepherd from the Bengal district, also in Mauritius for his health, and he "informs that the missionaries at Ceylon are doing very little . . . that the schools there have Congalee instructors, are examined monthly when one of the instructors delivers a sermon . . . That there is a positive order from Government to send home all who come out to Calcutta without leave from the Director to settle there . . . that the Government are extremely jealous of missionary labors, lest the natives should be disturbed . . . That no respectable Hindo or Musselman has been converted. . . . That the Burmans are in a state of war and have some difficulty with the company."[33] These were discouraging words to the group who were headed for Calcutta with Burma as their ultimate destination.

On July 2 the *Harmony* "put to sea in the evening" and Rice immediately succumbed to seasickness, this time with symptoms of a more distressing nature—backache, headaches, general debility. Their first night out, sudden gales rose and the crew, desperately pulling on the ropes, were unable to correct the ballast in time and "the fore topmast broke away."[34]

Heavy seas and rain continued throughout the voyage to Calcutta; otherwise it was uneventful and swift, and they arrived off Balfour Roads on July 28, where they were delayed many days in securing a pilot to navigate the entrance. One was finally hailed, came aboard, and promised to return the following day, only to appear five days later. The *Harmony* passengers began to perceive something of the Indians' differing value of time.

On the eighth, they finally obtained a pilot and proceeded up river toward Calcutta, the lush banks of green on each side dotted with native huts resembling the haystacks back in New England. The ship anchored on the night of the ninth, and early the next morning the supercargoes went ahead in a small boat to arrange details of docking and unloading. Rice begged a seat in the budgerow and was in Calcutta "very early this morning . . . met with Br. Judson between 9 and 10 o'clock and learnt that Br. Newell had departed for the Isle de France."[35]

Judson's news was discouraging, for he told how they had hardly disembarked before the authorities ordered them to return to America

69

on the *Caraven* or leave the company's territory on some other vessel. The *Gillespie,* bound for Isle de France, offered a berth for two in late July. The Judsons and Newells debated about which couple should contract the passage. Harriet wanted very much to await the other missionaries' arrival. She had corresponded for months with Roxana Nott, whom she was never to meet, and wrote: "Halted long between two opinions. . . . If we go we shall relinquish the pleasure of meeting the dear brethren, and sister Roxana."[36] It was decided that because of Harriet's approaching confinement it would be wise for them to make the voyage immediately and the Judsons to follow as soon as another passage became available. Dr. Johns filled in something of the day's happenings:

About 11 o'clock in the forenoon, the tide serving, we weighed anchor. At 2 we are abreast of a pretty place called Garden Reach. The villas appeared delightful. On our left is the botanic garden with the house of Dr. Roxburgh. Objects now press on us, so that we can scarce record them. The crows and vultures are very numerous and noisy; the gigantic crane is seen standing on the house tops, as though it were inanimate. Nothing can exceed the meanness of the sails of the country boats, all mere rags. We have just passed Fort William and now at 4½ have anchored. Soon after, Mr. Rice who had gone up to Calcutta, with the supercargoes in a country boat, came on board, accompanied by a gentleman from thence. The information we received was 'that all the missionaries have been ordered away; Newell who came out with Judson before us is gone to the Isle de France' . . . we were all landed by 8 o'clock and safely conveyed in palanquins to the house of Mr. Rolt. The same evening we slept at Dr. Carey's house in Calcutta; by 4 o'clock in the morning, our sister Lawson was delivered of a fine girl."[37]

9. India and Change

They found Dr. Carey's Calcutta house large and spacious, a huge stone building, rooms high-ceilinged and balconied, with many shuttered windows for cross ventilation. Dr. Carey resided here during the middle of the week when as Professor of Bengali he taught languages at Fort William College, preaching at the nearby Lall Bazar Church in the evenings.

Carey was a delight and a marvel to the new men. He was small, neatly dressed, bald and kindly, easy to converse with and unaffected by his growing fame as a linguist and botanist. Brainerd and Eliot, American apostles to a dying race, had kindled his missionary interests and now, here were Americans who in turn had been greatly affected by the Serampore triumvirate. He warmly welcomed them, along with the Lawsons and Johns from his own society back in England, inviting them to visit at Serampore while deciding what they could do.

The next day they reported to the police and received the much dreaded interdict; they were to leave India and were forbidden to enter any other British possession in the East, or the possession of any British ally. So they found it true that "India was a close preserve in the hands of the East India Company. To go there without a license from the Company was to become a poacher, and to incur the risk of being sent ignominiously home. A man without a covenant was in the Company's estimation a dangerous person; doubly dangerous such a one with a Bible."[1]

Discouraged but not disconsolate, for they had expected this after Judson's report, they went to the bazaar and bargained for linen and other cloth and hastened to a tailor. Their woolens, so necessary in New England's February, were unbearable in the heat and humidity of Calcutta's monsoon season.

Calcutta presented great contrasts. The Government House, parks, and estates of the British officials appeared more elegant than anything the Americans had ever seen at home, but the squalor of the poorly drained Bengali quarters was appalling. Sanitation was nonexistent and it was a most unhealthy city. But it was the capital of India and its largest port. Ships from all over the world were moored at the extensive docks ranging for miles down the Hooghly River, and the ghats, bazaars, and teeming hordes of Bengali fascinated Rice and his associates.

In the cool of the evening, they took a budgerow up the Hooghly to Serampore, two hours' rowing distance, and were cordially greeted by William Ward and Joshua Marshman, Carey's two colleagues. Serampore was a different world from the raucous noise and crowds of Calcutta. The Danes had made this settlement a model colony with wide streets and beautiful homes along the brown Hooghly, a healthy site for the cosmopolitan population of Danes, Germans, Portuguese, Greeks, Sikhs, and Bengali.

The Baptists' settlement was such as the young men were never to see repeated. Carey, Marshman, and Ward had fashioned a unique community, living in separate homes in their compound but eating together in the commons where the new arrivals were quartered. Hall and Rice probably took the two front rooms just vacated by the Judsons, who had moved into the Rolts' house in Calcutta.

This threesome pooled their earnings, apportioned to each family as it had need, and gave all surplus earnings from Carey's teaching, Mrs. Marshman's schools, and Ward's printing, back to the mission, a plan that though patterned after the earlier Moravian missions would surely have failed had not the three men been "worthy of their task and worthy of each other."[2]

In addition to the three homes and commons facing the Hooghly, the mission housed a type-foundery, a paper-mill, and the printing plant, already rebuilt after the 1811 fire. The most notable feature was the elegant gardens of Dr. Carey, Ann Judson reporting, "The garden is as superior to any in America, as America's best is to a common farmer's. It consists of several acres, under the highest cultivation. Fruit, flowers and vegetables grow in abundance. The pineapple grows on a low bush, the plantain on a tall stock, and the cocoanut on a high tree."[3]

Mrs. Ward, "a motherly woman, very active and kind,"[4] supervised the meals, serving as many as one hundred people in the commons dining room, and Mrs. Marshman was headmistress of the school for girls. Mr. Ward was in charge of the printing while Mr. Marshman, linguist and scholar, worked closely with Carey in directing the mission.

On Friday Dr. Carey returned from Calcutta for the weekend, and the men had a conference that lasted far into the evening. The Serampore missionaries were as apprehensive as the Americans about the deportation order. The British arrivals had been given a temporary reprieve, being told they could stay as long as the Director permitted, but there seemed no way to prevent the ejection of the Americans. Yet they were determined not to return home in inglorious defeat. After discussing the rather limited alternatives, "Dr. Carey and Dr. Marshman both think Madagascar the most eligible spot for attempting a mission."[5]

On Sunday Rice's illness returned, aching back and headaches, accompanied by a yellowish caste to his skin and eyes, and the attending physician diagnosed it "the liver complaint." Still ailing, he went the following day to Calcutta and on Thursday he "received a line from Capt. Brown informing me that he is ordered to carry the missionaries back to America, and likewise an order to attend at the police."[6] So he, Hall, and Nott did "attend at the police, hear the Order of Govt. to return on the *Harmony*," but they petitioned once again "to Govt. for leave to depart for the Isle of France (Mauritius)."[7]

On Friday, the twenty-eighth of August, Judson came to Serampore, evidently to consult the Baptists; for the next evening Dr. Marshman informed the others of Judson's intention to be baptized. Already beset with worry about eviction, Judson's decision came as a jolt to the other men. They felt his action was hasty since he had hardly discussed it with them.

But Judson's decision was not as precipitate as it appeared. On the *Caraven* he had begun investigating and had "candidly examined the subject of baptism, but I had strong prejudices against the sect, that is every where spoken against."[8] Of this study, he wrote:

I was going forth to proclaim the glad news of salvation through Jesus Christ. I hoped that my ministrations would be blessed to the conversion of souls. In that case, I felt that I should have no hesitation concerning my duty to the converts, it being plainly commanded in Scripture, that such are to be baptised, and received into church fellowship. But how, thought I, am I to treat the unconverted children and domestics of the converts? Are they to be considered members of the church of Christ, by virtue of the conversion of the head of their family, or not? If they are, ought I not to treat them as such? After they are baptised, can I consistently set them aside as aliens from the commonwealth of Israel, until they are re-admitted? If they are not to be considered members of the church, can I consistently administer to them the initiating ordinance of the church?[9]

When Adoniram first broached the subject to Ann, she was adamant in stating that she'd never become a Baptist, even if he were to do so. The day they arrived in Bengal, she recorded in her diary that Adoniram was studying baptism and "if he should renounce his former sentiments, he must offend his friends at home, hazard his reputation, and, what is still more trying, be separated from his missionary associates." But later she admitted, "I have been examining the subject of baptism for sometime past, and contrary to my prejudices and my wishes, am compelled to believe that believers' baptism alone is found in Scripture . . . If ever I

73

sought to know the truth; if ever I looked up to the Father of lights; if ever I gave up myself to the inspired word, I have done so during this investigation."[10] So the Judsons found their way to the Baptists through a study of the Scriptures and largely through that alone.

Their baptism forced another decision upon the distraught group, for it would hardly be feasible for them to stay together now. There must be two American missions. So when a ship bound for Mauritius, the *Adele,* was found, Rice, Hall, and the Notts booked passage, thinking to join the Newells on the island and expecting the Judsons to go elsewhere to work.

A few days later Felix Carey arrived from Burma. Each of Carey's sons was a tentmaker, having needed an occupation to support their missionary labors. Each had gone to a pioneer and difficult field—Jabez to Amboyna, William to Katma, Felix to Rangoon. The officials and viceroy of Burma, loath to accept missionaries, suffered Felix to stay because of his medical knowledge—he had vaccinated the royal children—and also because he had taken a Burmese for his second wife. Still later he had entered the king's service, his father lamenting, *"Felix is shriveled from a missionary into an ambassador."*[11]

Felix was taller than his father and spoke animatedly. There was a dualism about him. He was at once dreamy and impulsive; adventurous, yet something of a mystic. He was unlike any missionary the new arrivals had ever seen or dreamed about—part Oriental and part English—and now as he talked, they were both fascinated and repelled by his description of life in the empire to the east. All actualities—no glossing over was done. The viceroy was capricious and cruel, an absolute despot with life and death in his hands; the people were childlike and vicious; the cities swarmed with vermin and were unspeakably filthy, the houses unsanitary, prices exorbitant. Felix spoke with his eye on the Judsons, later revealing to his father, "They are just cut out for this Mission. I thought so, as soon as I first met them."[12] Still, his portrayal filled them with dismay.

But where were they to go? Surely an all-wise God did not allow them to come all this distance only to return home in humiliating defeat. Yet every door seemed closed; the time when Wilberforce would stand in Parliament and staunchly defend the corps at Serampore was still a year away.

Even the submissive Hall cried out, "Eighteen hundred years ago, it was solemnly commanded by Jesus Christ, that his gospel should be preached to every creature, but now the British parliament is debating whether it may or may not be published to 60,000,000 of their heathen subjects in Asia. Is not this something like what Dr. Backus says 'that men sometimes form themselves into a lower house to check the proceedings of the Almighty.' "[13]

Day after day the *Adele* did not sail and Rice began studying baptism again. Here was another in the strange—or was it providential?—series of events which guided him toward the Baptists.

Upon arrival in Calcutta, he certainly had not become a Baptist. Johns thought he sensed some anxiety on Hall's part regarding their position but never suspected Rice's doubt. Johns had not converted Rice to his side, being totally unsuited to do so, but their lively sessions had forced Rice to reexamine his position on certain points.

Judson said Rice "arrived in Calcutta about six weeks after those of us who sailed from Salem. At that time, I was deeply involved in the subject of baptism, which I had begun to investigate on board ship, and I soon learned that some of the passengers from Philadelphia, were in a similar position, and that Mr. Rice had rather distinguished himself, by reading every thing within his reach, and manifesting uncommon obstinacy in defending the old system."[14]

Even the perceptive Judson did not detect that Rice's "uncommon obstinacy" covered inner uneasiness. Rice signed a joint letter, with Nott and Hall, to the Board expressing regret at Judson's decision and stating that it was a "trying event." When Rice did make his decision, this recently posted letter to the Board left him vulnerable to the charge of impetuosity and being too easily swayed.

On September 27, in the Lall Bazar Chapel, Judson preached his famous sermon on baptism. With all the scriptural backing, logic, and appeal he could muster, he discussed the word "baptize" and its New Testament meaning, citing concessions of imminent theologians such as Luther, Alstedius, Beza, Casaubon, and Baxter. He then dealt with objections, such as the baptism of the Philippian jailor's household. Carey's appraisal: "The best I ever heard on the subject."

To his father, Judson wrote that Rice was "influenced, I am certain, not by my persuasions, but by the operations of his own independent mind."[15]

Perhaps Judson was correct in surmising that his decision did not sway Rice, but it doubtless impressed him for he held Judson in deep regard. And whatever Judson's purpose in preaching his sermon on baptism, he would have been intrigued by Rice's entry that night. "I have some difficulty upon this subject," he confided for the first time, "which I find some reluctance to disclose to my brethren. May the Lord himself lead me in his own right way."[16]

Rice still might have remained a Congregationalist had not several events forced his confinement, giving him time to study.

The *Adele* did not sail for week after week and Rice suffered a relapse of the hepatitis. By nature an activist, he began moving about each time he felt better and each time the illness returned. To receive better care, he moved from the commons in Serampore to Calcutta. And he moved into the Rolts' house with the Judsons. Mr. Rolt was an architect and Mrs. Rolt's first husband had been a Baptist minister whose fine library was in the home and had played a part in Judson's change to the Baptist faith.

Dr. Russell, Rice's physician, ordered him to avoid the enervating midday heat and to remain in his room except in the early morning and late evening. So he spent his days in study, the Judsons seeing him only at meals. Rice wanted to discuss baptism with Judson who remembered, "At first he was disposed to give me fierce battle; but I held off, and recommended him to betake himself to the Bible and prayer."[17] Since the Greek New Testament had been the deciding agent in Judson's change of sentiment, authorities he later read merely confirming what he found, Judson advised the same for Rice.

Throughout September Rice was undecided and on October 8 he noted that he was "still pursuing investigations respecting baptism."[18] But the following Sunday he added that he had revealed to "Bros. Hall and Nott this morning some of my apprehensions respecting baptism, made it a subject of united prayer with them," and also "told Dr. Marshman some of my late views on baptism."[19]

That very day Carey wrote William Staughton in Philadelphia, with whom he had corresponded since their days together in Leicester, England, recounting how Rice came early one morning before Carey had arisen to borrow a Greek New Testament and to ask questions. Carey concluded that he thought Rice had "fully made up his mind on baptism."[20]

So, in the solitariness of his own room Rice came last to what

Judson studied first, the Greek New Testament. The next day he wrote his brother Asaph:

I have just mentioned that brother Judson has become a Baptist. As I have here with him considerable means for the purpose, I am endeavoring to investigate thoroughly, the subject of the sacred ordinance of baptism . . . I conceive it to be *possible,* that a revolution in my own mind, similar to that which my dear brother and sister have experienced, may take place. Should this be the case, I shall in all probability, go with them to Java. It would be peculiarly pleasing to me, to be associated with them in the mission; but my affection for them can by no means determine me to become a Baptist, without the conviction that Baptists are in the right; nor can I on the other hand be deterred from conscientiously examining the subject, nor from following what really appears to be the truth; notwithstanding any unpleasant considerations attending such a change of sentiment in my situation. And it is a principle with me, that truth can be no loser by the most rigorous examination, . . . May the Lord himself lead me in the way in which he would have me to go.[21]

Yet eight days later Rice was "not yet satisfied on the subject of baptism."[22] But October 23, he wrote Dr. Worcester "informing him, and thereby the Board of my late change of sentiment upon the subject of baptism," and the following day he "held a pecuniary settlement with Brs. Hall and Nott."[23]

He told the Board that his detailed study of baptism had resulted in a "conviction, that those persons only, who give credible evidence of piety, are proper subjects; and that immersion is the only proper mode of Christian baptism."[24]

Two days later, he "addressed a letter to Rev. Drs. Carey and Marshman, and Rev. Mr. Ward, requesting baptism," and noted that "Br. Nott thinks I have done wrong in requesting baptism so soon. Br. Hall of the same opinion to whom I communicated the design to do so, this morning."[25]

"Little did I think, dear brother," he wrote to Asaph, "when conversing with you respecting Mr. G. [Grout], that I should so soon belong to the same denomination with him; a denomination, which I had thought, in no small degree, reprehensible for party feeling, and sectarian conduct . . . It has, indeed, been no small trial to me to change my sentiments, in a situation so conspicuous and delicate, and so highly responsible: . . ."[26]

Rice was baptized by William Ward in the Lall Bazar Chapel in Calcutta on Sunday, November 1.

10. Return Home

It was the most unpropitious time of their lives to make the change, for they were half a world and many months' voyage away from America, and they did not even know if the Baptists would accept and support them. American Baptists were not organized as a national group; they had few associations and less money than the Congregationalists.

But there was little time to mull over this anxiety. Each day brought more harassment from the police. In August the authorities had deferred the Judsons' departure on the missionaries' promise that as soon as their colleagues arrived, all would leave company territory. Now matters must be faced, for the authorities could no longer be placated. Even Carey thought their mission doomed to frustration and suggested they return to America and go as missionaries to the Indians in the West or into the Mississippi Valley. However, he had written Thomas Baldwin in Boston and William Staughton in Philadelphia, commending the Judsons to the Baptists' watchcare and urging their support; and now he wrote them with the same plea for Rice.

Rice was still bothered by fever, headaches, and ague as the evenings came on. He was beginning a long epistle to Hall and Nott concerning baptism when, on the seventeenth of November, they received a summons from the police to send "Brs. Hall, Nott, Judson and myself to England"[1] in the fleet which was leaving shortly. Action was expedient but there were few alternatives. The *Adele* had tarried in port so long that Hall, Nott, and Rice had canceled their passage only to see it sail almost immediately.

Having heard that the new governor at Bombay, Sir Evan Nepean, was friendly to missions, Hall and the Notts now engaged passage on the *Commerce,* bound for that place. But the Calcutta authorities were adamant, and it was only by the most ingenious contriving on their part and the collusion of Captain Arbuthnot that they were able to evade the order—a tactic alien to Hall's nature and one he felt obliged to explain in later years. But they were desperate. Better stowaways than return to England and ignominious defeat. They hid aboard the *Commerce* in the harbor while the Judsons and Rice were eluding the police to board another vessel, *La Belle Creole*.

Brother Judson and myself engaged a passage for the Isle of France the next day after being notified of the order of government . . . the magistrate of police, Judge Martin, having promised Doctor Marshman that he would grant us a pass if we would actually engage a passage; and indeed, said that this was the best thing we could do. The next day after, he refused to grant the pass; but again promised it to the master of the ship with whom we had contracted for our passage, that he would grant it; but yet refused again the next day.[2]

Still hopeful of the pass, they spent Saturday in transferring their possessions to the *Creole,* barely escaping the clutches of the police "who were sent to put us on board a small craft, destined to take us down the river to the fleet. The officers went indeed to the house, while sister Judson and a part of brother Judson's baggage were still there; but they were gone when he returned for the remainder of his baggage."[3]

On Sunday the *Creole* began to go down river, which roused "strong hopes of getting away without falling into the hands of Government."[4] On Monday, though still only a few miles below Calcutta, they began to breathe more easily—only to be apprehended late in the evening with an order instructing the captain to weigh anchor and wait because he had taken passengers remanded to England. This portended a search of the vessel, so the captain suggested that Judson and Rice go ashore and remain until the police had visited. They rowed to a tavern on shore, spending Tuesday "in great anxiety at Budge Budge, but not without divine comfort."[5] Late in the evening, Ann rowed to the inn and the three decided on another effort to gain the coveted pass. Rice, though hardly able, was elected to go, and left that night for Calcutta. Vainly he besought the magistrate for the pass, returning to Budge Budge the next evening, empty-handed.

Favorable winds had risen; the *Creole's* captain and owner were now eager to sail, and the hapless missionaries were obliged to retrieve their baggage and with it their last hope of sailing to Mauritius. But they were determined not to return to Calcutta and defeat so proceeded downriver to Fultah, and Nancy supervised the transfer of their possessions from the *Creole,* the men fearing to board the ship, the captain assuring them that a woman would not be apprehended. Rice went up again to Calcutta, this time to beg a passport to Ceylon, but again his efforts were futile. Upon returning to Fultah, they were eating supper in the riverside inn when an envelope was delivered with the long-sought pass from Mr. Martin. What or who prevailed on him to issue the oft-promised permit they were never to know, for they hastened to overtake the *Creole* anchored at Saugur for refueling. Gratefully they sighted her and climbed aboard, almost exhausted.

For Rice it was another slow voyage, the ship plying against strong winds. But during the seven weeks, he and Judson came to know each other better and cemented a lifelong friendship. The crew and other passengers were not congenial nor even conversant, and the three were thrown back upon themselves for entertainment. Judson was moody and often despondent and Rice's affable ways were a foil for his dispirited musings over their plight. The insurmountable, which brings out the noble in some men, revealed Rice in his best self during their trials. His heroic exertions during the interval when they were so distraught, even though he was still half-invalid, impressed Adoniram. In all their adversity, he was cheerful and hopeful and now aboard ship he brought out his flute and played the hours and their worries away. Judson knew they would be a winning team and thereafter felt Rice and he were fitted to serve together.

Rice was still remembering Rebecca, and now that the three were to be associated in a joint mission, Ann wistfully longed for female companionship. Whatever the nature of their understanding about the broken engagement, it is evident that Rice did not think the decision irrevocable or final; for ten days before he was baptized, Ann wrote a friend back home:

Mr. Rice is engaged to a Miss Eaton in America, who he hoped would accompany him to India. But as she had so little time to prepare for so important an undertaking, she concluded not to come. Since our arrival here and change of sentiment, since it is probable I shall be the only female in the mission, we have written urgent letters to have her follow us as soon as an opportunity offers. . . .

Let me once more request my dear Mrs. C. you will do all in your power toward having Rebecca Eaton come out to us. She is eminently qualified to be in a mission and will be a very great assistance to Mr. Rice whose health is very delicate.[6]

To bolster his entreaties to Rebecca, Rice also wrote her former brother-in-law, Dr. Emerson of Beverly, a very long letter, telling of his change of sentiment and his illness and requesting his help:

That I may really be prudent and cautious respecting my health I shall probably need frequently the influence and advice of a dear and judicious friend. On this account—on account of sister Judson—from my feeling she would be greatly useful in the mission—and *especially from my attachment to her,* I very much wish that Rebekak were with me . . . as it is, I very much wish that she may follow me as soon as possible. And again I very much wish you to encourage, . . .[7]

Rice assured Dr. Emerson that it would not be improper for Rebekak to travel out alone; but he may have sensed that his becoming a Baptist would not enhance his position in Rebekak's eyes, for he added:

I hope that my change of sentiment may not be any objection to her coming, as I have the fullest persuasion that we should live happily together. I cannot expect the Board of Commissioners to pay her passage, but would hope that money enough for the purpose might easily be collected among the Baptists in Beverly, Salem, and Boston.[8]

Every time he saw the quickening look of fondness between Adoniram and Ann, his thoughts turned to Rebecca. But she was not the adventurous soul that Ann was, and it was difficult for those back home to understand the trio's seemingly sudden change of denominations. Ann had been reluctant to become a Baptist even when Adoniram explained in detail his reasons for becoming one, at first telling him defiantly that she would never become a Baptist even if he should. Now Rice was expecting Rebecca to acquiesce in his decision with him halfway around the world.

En route to Port Louis the three weighed their predicament from every angle. They did not know where they could eventually settle. They did not know whether or not they could depend on support from American Baptists. They did not know if Rebecca would join them.

At the end of the seven weeks' voyage, they were again at Port Louis, anticipating a joyous reunion with the Newells, only to have a grieving and stricken Samuel come aboard and sob out his tragedy.

Like the *Creole,* the *Gillespie* had encountered contrary winds, had sprung a leak, and the first week in September when they had been at sea a month, had put in at Coringa on the Coromandel Coast. Harriet had been ill with dysentery and fever but seemed to regain her strength at Coringa before they sailed again on September 17. On October 8, on the floor of the small cabin and attended only by her husband, she gave birth to a baby girl. Five days later a sudden storm caught the *Gillespie,* and Harriet and the baby were drenched with rain. Her baby, frail and premature, caught cold and died and Harriet also became ill, soon evincing the symptoms of tuberculosis that had claimed so many victims in her family. She gradually weakened and upon arriving in Port Louis, Samuel rented a small house, engaged two physicians to attend her, and did all he could; but it was obvious to everyone, including Harriet, that her short life was nearly over. Touched by a euphoria that softened the parting for her, she assured her husband of devout faith and resignation in going so soon and died seven weeks after her confinement. Brokenhearted, Samuel wrote her widowed mother back in Haverhill, detailing the last moments of her life, trying to explain the series of events leading to her death and why they elected to journey at such a time.

Missionaries' wives paid oftenest with their lives or those of their little ones in those pioneer years. The graves were to outnumber the converts in the Eastern mission in the first years, and lovely Harriet, barely nineteen, was the first of the group to lie beneath Asian soil.

Rice and the Judsons moved into the small rented home with Newell and they all looked daily for a passage to Java or Ceylon. Samuel preferred to go to Ceylon and finally sailed for the island on February 24, from whence he eventually joined Hall and Nott in Bombay.

As Judson and Rice discussed the limited possibilities, a new idea began to form in their minds. They began to think that some contact with the American Baptists was desirable, and while they were waiting for passage to another land, why not let one of them return to America and feel out the Baptists about support, rally help if it were not immediately forthcoming, and then return to the field of labor on which the other had settled? Obviously it would be easier and less expensive for Rice, unmarried, to do this than for Judson. Also, he could personally persuade Rebecca to return with him and she would not have to undertake the long voyage alone. On the eleventh of March, four days before he embarked for America, he wrote to Marshman:

An opportunity of a cheap and probably quick passage to America offers, and we are all of the opinion that it may, to a considerable extent, subserve the missionary cause for me to visit our Baptist brethren in that country. I have indeed some private reasons for wishing to make such a visit.

He tells Marshman that private reasons alone would not justify the time and expense of the trip, but he hopes

to kindle the zeal or if it be already kindled, to increase its ardour, of our brethren in the United States; bring about the formation of a Baptist Missionary Society . . .
Being already about one-third of the way from India to the United States, I hope to be able to pass to that country, effect the objects in view there, and rejoin Brother Judson in a year and a half, possibly less time; at farthest, within the compass of two years, if it please God to make my way prosperous. Our views of different missionary fields at present are such, that on my return I shall expect to find Brother Judson at Penang . . . But if calculations deceive me, and, on returning, I should find Brother Judson at Rangoon, instead of Penang, I shall not be greatly disappointed if only his situation shall be such that I can rejoin him in the mission, this last consideration I cannot think of relinquishing.[9]

Rice left with the Judsons all the small pieces of furniture, books, and other supplies which they had bought together and on March 15 bade them farewell, embarked on the *Donna Maria,* and arrived at St. Salvador, Brazil, on May 4. Here he found a small group of Americans and stayed in the home of the American consul, Henry Hill. Nothing of moment happened while he was in St. Salvador except that the Hills arranged for baptismal rites for their children and became piqued when Rice informed them that he could not administer baptism to an infant.

He remained in St. Salvador two months, for "the vessel in which I proceeded from the Isle of France [Mauritius] to St. Salvador, after a few weeks, set sail for Salem: but I was not permitted to join her. She had a quantity of salpetre on board, which was a contraband article, and the proprietor conceived it not safe for a person to be taken as a passenger, who would not, as he supposed, swear for the truth, in case the vessel should be overhauled, in order to save the cargo."[10]

On July 17 he sailed for New York aboard a vessel carrying about a hundred prisoners of war and several other passengers. He conducted divine services each Sunday and "about a fortnight after leaving the harbor, one of the sailors died, I made an exhortation . . . one of the sailors . . . was awakened by that exhortation . . . not long after arriving in this country, he became a member of a Baptist church in Philadelphia, and has since become a preacher."[11] Another sailor was converted under his shipboard ministry. Rice arrived in New York, September 7, 1813, and was warmly welcomed in the Baptist churches.

11. Convention

Rice's ship docked in New York on the seventh of September and the following Sunday he preached in the Oliver Street Baptist Church. Among the squirming lads in the audience was one William Hague who remembered the silence and awe of the Sunday long afterward when he had become a prominent minister: "Never did an audience gather with a more curious interest combined with profound emotions than did the assembly in Oliver Street to listen to the narative and appeal of Rev. Rice."[1]

Early in the week Rice hurried to Boston to appear on Wednesday before the annual meeting of the American Board of Commissioners, for he "had determined not to have any thing to do with the Baptists: nor to enter into any arrangements implying a dereliction of my connection with the American Board of Commissioners for Foreign Missions, till my relation with that body was adjusted, or rather regularly dissolved."[2]

In what surely was one of the most difficult speeches of his life, Luther spoke for an hour and a half and placed a formal statement of his change to the Baptist position in the hands of Dr. Worcester; however, he was dismissed from their presence without receiving a reply to either his speech or his statement. Lingering several days for a formal termination of his relation to them, Rice finally learned from Dr. Dwight that measures "to the effect of severing the relationship" had been taken. Jeremiah Evarts conversed with him early the next week, saying the Board members "had voted that they considered the relation between me and the Board dissolved from the date of my letter from Calcutta, announcing the fact of my change of sentiment,"[3] adding that they wished Rice to refund the money expended on his outfit and passage to India. This *viva voce* request from the secretary was the only one he ever received and since he raised most of his own passage and outfit money across denominational lines, he seemed to feel no obligation to return it.

Though Rice remained friends with many of the men on the American Board, corresponding with Dr. Morse, Dr. Stuart, and others, he was not viewed kindly by some of them. It was easier to forgive Judson who was many miles away than Rice who was present and constantly working for the Baptists. The following year their annual report stated:

The Committee has no disposition to impeach the sincerity of these men, but they regret that the subject was not examined before so late a day. Nevertheless the foundation of God standeth sure. We repose our hopes on this in spite of the instability which we regret to record, but against which no human foresight could provide.[4]

After seeing the American Board, Rice then called on Rev. Thomas Baldwin of Boston's Second Baptist Church and Rev. Lucius Bolles of Salem, whom Judson had written as soon as he and Ann were baptized. Upon receiving Judson's startling news, Dr. Baldwin had led the Boston Baptist Missionary Society to underwrite the Judsons' support; and now this group welcomed Rice warmly and graciously. Dr. Baldwin invited leading Baptist ministers to his house to discuss the situation. Outside Boston, there were missionary societies in Haverhill, Providence, and in Salem where Dr. Bolles had led in forming the "Salem Bible and Foreign Mission Translation Society" in April, 1812. Dr. Bolles had been present at the Salem Tabernacle ordination and had conversed with Judson, who suggested that the Baptists organize such a society. Upon hearing from Adoniram, the Salem Society had voted to divert one half of their funds from the Serampore translations to Judson's support.

In September the Salem and Haverhill Societies sent representatives to Boston where, in Elder Ensign Lincoln's home, they conferred about bringing the existing societies or associations into cooperation. Dr. Daniel Sharp and Dr. Baldwin revealed that they had contacted the New York and Philadelphia Baptists in an attempt to secure their cooperation but had received no response.

This news did not faze Rice, since another man's failure was often his challenge, due not so much to an exaggerated opinion of his ability to persuade as to his optimism about other people's willingness. He told them of his warm welcome in the Oliver Street church and of its personable Welsh pastor, John Williams. He had also been introduced to several notable Philadelphia Baptists prior to his sailing the previous year. The Philadelphia Baptist Association, America's oldest, had societies within it that had donated generously to the English Baptist work at Serampore. Certainly they would participate if rightly accquainted with the purpose and plan.

These mission society representatives instructed Rice to travel south to New York and Philadelphia to solicit the churches' interest and cooperation in a joint enterprise, and to suggest that delegates convene in the near future to formulate the plan and federation. They reckoned that only New England, New York, and Philadelphia societies could be depended upon; but Rice became convinced, either before leaving Boston or as he journeyed, that the southerners would respond if the appeal was carried to them.

Rice left Boston on September 29 on this first southern trip, with credentials and letters of introduction from the Boston-area Baptists. En route he stopped in Northborough to spend the Sabbath and visit his parents, of whom he wrote: "Glad to see my parents once more, and to find them in comfortable health. My brother, anxious to know the ground of my becoming a Baptist, is I hope, satisfied; after some conversation on the subject that I am able to render a reason in this matter."[5] Luther coveted Asaph's understanding, well knowing that his change must have seemed abrupt and embarrassing to the family since they were unaware of any contemplation of such action before hearing of his decision. As Judson admitted to his own father, "I well knew that when I descended into the baptistry I left my former character at the bottom of the water."[6]

On this visit the Rev. Mr. Whitney invited Rice to preach in his boyhood church, and Rice revealed his awareness of the local attitude by his text from Paul: "I am not mad."[7] Rice and Whitney remained friends and on a subsequent visit, Luther stayed overnight in the Northborough minister's home. Always he mailed Mr. Whitney copies of the missionary papers.

Again in New York City, Rice found the churches eager to join the New Englanders in a general meeting. The Rev. Mr. Williams was the most eminent pulpiteer among them, and he enthusiastically supported the proposal Rice brought. Judge Matthias Tallmadge, in whose home Rice stayed thereafter when in New York, was another leading Baptist. He was a district judge, affluent and cultured, Yale-trained, prominent in Baptist councils, and the son-in-law of Vice-President George Clinton. Frail in health but vigorous in spirit, he spent his winters in Charleston and was an intimate friend of Dr. Richard Furman there. He could assist Rice in persuading the southern churches to send delegates to a central meeting, and it may have been Judge Tallmadge who confirmed Rice's resolution to venture southward beyond Philadelphia.

He arrived in Philadelphia the first day of their annual associational meeting and was invited to take a seat in the deliberations and to speak.

American Baptists had never heard such a challenge as Rice brought. In the unique way that Rice and Judson had been thrust upon them as already-commissioned missionaries, it was as if Providence was speaking. They dare not reject the appeal. A committee of eleven was appointed to consider its import and they reported favorably, urging the churches to plan a meeting of delegates to form some kind of general organization.

Among the Philadelphia societies and churches that had forwarded funds to aid the Serampore translations, the implementer and mover was Dr. William Staughton, pastor of the Sansom Street Baptist Church. An Englishman who had been associated with Carey, Fuller, Pearce, and Knight in the Kettering meetings and present when the English Society was formed in Widow Wallis' parlor, Staughton was cosmopolitan in his thinking. Educated at Bristol College, he had immigrated to South Carolina upon the invitation of Dr. Furman of Charleston and from there had moved to Burlington, New Jersey, then to Philadelphia's First Baptist Church, and still later to the Sansom Street Church. In each place he kept a school for young ministers, preached to crowds, and led in every missionary endeavor. During this October, Rice and William Staughton formed a friendship that was to bridge many years and weather many vicissitudes.

Rice also met Dr. Henry Holcombe, the immense, burly pastor of the First Baptist Church, a southerner who had come to Philadelphia only a few years before, a forceful and energetic man who readily assented to the call for a general meeting of American Baptists.

Another former pastor of the First Baptist Church, elderly William Rogers, then professor of oratory and belles lettres at the University of Pennsylvania, was a third distinguished Philadelphian who offered his support. And a fourth who expressed cordial interest was a handsome young man, Horatio G. Jones, pastor at Lower Merion and one of Dr. Staughton's former pupils.

These four joined other Philadelphia Baptists in assuring Rice of their support of the proposed plan of union and tendered Philadelphia as an ideal place for both northern and southern Baptists to convene, since it was accessible by both land and sea.

Taking the stage to Washington and Baltimore, Rice found there the same readiness to unite in missionary work. It seemed that Baptists were awaiting his coming to congeal sentiment and thrill them into action. No one was better suited than he to arouse churches and persuade individuals of the needs of the mission fields, for "he was the only American who had gone out into the darkness of paganism and had returned to tell us what existed there."[8] Of the five who ventured out to India, Rice was the most accomplished as a speaker. Not the scholar Judson was, he surpassed Judson in poise and pulpit magnetism; it was a happy stroke of fate or providence that turned Rice homeward to make the sweeping appeal for their mutual support and left Judson in the Orient to perform the tedious and exacting translating.

In Washington City, Rice met Obadiah B. Brown, a post office clerk during the week and pastor of the First Baptist Church. Brown ardently favored the proposed convention and proffered Washington as the logical site since the Federal Government was there and it was centrally located. They sketched plans for a local missionary society and soon after Rice's departure from the city, "The Washington Baptist Society for Foreign Missions" was organized.

On a cool evening in mid-October, William Crane, a young businessman recently moved to Richmond, was instructing illiterate Negro members of the First Baptist Church. This evening school was held in the schoolroom of Rev. Jacob Grigg, an Englishman who had served briefly as a missionary to Sierra Leone and who immigrated to Richmond after becoming embroiled in a political dispute for which he was banished from that country.

Into this gathering strode a "tall, interesting stranger on his way to Georgia."[9] Rice told this group of his journey to India, how he became a Baptist, and of his return home and effort to gather support for himself and Judson on the foreign field. Among his patient listeners were two Negro men who would be the first American Baptist missionaries to Africa.

The Bostonians had written letters ahead to Rev. Robert Baylor Semple, longtime pastor of the Bruington Church in nearby King and Queen County; to Rev. Andrew Broaddus, beloved pastor in Caroline County; and to other Baptist leaders in and near Richmond, apprising them of Rice's coming and the purpose of his tour.

Two weeks later, on October 28, local Baptists formed "The Richmond Baptist Society for propagating the Gospel in India and other Heathen Countries."

By this time, one month after leaving Boston, Rice was hurrying south to the Charleston Associational meeting, held at Society Hill that year. Here he met Esquire John Wilson, a friend for the rest of his life, and the distinguished Dr. Richard Furman. Wealthy and highly esteemed for his character and pulpit abilities, Dr. Furman introduced the subject of Rice's coming at this annual meeting; his support tendered to the proposal was tantamount to acceptance by the body. Measures were adopted to bring the scheduled meeting to the attention of all the churches in the tidewater area. The Charleston Association had fostered missionary work in the back country and among the Indians, and for half a century had maintained an education society, sending ministerial candidates to Brown or elsewhere to study, sometimes privately under trained ministers.

For many years Dr. Furman had corresponded with English Baptists and with those in other parts of America. In him Rice sensed a preeminent leader for the whole denomination and immediately urged him to be a delegate to the spring meeting. But "Mr. Madison's War," so unpopular along the seaboard, was still disrupting sea passage to the north and Dr. Furman indicated he could not be absent from his congregation the many weeks required to make the trip by chaise or stage.

Rice had used public conveyances until he came to Charleston, but he now rented or bought a chaise. He had decided to itinerate in the Charleston-Savannah district and to visit other leading ministers and churches.

This circuit took him north, first to Georgetown where lived the venerable "flying preacher," Edmund Botsford, a founder of the Baptist denomination in both Georgia and South Carolina. The talkative and affable Reverend Botsford gave Rice much sanguine advice from his own days of circuit riding among the churhes in the area.

Rice visited the Vernon, Augusta, and Savannah churches,[10] meeting in Georgia two men destined to be caught up with him in the vanguard of Baptist organizational life. His most cheering surprise was young William Bullein Johnson, a South Carolinian whom he met in Savannah. To Rice's delight, Johnson was a man who viewed Baptists with the eye of a seer and a statesman, having already drafted a constitution and bylaws for a national convention. He proposed that the delegates meet to plan a general union on a convention basis, not simply to form a board, as some had felt was the only possibility.

The other person with whom Rice was to share long and intimate accord was Jesse Mercer, destined to be "Mr. Baptist" in Georgia.[11]

"How is Mr. Mercer?" asked Dr. Staughton of a Georgian in later years.

"He is well," came the reply.

"He exerts a great influence in your State," continued Dr. Staughton.

"His word is *law*," the Georgian replied.

"I am sure," said the doctor in return, "it is *gospel*."

Mercer's residence at Powelton and Washington served as Rice's southern home in later years, and Rice designated Mercer as his favorite pulpiteer. Mercer's life and wealth—acquired through his second marriage to the Gentile widow of a Jewish merchant—was to be wholly expended in the Baptist cause. Every object dear to the heart of Rice was remembered by Mercer, for "aside from his father, the one who most influenced his interest in missions and Christian education was Luther Rice."[12]

Johnson and William T. Brantly, as officers of the Savannah Baptist Society for Foreign Missions, aroused public interest through the distribution of a "Circular Letter" which was republished in the North in the *Massachusetts Baptist Magazine*. Readers were asked if "the Divine Providence, so evidently marking out the path for us, be mistaken? Can the Lord's work so clearly made known in this dispensation, be misinterpreted?" The circular continued:

Since the defection of our dear Rice, Judson and Lady . . . several Missionary Societies have been formed by the Baptists in America. These societies have as their object the establishment and support of foreign missions and it is contemplated that delegates from them all will convene in some central situation in the United States for the purpose of organizing an efficient and practicable plan, on which the energies of the whole Baptist denomination in America, may be elicited, combined and directed, in one sacred effort, for sending the word of life to idolatrous lands. What a sublime spectacle will this convention present! A numerous body of the Lord's peoples, embracing in their connexion between 100,000 and 200,000 souls, all rising in obedience to their Lord, and meeting, by delegation, in one august assembly; solemnly to engage in one sacred effort for effectuating the great command, "Go ye into all the world and preach the Gospel to every creature" . . . we affectionately and cordially write you, to embrace the privilege of uniting in so glorious a cause so divine a work.

In a similar circular letter the Philadelphia Society stated:

On the conviction wrought upon the minds of our brethren Judson and Rice, in India, respecting Christian baptism, and their cheerful submission thereto, you have already been apprised. This change of sentiment in those men of God, must convince us of the necessity of imitating the laudable examples already set us by others of the American Baptists, in giving every encouragement and assistance towards the furtherance of such benevolent designs, as are connected with the bringing into the fold of Jesus, the far separated, and distant members of the same redeemed family.

As Rice traveled, met the men, and recorded their response, he wrote his findings to the Boston group which had commissioned him, apprising them of his cordial reception and inquiring about a possible time and place of the proposed meeting. Would the third Wednesday in May be a propitious time? Both Philadelphia and Washington had offered to be hosts. Which place seemed the best site?

While the New England Baptists had initiated the proposed meeting and had already underwritten Judson's support, Baptists in the South far outnumbered them. The site of the meeting should be a place to which they could easily travel.

Bolles answered Luther's query, expressing gratitude for his strenuous exertions and proposing:

For myself I think Philadelphia must become the central point, and the residence of most of the executive members of the general society. We must have in some one place, a few men, to whom the immediate management of the whole concern may be intrusted. Brethren widely separated, cannot act with that concert, promptness, and decision, which a concern of this nature and importance demands. Will each of the societies formed at the south, send *one* or *more* to the contemplated meeting in Philadelphia? I think the time you have proposed for the meeting will be as favorable as any one that could have been named.

He further inquired:

Do you hear any thing from Kentucky and the western states? There are many Baptists in those parts. Take some measures, if you can, to excite them to co-operation.[13]

Rice was soliciting for the mission during all this time, reporting to Furman that since leaving Charleston the collections were not large, "ammounting in four Sabbaths only to about $250, as in these times of difficulty, however, are well not [sic] to despise the day of small things."[14]

While Rice was in Augusta, his horse was frightened and ran away, wrecking his chaise, but the kind people raised $166 to replace the vehicle.

Leaving Savannah in mid-January, he spent another weekend in Charleston with Dr. Furman and his church. The congregation voted to give their pastor a leave of absence extending through the summer so that he could attend the May convention. Soon Dr. Furman was writing the Washington group that although their invitation was welcomed, the South Carolinians "consider Philadelphia as the Place designed by Providence as where a Board of Directors should be formed to be the seat of the mission and there the most proper for the Meeting of the Convention." He added, "Our body have nominated and are about to delegate the Honorable Judge Tallmadge of New York and myself to be delegates."[15]

So, the prevailing judgment deemed Philadelphia the proper place to meet. This was a fortunate decision, although forethought could not have known that Washington City would be entered by the redcoats during the summer, its capitol and White House burned.

By the first of February, Rice was again in North Carolina where he wrote Judge Tallmadge from Raleigh on the eighth: "In this place, I am happy to learn that measures have already been taken to bring about the formation of a 'North Carolina Society for Foreign Missions.'"

He urged Judge Tallmadge to be in Philadelphia for the May Convention and, still apprehensive about Dr. Furman's coming, added:

I am particularly solicitous that Dr. Furman shall be among the number of delegates . . . His weight of character will very much contribute to make that impression of the importance of the business which ought to be made . . . his wisdom and experience would equally contribute toward devising the best practicable plan.

The Savannah Society of whose Circular Address and Constitution your kindness allowed me to beg your acceptance, have appointed as their delegate, the Rev. Mr. Johnson of Savannah, who is also the President of that Society and a man of distinguished worth. The Boston Society also have appointed as their delegate the Rev. Mr. Baldwin, President of the Boston Society.[16]

In North Carolina at the Still Bank Meeting House on March 19, "The North Carolina Baptist Society for Foreign Missions" was formed. Stopping in Washington on April 10, Rice addressed Congress, whose members slipped $67 for the mission into his pocket.

As May drew near there was an air of excitement in many a Baptist household. From Virginia Robert Semple wrote Rice, "I shall go if possible . . . I'll try especially to come if Grigg comes . . . Old Father Leland is among us at present."[17] Both Semple and Grigg came and brought "Old Father Leland," who preached a "very long sermon" the evening before the delegates convened.

Those traveling from the deep South were on the road several weeks prior to the convening of delegates; roads were poor in the that part of the country where the waterways were more frequently used. The first day of April, Dr. Furman wrote Edmund Botsford that since so many had urged him to attend, he had reversed his earlier decision: "I have fully determined to attempt it; and shall probably set out on next Wednesday taking Statesburg in my way. It may be I shall be delayed till Monday following. Judge Tallmadge and his Lady intending to leave Town on Wednesday and having delayed their setting out a few Days, probably, with a View of having my guidance to the Hills, (of Santee), operate as a reason."[18]

Pecuniary reasons prevented Botsford's attending, but he went in spirit, writing his young Timothy at Columbia, William Bullein Johnson, some candid and charming advice:

Georgetown, April 16, (a cold day) 1814 Dear Son Johnson. . . . Art thou on thy way to Philadelphia? May thy God be with thee, then thy journey will be prosperous. You will recollect, my son, that this journey may be of singular advantage to you, if you wisely improve it. You will see, and have an opportunity of forming an acquaintance with, several valuable men, servants of our Lord. You will also observe a great difference in the manners and customs of the people. You will recollect the people, among whom you are going, are a free, plain people. No doubt you may meet with some eccentric characters; yet even from these, you may obtain useful knowledge. Old men are oft-fond of giving advice; you know this is one of my foibles; you will, therefore, bear with me on the present occasion. Now mind what I say Be careful to carry a praying heart, that God may direct you in all your ways, and meet with you when you meet the brethren. Be not so forward, at any time, to give your opinion; either be backward where it appears duty. Remember you are a young man; you will, therefore, duly attend to the observations and reasoning of those, who have the advantage of years and experience. They may deliver their sentiments in a very plain way, yet they may be really weighty, and more to the purpose, than at first may appear. You will, also remember the cause of Christ requires *doing* as well as *saying*. Now you must try to discover the secret how to get the doing part accomplished. Various plans may be proposed, but some one will be the best, and the best judge is the Lord: this shows the propriety of constant recourse to Him by prayer, to be directed in the right way. See to it, my son, for yourself. Once more: remember, the Carolinians are remarked, and I think very justly, as a very generous people; and it is possible, if you are not on your guard, you may be prejudiced against some, who, to you, may seem not so generous, who yet, owing to a different education, may not be esteemed niggardly or covetous—Mind this. People, who labor hard, set more value on money than those who have others to labor for them. That, which you, and many in our State would esteem a trifle, is, by many, esteemed a considerable matter. A Carolinian, with all his generosity, is a proud man. If he cannot do something, as he thinks, clever, he will do nothing; I now have reference to pecuniary matters. You'll take the hint. I'll now leave you in better hands. You'll see Dr. Staughton, Dr. Rogers, and Dr. Holcombe; Mr. Benedict, Mr. Rice, Dr. Baldwin and Dr. Gano,—my kind regards to each of them. One word more; be sure consult Dr. Furman on every occasion.

There now; if you remember these, enough is said; if you do not, more would be needless. I shall expect a line from you when you can make it convenient. I remain, my dear Son, yours affectionately,[19]

EDMUND BOTSFORD

In 1814 Philadelphia ranked second in size among the nation's cities and claimed itself first in cultural leadership, these claims bolstered by its red-brick look, its wharfs, ropewalks, fast sailing fleets, rich merchants, diversified crafts, parks, and museums.

The newspapers hardly noticed the meetings in the Baptist church which began on May 18 and convened for more than a week. For although observers, local Baptists, and wives who accompanied delegates swelled the audience at times, it was not an immense gathering. They came by twos and threes or singly, turning from brick-paved Second Street into Fromberger's Court and to First Baptist's double entrance doors, where Dr. Henry Holcombe's massive hand grasped theirs in hearty welcome.

By chaise from Boston came Revs. Lucius Bolles and Thomas Baldwin; from Maryland, Revs. Lewis Richards and Thomas Brook; from South Carolina, Dr. Richard Furman and Judge Matthias Tallmadge. Rhode Island's lone delegate bore the famous Baptist name of Gano, *Stephen* Gano. Rev. Daniel Dodge, a Nova Scotian by birth, represented Delaware; young William Bullein Johnson, loaded with advice and his drafts of a proposed constitution, reported for Georgia; and from North Carolina came Scotsman James A. Ranaldson, who would serve the denomination admirably and then defect to the Campbellites in the years to come. There were eight delegates each from New Jersey and Pennsylvania and four from New York. Thirty-six delegates from eleven states and the District of Columbia had been appointed. Only thirty-three men, twenty-six ministers and seven laymen, appeared. William G. Moore and O. B. Brown could not attend from Washington and Luther Rice signed for that society; John Bryce did not appear from Virginia.

These men were different in background and training as well as in age and geographical locality. A few, such as Dr. Furman and Judge Tallmadge, were men of wealth. A third of the ministers were foreign born or trained,[20] evidence of the fact that though Baptists were indigenous to American soil two hundred years after Roger Williams, they were still depending, in part, on other Baptist groups for leadership. Three Englishmen—William Staughton, Richard Proudfoot, and John P. Peckworth—were to play vital roles in the new organization. The Welsh, who had swelled the stream of Baptist migration to America since Williams' day, were there in the person of John Williams, Edward Probyn, Lewis Richards, and many Pennsylvanians of Welsh ancestry, such as Horatio G. Jones.

Certainly there had never been such a meeting of American Baptists before and only one man, Rice, had met each delegate previously and knew something of the society he represented. "Tall, nervous, anxious, counting too much upon the cooperation of others,"[21] he was now busy working out details, acquainting the men with the unique qualities of leadership each man possessed, endeavoring to modify variances and to move proceedings along harmoniously.

The delegates convened in the center section of the sanctuary between the two aisles, the side pews occupied by friends and relatives. The elder clergymen sat on the pulpit facing the young clergymen and layman-delegates in the center pews. Dr. Furman was called to the chair; Dr. Baldwin was asked to act as secretary. The delegates produced testimonials and their names were enrolled in the record book. It was agreed to have a prayer meeting the following Saturday in behalf of their deliberations. Since no one had been appointed to preach the convention sermon, Dr. Furman was chosen.

Dr. Furman was "six feet tall, hair and eyes dark, stern voice. His dress to the last like that of older men of Charleston of that day—coat with pockets in the skirts opening outwardly under a lapel, waistcoat reaching to hips, kneebreeches and long stockings."[22] But he wore a Genevan gown when he preached that evening, in his introductory remarks saying, "At the present Convention, the sight of brethren who had never expected to meet on earth, afforded mutual and unutterable pleasure. It was as if the first interviews of heaven had been anticipated."[23]

On the first day, Wednesday, there ensued discussion as to the most eligible plan for the formation of a convention and they appointed a committee to prepare a constitution and report to the larger body. This committee included one man from each state and two additional men from Philadelphia. Drs. Furman, Baldwin, and Staughton were asked to prepare an address on missions to be circulated among the states and the first day's meeting was ended.

The size of the committee (fifteen men) to propose a plan of organization encumbered the writing of a constitution, but both Johnson and Furman had brought drafts; from these they were able to write a constitution acceptable to a majority and to report Thursday morning. The convention went into a committee of the whole to discuss this proposed constitution and there was protracted discussion. Even at this early time there seem to have been closely contested disputes, perhaps with personal overtones, among the Philadelphia men. Many policy questions affecting the future of the whole denomination had to be considered and a course recommended. Would the convention limit itself to missions, and if so, to foreign missions only?

Men from the South, particularly Johnson and Furman, wished from the beginning that ministerial education, and perhaps home mission work also, might be encompassed in the national plan. Staughton of Philadelphia seems to have joined them in this desire. The Philadelphia, Charleston, and Warren Associations had joined to found Brown University. Thus it seemed appropriate that the national union would include other schools. In his address Furman said that the "efforts of the present Convention have been directed chiefly to the establishment of a foreign mission; but it is expected that when the general concert of their brethren, and sufficient contributions to a common fund shall furnish them with proper instructions and adequate means, the promotion of the interests of the churches at home, will enter into the deliberations of future meetings."[24] He also lamented "that no more attention is paid to the improvement of pious youth who are called to the gospel ministry."

Until this time the basis for organization was associations. Would the national convention be made up of delegates from churches, associations, state conventions (which were yet to become a reality), or from societies?

Of his own opinion Rice wrote:

While passing from Richmond to Petersburg in the stage, an enlarged view of the business opened upon my contemplations. The plan which suggested itself to my mind, that of forming one principal society in each state, bearing the name of the state, and others in the same state, auxiliary to that; and by these large, or state societies, delegates be appointed to form one general society.[25]

The delegates had been designated and sent by the societies and these societies were not confined within one church nor even one association, nor did they include all the members within the churches. Thus the delegates were representing not their churches but the societies which sometimes embraced several churches and crossed associational lines.

On Thursday afternoon the committee reported again, but unanimity could not be reached and they met again. At 3 o'clock on Friday the first plan, evidently drawn by Furman from Johnson's draft and including work other than foreign missions, was laid aside and a smaller committee consisting of Furman, Baldwin, Gano, Semple, and White was appointed.

They reported on Friday and the constitution was adopted as far as the sixth article. By this proposed plan, the body was to be styled "The General Missionary Convention of the Baptist Denomination in the United States of America, for Foreign Missions." It was to meet in convention every third year and thus became known as the "Triennial Convention," its membership "consisting of Delegates, not exceeding two in number, from each of the several Missionary Societies, and other religious bodies of the Baptist Denomination, now existing, or which may hereafter be formed in the United States, and which shall each regularly contribute to the general Missionary Fund, a sum, amounting, at least, to one hundred Dollars, per annum."[26]

During the interim between conventions, the business was to be conducted by twenty-one "Commissioners, who shall be members of said Societies, Churches, or other religious bodies." This executive committee was to be known as the "Baptist Board of Foreign Mission for the United States." This board was given the authority to appoint missionaries and "if necessary, to take measures for the improvement of their qualification, to fix on the field of their labours, and the compensation to be allowed them for their services."

Officers were to be chosen by ballot and their duties were specified. The board was given "power, to elect honorary members of piety and distinguished liberalists, who on their elections, shall be entitled to a seat and to take part in the debates of the Convention: but it shall be understood that the right of voting shall be confined to the delegates."[27]

Reading the minutes, one perceives that Rice was not a prime mover, but at times his handling comes through, as on Saturday when it was "agreed that the members in their individual capacity, furnish Rev. Mr. Rice with the names of Persons whom they conceive most eligible for members of the Board of Commissioners, with a mind to assist the convention in the choices about to be made."[28]

The following Tuesday with fifteen men present, the Board proceeded to elect officers according to the provisions of the constitution, Dr. Baldwin presiding and William Johnson acting as secretary. On the first ballot Dr. Furman was chosen president but he declined "on the account of his distance from the seat of the board."[29] Dr. Baldwin was elected president of the Board on the second ballot, Drs. Holcombe and Rogers vice-presidents, and Judge Tallmadge treasurer, which he declined for health reasons. John Caldwell, another New York layman, was chosen in his place. William Staughton was elected corresponding secretary and William White, recording secretary.

Wednesday the group moved to the Sansom Street Church on the corner of Ninth and Sansom. This unusual edifice had been erected in 1810 when Dr. Staughton and part of the First Baptist membership formed a new congregation. The baptistry was in the center with the seats rising in amphitheater.

In one of the first actions of the Board, it was resolved that "Mr. Rice be appointed, under the patronage of this board, as their Missionary to continue his itinerant services in these United States for a reasonable time, with a view to excite the public and more generally engage in Missionary exertions: and to assist in originating societies, or Institutions, for carrying the Missionary design into execution."[30] A subsequent motion stated that Judson "now in India, be considered as a missionary, under the care and direction of this Board", with instructions "to pursue his pious labors in such places, as, in his judgment, may appear most promising."[31] They voted to assume Judson's support and appointed a committee to consult with Rice about his compensation. Following the American Board policy, they set eight dollars a week plus expenses as his salary, retroactive from the previous September.

Rice made his report at this time, recording $1,836.67 as the amount collected on his recent tour, noting that "as the point of responsibility, furnished by this Board, did not exist at the time of receiving the monies . . . they were marked in my memorandum book to be accounted for to the various missionary societies."[32] The report revealed that the money had come from Baptist Churches, a surprising $345 from Presbyterian congregations, nearly $300 from individuals, including twenty-five cents from a Negro ferryman, and it listed a gift of $166 from individuals to "restore his borrowed chaise destroyed by run-away horse, near St. Paul's church, Augusta and two pairs gloves, one pair shoes." He noted that there were seventeen societies then existing and concluded: "I cannot but feel myself to be under grateful obligations, nor refrain from expressing my unfeigned thankfulness, to many individuals, for aid in travelling over portions of country in which I could not avail myself of conveyance by stage; for entertainment at several public houses free of expense; and for numberless instances of hospitality, attention, courtesy, politeness and kindness."[33]

The convention ended on a note of thanksgiving that unanimity had been reached and all had gone harmoniously. Though there were those who were disappointed that the Convention limited its works exclusively to foreign missions, they doubtless felt this could be adjusted in time as state conventions were formed or as education societies became more generally supported. Some thought the society method of representation was a regressive step in that it relegated missions, the chief duty of the church, to a group within the church, even in some cases to one sex since the Female Societies were its sole support in some instances. But the delegates could be from churches or "other religious bodies," as the constitution clearly stated, and so most delegates who would have preferred the constitution otherwise were mollified.

"Devout thanks were given to the God of all grace for his special favor in securing such cordial unanimity; and fervent petitions were offered that the new organization might be a blessing to churches, the country, and the world. In all the devotional group, Mr. Rice appeared to be one of the happiest and his prayer of thanksgiving was long remembered as especially spiritual."[34]

Soon Dr. William Staughton wrote Joseph Ivimey in England:

A Spirit for foreign missions, vigorous . . . and spreading, has gone forth in America. American Baptists appear resolved on supporting men whom God has so remarkably thrown in our hands. Mr. Rice is at present an inmate of my family. He is a man of considerable talents—a good scholar, of an easy, popular, pulpit address. His heart is consecrated to the work of the Lord. His spirit is catholic, but in relation to what he values truth or duty, he is a perfect Fabricius. He knows how to bear indignity without resentment, and fatigue without complaining.[35]

12. Enlistment and Expansion

The years 1814 to 1817 were the busiest and perhaps the happiest Rice ever experienced. Traveling up and down the seaboard, across the mountains into the Mississippi Valley, on to his native New England, visiting the cities and the small hamlets, he began to form plans for the Baptists in America. Not all these schemes originated within himself, for many men shared their ideas and dreams for the denomination with him, and he often appropriated their plans. But one trait which distinguished Rice from many a dreamer was that he not only dreamed, he implemented his dreams.

In addition to the already inaugurated foreign mission enterprise, his designs grew to include a home mission to the Indians, the Negroes, and the pioneer areas; a newspaper with a national circulation; a tract society; a publishing house which would print periodicals and religious books; and a university comprising a fine arts college and professional schools of theology, medicine, and law. In its entirety, Luther's dream was a "permanent, national program of a cultural pattern sufficiently flexible to meet the constantly changing conditions in our American life."[1]

Since he felt men were the key to any new venture, he was always seeking them—committed men of ability and dedication, men willing to build for the future. He recruited many who led the denomination for the next half century, for his friends were legion. And though in time his enemies may have formed a sizable regiment, the men he enlisted supplied the outposts in each of the denomination's new undertakings.

Among the delegates to the Warwick, New York Association, gathering at Lattintown in June of 1815, was John Mason Peck, the twenty-six-year-old pastor of Amenia Church.

Rice "with characteristic ardor was posting from one association to another fanning the flames of missionary zeal."[2] He presented his credentials as agent for the Board and was invited to preach. When "the mind of Peck heard the voice of Luther Rice appealing for the vast world, it knew a crisis had come."[3]

After the meeting Peck persuaded Rice to go home with him, where they talked far into the night. Peck's "heart burned with love and his purpose was fired with determination as Rice pictured India's need to him. Rice—the flaming evangel—helped turn Peck's enthusiasm into mission channels."[4]

Burdened with the needs of a growing family and hampered by a scant education, Peck never hoped to become a foreign missionary. Yet, to Rice he revealed his willingness to endure hardship and a yearning to preach the gospel in an enlarged field. In turn, Rice told him of the vast unchurched areas on the frontier, of the need for a concerted effort to evangelize the Indians, of the plan to establish a mission in the Missouri Territory.

"Is it contemplated to form a permanent mission-station in the West?" inquired Peck."

"Yes, certainly."

"Would it be best to have schools connected with the mission?"

"Yes!"

"Any particular place in view for the seat of the mission?"

"St. Louis, probably."

"What literary attainments would be indispensable?"

"A good English education, to say the least, so as to be able to conduct a school to advantage . . . an acquaintance with the Latin and Greek, if not the Hebrew; and indeed it would be desirable that a missionary should be a graduate of some college . . ."

"Would it be thought necessary for some person to accompany you in this Western tour?"

"Should some suitable person find his heart moved to offer himself to the service of the Board, as a missionary to the West *for life.*"[5]

Rice asked Peck if he would assist in distributing the Annual Report in upper and central New York that summer and received a ready assent.

The immediate rapport between these two issued from a similarity of natures. Each had traveled the theological route from Congregationalism to the Baptist position on the doctrine of baptism. Each possessed an abiding zeal to evangelize, combined with the insight and patience to be foundation-builders for the future. Each had a national concept as against the narrow sectionalism typifying many of their fellow members.

Peck was to render many services during his tenure on the frontier: a decisive voice in the anti-slavery stand of Illinois; a founder of Bible societies, associations, and Shurtleff College; an editor and the general secretary of the Publication Society; and eventually one of the men who held the western states to the east within the Baptist denomination.

He visited the Franklin, Otsego, and Madison Associations that summer, distributing the report and collecting for missions, and was elated with the response. "What a checkered scene is human life," he wrote, "but a few weeks since I was repining my lot. Now I share and rejoice in the light of life."[6]

From this encounter Peck and Rice began corresponding. In Kentucky in the autumn, Rice met another young man, James Welch,

102

and found that he had done some itinerant preaching in unchurched areas and was interested in becoming an appointed missionary on the frontier also. From Indiana Territory Rice wrote Peck: "Possibly you may be fellow-laborers in this great field."[7] He thought both of them should secure some theological training, advising: "It would afford me great satisfaction to see you in Philadelphia next spring and I believe you might be highly useful in this western country, whether as a missionary or otherwise."[8]

This suggestion was followed by a letter from Dr. Staughton to Peck stating that he should come to Philadelphia, live and study in their home. The New York Education Society examined him and agreed to underwrite part of his theological training. Peck resigned his church in Amenia, left his wife and small children there, and entered Dr. Staughton's seminary where, though having little formal education, being an apt scholar and possessing great determination he acquired skills which later enabled him to become the best chronicler of the West in his day.

Welch soon joined him as did several other Rice protégés, all residing and studying in the Staughtons' brick home on the northwest corner of Filbert and Eighth Streets. Peck and Welch decided to apply for appointment at the Board's annual meeting in 1816.

At this meeting, Drs. Bolles, Staughton, and Burgiss Allison were appointed as a committee to take the subject of a western mission into consideration and they reported that "an effort of this kind deserves an early and zealous attention"; but it was deemed best that such an important undertaking, requiring a change in the constitution, should be deferred until the Triennial meeting the following year.

In the Board's "Address to the Convention," they suggested "that the powers of the convention be extended so as to embrace home missions and plans for the encouragement of education."[9] The Board also stated that they were "deeply convinced of the propriety of immediate attention to the Indians of our own country . . . they are heathen which from their proximity have a special claim on us."[10]

In 1814, as soon as the Board voted to retain him in the States, Rice had begun seeking someone to join Judson in Burma in his stead. He found George Hough, a schoolteacher and printer, in Rhode Island. There was some delay in Mr. Hough's appointment, possibly because Phebe Hough was not a church member. Rice heaved a sigh of relief when he knew they were going and the Judsons would have co-workers.

In the winter of 1815-16, accompanied by Mrs. Charlotte White, a widow going out at her own expense, the Houghs sailed from Philadelphia in the "newly copper-bottomed" *Benjamin Rush,* by compliment of the owner, Edward Thompson.

Another man who offered his services to the Board at the same time Welch and Peck did and who also hoped to be appointed to the St. Louis mission was Isaac McCoy.

On the same trip West when he met James Welch, Rice had met the McCoys in Kentucky and Indiana Territory—all involved in pioneer Baptist life along the Ohio and its tributaries. William, the father of the large family, lived in Shelby County, Kentucky.

Isaac was living on the banks of the Maria above Vincennes in Indiana Territory, working as a wheelwright and preaching at every opportunity. Rice met him at Liverpool on December 2—"Isaac McCoy having come here to attend a church meeting"[11]—and McCoy arranged for Rice to visit and preach in his home at Maria the next day.

Born in Western Pennsylvania and reared in Kentucky, Isaac had come to Indiana Territory in 1804 with his fifteen-year-old bride, Christiana, to do pioneer work. Restless by nature, he had moved several times in the intervening years and had thought of a "Domestick Mission to the Missouri Territory," lacking only the means to engage in the work.

Of all Rice's recruits, Isaac was surely the most unusual. Tall and thin, his even features bespeaking something effeminate despite his angular frame and wiry physique, he had two forefingers missing from his left hand and a compelling intensity in his blue eyes. He was a man of contrasts; mercurial in temperament, he would be soaring one day, despairing the next. His fortitude was amazing; he would travel by horseback to Washington thirteen times to plead his beloved Indians' cause before three Presidents and many Cabinet members. Yet he was addicted to hypochondria. A peacemaker, believing that argumentation, so popular in frontier churches, might win an argument but rarely an opponent, Isaac said: "Judge of other men's feelings by your own, and you will find that a soft answer turneth away wrath, and that the maxim is true, it is more difficult to drive than lead."[12] Yet he was imperious in his dealings with the Board: "They knew little more about this than they did the geography of the moon."[13] Often filled with self-pity but rarely with self-blame, remorseful as a child but seldom repentant: "I knew the

Board had told me not to draw more than $500 but nevertheless I did."[14] Never much of a team man, in 1842 he would head the American Indian Mission Association which helped precipitate the cleavage between Northern and Southern Baptists.

Withal, a noble man. A compassionate man. A tenacious advocate, possessing restless energy which would keep him going when physically ill, many times riding the hinterland where a man was not safe, crossing hostile Indian country, his diary filled with jottings to the lonely inhabitants: "Enquire for John Dougherty, trapper, son of Michael Dougherty. Living high up on the Missouri. His friends have thought him dead till latterly."[15] Or, "Enquire for Jacob Wise and wife, Baptist, Missouri Territory, opposite the American bottom . . . compliments to him from Thomas Piety who requests him to remember that 'it is *by Grace he is saved.*'"[16] Traveling all day to preach to a handful of indifferent backwoodsmen, he often must have claimed the Lord's promise to little congregations, as in the dead of winter, 1821: "Yesterday I swam my horses across Maumee River, reached Fort Defiance and preached by candle light to about a dozen hearers. I have traveled all day along a dreary wilderness, have seen no one since I left Defiance except four Indians. Much wearied with the day's travel, I have just finished my supper, tied up my horses to trees, and now sit all alone by a little fire in the wilderness, where I make this note."[17]

And Isaac possessed a rare asset in Christiana, a woman whose "uncommon fortitude and mild disposition"[18] were a foil for his own volatile nature. A remarkable woman—once going down the Wabash three or four hundred miles with her small children in a pirogue "almost the whole distance through a wilderness and leading by several Indian Towns"[19] to reach a settlement before bearing another child—she shared without quibbling the hardships and loneliness, the malaria and other fevers which plagued all settlers along the bottomlands.

This couple sat across from Rice in the glow of their fire in the small house on the Maria, and he sensed their innate rightness for pioneer work. The meeting changed the whole course of McCoy's life.

The following spring, McCoy and Hansom Hobbs were employed by the Long Run Association in Kentucky for a three-month stint of itinerating in the Illinois and Missouri Territories but nothing permanent ever came of the appointment.

Soon Rice inquired by letter: "I should be glad to know if you would be willing to perform missionary service under an appointment by the General Convention and what plan you would suggest as most agreeable to your views and wishes in the event of such an appointment."[20]

Elated, Isaac replied: "You can hardly guess what my feelings were, when I read your request to know if I would be willing to perform missionary service . . . I had thought that for the obscurity of my character and many other reasons, I had no right to suppose I should be thought of."[21] His many reasons included: "I am now a little turned of 33, and have 8 small children." He wrote Rice that he would prefer "to make choice of St. Louis for the residence of my family while I would itinerate as far into the adjacent regions as circumstances would admit."[22]

The correspondence between the two reveals that McCoy preferred to become a missionary to the settlers on the frontier, yet he was to become the apostle to the Indians in the West and a determiner of the whole course of government policy toward those west of the Mississippi. This change in the direction of his labors was due to the Board's action.

The Second Triennial Convention, meeting again in Philadelphia in May of 1817, passed two amendments to the Constitution, the first stating that the Board "have full power at their discretion to appropriate a portion of the funds to domestic missionary purposes, in such parts of this country where the seed of the Word may be advantageously cast, and where missionary societies on a small scale do not effectively reach."[23]

This opened the way for beginning domestic missions. James A. Ranaldson, a North Carolina minister who had been a delegate to the first convention, was appointed in June as a missionary to New Orleans with instructions, if practicable, "to visit such Indian settlements as shall not be found too remote, and to inquire, and ascertain as accurately as you can, what prospects offer for the enlargement of the mission, and what for the establishment of schools among the settlers and natives."[24]

At the May meeting Peck and Welch were appointed as missionaries to the Missouri Territory "during their and our pleasure" with "the sum of one thousand dollars to defray expenses in getting to St. Louis and for the support of the mission," and instructions that they were "particularly desirous that the Fox, the Osage, the Kanses, and other tribes of Indians, should engage your peculiar zeal."[25]

Before the convening ministers departed the city, Welch and Peck were set apart for domestic missions in an ordination service, Drs. Furman, Mercer, Baldwin, and other Convention delegates participating and Peck confessing: "When I came to take the hand of my ever-valued and much endeared friend, Rice, my heart well nigh failed."[26]

The two appointees set out immediately for St. Louis. Peck, his young wife, and three small children made the arduous overland trip to the Ohio Valley in a one-horse covered wagon. In Kentucky they were joined by the Welches and the last leg of the 125-day trek was by a keelboat which nearly capsized below Shawneetown. In late November, Peck gravely ill, they arrived in St. Louis, then a rough frontier town inhabited by Negroes, French atheists, devout Catholics, pioneers of Anglo extraction, and every breed of ruffians who flouted law and conformity and boasted that the Sabbath would never cross the Mississippi. It was largely a shanty town sprawling in mud, with churches and schools nonexistent; but though the new missionaries endured dire living conditions and found groceries and other necessities exorbitant, they soon opened Sunday Schools, a weekday school, and by February had constituted a church.

Meanwhile, McCoy, waiting in Indiana, was disappointed when he learned that the St. Louis mission did not include him. Earlier, he had journeyed into Missouri on his own and had advised the Board, via correspondence with Rice, about beginning a mission there. At the fall quarterly meeting, the Board gave him an appointment on a *yearly* basis—a fact that grated on his sensitive feelings—to the Wabash and White River area with instructions to minister "to the aborigines in that quarter."[27]

This same meeting appointed Humphrey Posey to work among the Cherokees. In 1816 in Buncombe County, North Carolina, Rice met Posey, a minister three years older than himself who "among the Cherokees inhabiting the wild mountainous country which lies on the borders of North Carolina and Tennessee . . . has communicated evangelic instruction with acceptance, and has established several schools for the education of their children."[28] Posey was given a like appointment to that of McCoy's and soon was communicating from Valley Towns that he had set up four schools on the Lancastrian plan "for the instruction of Indian children, at an expense of forty dollars per quarter for each assistant teacher."[29]

McCoy moved toward establishing schools in his area, first visiting General Thomas Posey, Indian agent, finding him "truly friendly," and proposing that the school be among the Indians where they lived since the tribes objected to "let their children go to Kentucky because they would lose their mother tongue, and be unable on their return, to communicate to their kindred anything they had learned."[30]

The Kentucky Missionary Society had sponsored a boarding school for Indians at Great Crossings, one of the founders being Richard Mentor Johnson, Congressman, Senator, and later Vice-President.

Posey's death shortly thereafter was a blow to McCoy's plans, but he pursued the Indians' friendship and an entry into their lands, visiting and talking with their chiefs, pleading the cause of a school for their children. He opened a small school at Maria Creek and spent much time visiting the settlers, making tours along the rivers, soon reporting that he had aided in constituting the White River Church, "the first in Pike County, Indiana."[31]

As McCoy came to understand something of the Indian situation, he was appalled at the havoc wrought by the white man and his whiskey. He witnessed the trappers and traders plying their trades to the detriment of the red man, often visiting where whole villages were inebriated and in squalor, and came to feel that the "white man's influence was always corrupting to the Indian."[32] And though this supposition was later refuted in states such as Oklahoma where the two lived amiably together, it became a passion with McCoy. He began badgering Rice to work through his Congressional friends— Richard M. Johnson, Joseph Johnson, Chaplain Burgiss Allison, and others—to implore the Secretary of War, whose department governed Indian affairs, for a Baptist share of the ten thousand dollars which the government allocated annually. By the 1819 treaty, the government assumed responsibility for educating the Indian children and set aside lands for their exclusive occupancy.

Both Posey's and McCoy's missions proved costly to maintain, and Rice was strained to provide funds to keep them operating. Dr. Staughton informed McCoy that "the whole convention, together with the Board were unacquainted with the sums your situation would require."[33] The Indians came and lived at the site of the schools and had to be fed and clothed, the cost of each mission equaling that of the entire Burman mission some years. This fact dampened the ardor of some who had voted to begin home mission work on a Convention-sponsored basis.

Nevertheless, the work among the Indians was more appealing than that among the frontiersmen. Many easterners felt that ministers within the frontier churches could supply itinerating services among the settlers in unchurched areas, as many of them had done for years, and that competent ministers would migrate to the expanding frontier. This group began to press for short-term support of the frontier mission, unless the appointees would devote their entire service to the Indians. Thus in 1820, the Convention "having listened with concern to some anti-mission complaints from the West, proceeded to direct the Board to discontinue the missions at St. Louis."[34] They suggested that Welch remain in the St. Louis area without their support and instructed Peck to join McCoy in Indiana.

This was a blow to Rice's dream of a unified program under the direction of the Convention and he, along with Peck, felt that the work in St. Louis should not be abandoned.

But there had not been entire satisfaction between Peck and Welch in their mission, at least not on Peck's part, though they remained friends throughout life. Perhaps they disagreed about their schools or how to handle the hostility toward a paid ministry. Whatever the cause, Peck kept writing Rice and in February before the Board severed its relations with Peck and Welch in what seemed an abrupt fashion, Rice wrote Peck about the underlying factors:

I have your letters 1, 2, 3, & 4. . . . My opinion is decided that the sooner Bro. Welch becomes totally disconnected from the Board the better. The Board is of this opinion too; but we are desirous on all hands that the separation should take place in such a manner if possible as neither to wound his feelings or inflict injury upon him. With your situation, my dear brother, I do most sincerely sympathize. I earnestly wish it was in my power to minister to your relief . . . Don't give up that mission . . . if we had some one to take your place, I should be willing you should join McCoy among the Indians.[35]

McCoy wrote Peck "in the most meek and affectionate manner that I was master of and invited and welcomed him"[36] to Fort Wayne. But Peck took Rice's advice and resigned from the Board rather than leave his post. He conceived the station among the settlers near St. Louis as too important to justify leaving it, even at the Board's behest.

Peck had begun to plan for the academy which was to become Shurtleff College, unalterably convinced that the education of the ministry is of primary importance in all new countries . . . The mind must be trained to habits of thinking; to logical reasoning, to readiness of speech; to systematical arrangement of gospel truth, and to a practical application of Christian duties. Mere declamation is not preaching the gospel. A man may stand up, rattle off words, tear his voice to tatters, and foam at the mouth, and yet not communicate one Scriptural idea, nor excite one spiritual emotion in his hearers."[37]

He lamented the dearth of learning among the Baptist clergy on the frontier and was skeptical of the dividends from a ministry among the roving bands of Indians on the always retreating frontier. Both these convictions, plus the advice of Rice, led him to stay in the St. Louis area.

Ranaldson in New Orleans was finding the climate intolerable for his family and moved them to Feliciana Parish, but he persevered in the work, visiting the Mississippi Missionary Society and forwarding their contributions to the Board.[38]

It appeared that the Convention was irrevocably committed to fulfil the dream of a concerted effort to evangelize the homeland, another milestone in Baptists' progress toward unity. These home mission accomplishments were constantly pushed through another of Rice's interests, the *Latter Day Luminary,* an official publication of the Convention begun in 1818 as a means of illuminating Baptist life throughout the nation.

In the autumn following the Triennial Convention formation in 1814, Rice wrote Judge Tallmadge from Vermont, pleading his aid in securing magazine rate from the postal department for the Board's reports. He and Dr. Staughton were making plans to publish and disseminate the proceedings of the Convention as widely as possible. Rice wanted each association to appoint a secretary to correspond with the Board and to receive and distribute the Board's literature and records.

I wish also to enable the Board to give the names of the association, together with the *number of the churches and their aggregate number* of members, of each association. A small statement of this kind, annually, which would occupy but a small place in the annual publication of the Board, would prove, I apprehend, a source of much gratification to the churches.[39]

But he had difficulty distributing this *Annual Report,* for though he personally conveyed many copies to the different associations, many had to be mailed and the postage was notoriously high for the country beyond the Alleghenies. Many of the Baptists who most needed the information in all sections of the land were unable to buy them. Also, the vast correspondence which was coming into the secretary's office in Philadelphia needed to be culled and some of it published, and important issues needed to be discussed in a manner available to all the Convention's constituency.

In 1817 Rice suggested that the Board publish a magazine other than the nonofficial but foremost *Massachusetts Baptist Missionary Magazine* "because the Missionary Magazine does not go to destitute areas."[40] He also expressed his desire that "funds be allowed to cover publishing and distributing"[41] this magazine, which would be more comprehensive, covering the Convention's expanding interests and including the *Annual Report*.

At the September, 1817 meeting, the Board stated that the *Baptist Missionary Magazine* "could not serve the purpose" and resolved:

That the Corresponding Secretary be instructed to write to the Editors of the Magazine on the subject, and that brother Rice also be instructed to proceed to the eastward as soon as practicable to see the members of the Board, particularly in New-York and Boston, about this matter; to acquaint them in detail with our views, and learn theirs, relative to the issuing of a periodical published under the auspices of the Board, designed to circulate missionary intelligence.[42]

Rice visited Boston, and the editors of the *American Baptist Magazine* graciously assented to the Board's request, sending a letter "explicitly announcing their acquiescence in the publication of a periodical work by the Board."[43] At the October meeting the Board appointed Dr. Staughton, Rev. Burgiss Allison, Rev. Horatio Jones, and Rice as a committee to supervise the new publication; by February Rice gave the Board a report "relative to the subscription papers and the means of extensively circulating the *Latter Day Luminary* . . . it is gratifying to state that near 8,000 are called for . . ."[44] It became a monthly publication promoting every endeavor of the Convention, publishing the Board's transactions, letters from the missionaries, and progress reports.

Through the *Luminary's* pages a glimpse is caught of all the Board fostered.

Rice had stated in his *Second Annual Report* that "the colored want to give to an African mission."[45] This was particularly true

111

of the members of Richmond's First Baptist Church, perhaps influenced in their decision by the witness of Jacob Grigg, who had lived in Africa. At the May, 1819, Board meeting, Dr. Obadiah B. Brown of Washington stated that among the pupils in William Crane's class for Negro members of the First Baptist Church in Richmond, there were two outstanding men—Lott Cary, manager of a large tobacco warehouse, and Collin Teague, harness-maker. Both men had purchased their freedom and that of their families by their own industry. These men presented themselves as candidates for appointment as missionaries to Africa, to be supported by the African Missionary Society but wishing the guidance and counsel of the Board. "Some letters published in No. VI issue of the Luminary, have served to awaken them effectually."[46] Said Brown: "Man is torn from his kindred, and dragged by barbarous hands to a distant, unknown country, to wear the shackles of slavery among men of strange language and complexions where no friendly hand can sooth his anguish, nor pitying eye mingle with his the tear of commiseration."

Realizing that "our cup has too long been sweetened with their blood,"[47] the Board voted in April, 1819, to accept Collin Teague and Lott Cary "as missionaries under their care; and that they be sent out in the fall in a vessel which the President of the United States is about sending to the western coast of Africa, or in one which the Colonization Society shall send and that these brethren be encouraged to improve their minds to the utmost, before they sail."[48]

These men sailed from Norfolk in January of 1821 aboard the *Nautilus,* a Colonization Society vessel bound for Sierra Leone.

By the end of the second decade of the nineteenth century Rice seemed to be well along in accomplishing, along with others who were of like mind, his dreams for the Baptist denomination in America. Although many of these plans were still in embryonic stage and it was true that the Board had rudely scuttled some of the domestic missions, it appeared that Baptists would never again revert to independent societies to promote and finance each separate endeavor. Though there were those who could not agree to a unified plan of action (and their voices were loudest in New England), Rice, Staughton, Furman, and others were exerting the kind of leadership which Baptists had lacked and to which they were responding in gratifying and ever increasing numbers.

Above all else, within Rice a conviction was growing which eventually consumed much of his thinking and all his best energies during the remainder of his life. That conviction was that Baptists must think in terms of leadership—educated, competent leadership. More and more of his interest and more and more pages of the *Luminary* were filled with his plan for a great national Baptist university in Washington.

13. Education—An Enterprise
for Eternity

Young Henry Keeling could hardly believe it was morning. It seemed the middle of the night, but every night since he had been in Washington and sharing Brother Rice's room had been the same—the hours of slumber were short. The sound of fireirons and poker grating in the fireplace was followed by the pungent smell of wood smoke, a crackling and sputtering, and then the flicker of light on the ceiling. Brother Rice had been stooped over a table writing furiously when Henry had drifted off to sleep at nearly eleven the evening before and now, a few minutes past four, he was padding around in a flannel wrapper, punching the fire.

Hope of further sleep dispelled, Keeling reluctantly rose and dressed. Brother Rice was sitting in a chair, pulling on his boots. They were so snug he could only get them on by soaping them and leaving off his wool socks. Pulling and yanking, his feet finally slid into them and Keeling marveled as Rice remarked that the thin boots were really too small but they were a gift and rather than dispose of them he "made do" by forgoing socks.[1]

Dressed, the two descended the stairs for breakfast with the Browns before daybreak, for Brother Brown went to work at his post office job before the inaugural ceremonies began at ten. Keeling and Rice walked with him down "E" Street to the General Post Office and then to Columbian College where Rice, in his usual energetic way, tended many things. This was a day of attainment for which he had given unflagging zeal and prodigious toil.

113

"The Susquehanna was frozen over so as to admit passengers on the ice. The Delaware was so firm that wood was hauled over in wagons from New Jersey to Philadelphia on the ice."[2] But weather could not cool Rice's ardor. Both his strength and his weakness lay in the belief that anything that was right to do, he could do. This belief had enabled him to set out in the frigidity of a New England winter and raise money for his passage and salary in nine days; it had fortified him to ride up and down the eastern seaboard, calling Baptists into a general union. Now it was being expressed in the founding of a national Baptist university; and if there were those who felt Rice was rushing ahead of the leading of Providence, and certainly of the Convention's mandate, he was not bothered. For him, it was never too early to assault any attainable objective.

Dr. Staughton had not yet moved to Washington but had come for the formal opening, and at the appointed hour

the procession formed at the house of Professor Chase and moved to the College Chapel. The solemnities were introduced by prayer by the Rev. Burgiss Allison, D.D., then Chaplain of Congress, one of the vice-presidents of the General Baptist Convention . . . Rev. Robert Semple of Virginia, not having been able to attend. The act of incorporation passed at the last session of the Congress was read, and from the records of the trustees the elections respectively of the members of the faculty. The Rev. Obadiah B. Brown, President of the Board of Trustees, then rose and addressed the President of the College, the Rev. William Staughton, in a few but very appropriate observations . . .[3]

Addressing the prominent ministers, cabinet members, and students, Dr. Staughton was dramatically eloquent:

Among the numerous considerations which afford pleasure to the patrons of our college, and inspire their generous hopes, its location must be mentioned. From this Hill, as from the eminence on which Enos stood, the frequent pupil shall look down and exclaim, 'O fortunati! quirum jam maeniea sargent!' He will behold a rising metropolis . . . not the city of Carthage, but the city of Washington.

And President Monroe's message read: "The opportunities which it will provide the students of hearing the debates in Congress and in the Supreme Court on important subjects must be obvious to all."[4]

As the oratory flowed on, the whole scene in Isaac McCoy's judgment was "orderly and interesting."

114

Rice's thoughts deviously wandered to mundane matters—the money to buy apparatus for the medical school, furniture for the boys' rooms, houses for the faculty. The speeches afforded him a moment to indulge in devout gratitude upon the realization of his most extravagant ambition for his denomination, a great national university to train ministers, missionaries, doctors, lawyers, and teachers.

On his first southern trip, Rice had observed the need for an educated ministry among Baptists. The Charleston Association had raised a fund for ministerial education as far back as 1757 and ever since Richard Furman had served in that association, the education society had financed a score of southern students at Brown. The Philadelphia Association had also supported an education society since the days when they led in founding Brown, though it was a rather loose organization until 1812 when they formed the Baptist Education Society of the Middle States, called the Philadelphia Education Society. About this time New York and New Jersey Baptists inaugurated the New York Education Society, which cooperated with the Philadelphia Education Society and fostered the small seminary under Dr. Staughton's tutelage from 1813 until 1818.

But the Baptists in the southern states were not benefited by this. In South Carolina, William Bullein Johnson spoke about the need for a college that would be accessible to the middle and southern states since Brown University was too distant to aid them materially. Baptists were becoming more numerous in the South, more in Virginia alone than in all New England. Their need for higher education was acute and a primary concern of many leaders.

Article 4 of the constitution adopted at the 1814 Triennial Convention stated that the Board could employ missionaries and "if necessary, take measures for the improvement of their qualifications." In the first General Address to the Convention, prepared by a committee of Baldwin, Staughton, and Furman (but usually considered the work of Furman and presented by him), he said,

It is deeply to be regretted that no more attention is paid to the improvement of the minds of pious youth who are called to the gospel ministry. While this is neglected the cause of God must suffer . . . let us never lose sight of its real importance but labour to help our young men, by our contributions, by the origination of education societies, and, if possible, by a general theological seminary, where some at least may obtain all the advantages which learning . . . can afford.[5]

In August following the 1814 meeting, William Bullein Johnson wrote Rice, "There is another subject which has occupied my thoughts since my return, to the furtherance of which I am willing to lend my exertions. It is the establishment of a central theological seminary."[6]

On his first western trip in 1815, Rice's impression about the dearth of an educated ministry was intensified. Not only was the ignorance appalling west of the mountains where a college-educated Baptist minister was hardly to be found, but there was even open hostility toward education. Many Baptists had come by this antipathy via their Virginia background with its prerevolutionary, state-supported clergy for which their fathers had been taxed. This Virginia clergy was educated but sometimes morally lax or incompetent. Seeing that Christian greatness was not always to be equated with prominence or education, they made the mistake of assuming that it was never so. Some ventured to state that education and piety were mutually exclusive.

This odd heresy, that learning was carnal and a minister was not to love God with his mind, was closely allied with another—that the gospel was free and therefore the ministry should be unpaid. As Peck said of the Baptists in his area, the frontier settler "made the egregious blunder that because the gospel was 'without money and without price,' therefore they might take the *time and the talents* of a minister of Christ for their own use, and rob him of the means of support due to his family."[7]

In the tradition of Squire Boone, many of the ministers were completely unlettered or, at best, self-taught, their grammar and homiletics unorthodox. But if they were weak in logic, technique, and academic training, they were unsurpassed in devotion to duty.

Rice, schooled in the New England concept whereby a minister took a text from the Bible and preached a doctrinal lesson, yearned for a college where his fellow ministers might trade their loud oratory for skilled interpretation of the Bible. He saw, as no other Baptist of his day was equipped to see, that Baptist churches were springing up all over the western states and that without trained leadership their foundations were on shifting sands. This was confirmed in their lack of skill in meeting the onslaughts of Alexander Campbell. Unschooled in the Scriptures, untrained in their theology, they were ill-prepared for error and could not counter the sophistry and erudition of a man such as Campbell.

Rice came to feel that the destiny of the denomination lay in the minds of its leaders and that to mold these minds was to guide and control the denomination's future for ages to come. If he could found a superior university where the best minds of the Baptists could be trained, this would have a more far-reaching power than any other work one could perform.

In his president's address at the 1817 Triennial Convention, Dr. Furman brought a long message on education, advocating the establishment of one or more centrally located seminaries. An amendment to the constitution was passed, stating that "when competent and distinct funds shall have been received for the purpose, the board from these, without resorting at all to mission funds, shall proceed to institute a classical and theological seminary . . ."[8]

At the meeting of the Board following the Convention, the president's suggestion was considered and a committee of Staughton, Burgiss Allison, and Horatio G. Jones was appointed to bring a recommendation for proceeding. Judge Tallmadge assured Dr. Furman that the "entering wedge for promotion of education has been so far driven that it may be hoped that another convention will be able to give effective organization efficacy to your excellent views on this subject."[9]

In May of 1818 this committee reported that they "approved in the main, highly, of the plan proposed, and are of the opinion that it will ultimately, in substance, probably in a few years be found in successful operation." They suggested that "until it can be accomplished, and for its accomplishment very ample funds must be found, something may be done that will prepare the way for more comprehensive measures." They felt that "no adequate reason can be assigned for further delay,"[10] and that a plan for collecting funds should be inaugurated.

The Philadelphia Education Society voiced its willingness to cooperate in a Convention seminary, and a meeting was held in New York in August so that Judge Tallmadge and other members of the New York Education Society could attend and lend their advice.

At this New York meeting, letters were received from Dr. Furman and several associations. A committee proposed ten resolutions for implementing the educational design of the Convention. It was voted that the Board would assume the seminary in Philadelphia as the official Convention seminary, with Dr. Staughton as principal and Irah Chase, "a young brother of piety, talents and learning," as tutor to assist him. The country was divided into three sections with two persons designated to raise funds in each area. A committee composed of Philadelphians was appointed to arrange the necessary student accommodations and another one to purchase books for the library as funds became available. A "Plan" was prepared and presented to the public, soliciting support and expressly stating that the seminary's establishment awaited "distinct and competent funds." They thanked the Philadelphia Education Society for making it possible for the Convention to begin immediately by merging the local seminary into the national one. The "Plan" stated that the national institution was to be theological rather than literary, and therein lay one of the causes of dissent in subsequent years.

Some felt that the Board was rushing beyond the Convention's action and protested the salaries allotted to Staughton and Chase, amounting to six hundred dollars per year. Dr. Furman led the Charleston Association to protest the haste with which the Board was moving. They lamented the fact that the Charleston Association's plan of supporting the students was not followed and suggested that the appointment of a seminary staff should have awaited Convention sanction.

Rice had been instructed "to encourage the formation of other education societies, auxiliary if they think proper to the Institution connected with the Board and make such collection and obtain such donations, as he may be able for the advancement of this interesting concern."[11]

He began to bring students to the seminary. As Irah Chase recalled, "The number which at first was only one or two, gradually increased to more than twenty. Most of them were to a very considerable extent sustained by the contributions which Rev. Luther Rice obtained for this purpose, not one of the agents who had been appointed at the meeting in the city of New York having engaged in the work."[12]

Rice thought from the beginning that the new school should be in Washington City. Wealthy men there were interested. During his presidency, George Washington expressed a desire for a national university and left a legacy of fifty shares in the Potomac Company for its endowment; but this company subsequently failed and the shares became worthless. Each succeeding President had favored the establishment of such a university, mentioning the need in their annual addresses.

118

Obadiah Brown, Spencer Cone, Enoch Reynolds, and Rice formed a Literary Association and began raising money to purchase a site for the new institution. During 1817, they purchased a forty-six-and-one-half acre lot extending north from Boundary Street between Fourteenth and Fifteenth Streets. A magnificent plot situated on a hill about a mile north of the White House, it commanded a view of Georgetown, Alexandria, and even Mount Vernon on a clear day.

The land was held in trust for the Convention in the name of Brown and his "heirs for a thousand years." Rice raised most of the money to pay for the ground, as for all other endeavors. Everywhere he went now, he was listing donations for "the lot in Washington City," and as he entered associational meetings he asked for funds for the new school in addition to gifts for the missionary fund.

The next few years were hectic ones, his *Journal* filled not only with subscriptions for missions, the lot, notations about his travel and home missions, but increasingly with concerns of the new Baptist college.

"Attended auction with a view to obtain some articles for the Theological Institution," he would write, or he would refer to "buying copies of Paley's Evidence" or "apparatus for the new proposed medical division."[13]

At the June 7, 1819, Board meeting, he inquired whether or not licensed ministers would be admitted to the new institution without a knowledge of Latin or Greek, and if they were admitted, whether or not they would be able to study English without taking classical languages. He also asked the Board to authorize the purchase of the Washington lot for the seminary whose campus was to be "ultimately connected with that of a respectable college."

The Board voted that the requirements for entrance and the curriculum should be left to the discretion of Dr. Staughton and that a decision about the proffered site should await Convention action in 1820.

In his 1820 report Rice confessed:

It has afforded me no small pleasure to find it convenient, incidentally to other matters on hand, to bestow some attention on the object of providing, at Washington, a site for the Institution to promote the education of the ministry and ultimately for the foundation of a College under the direction of the General Convention.[14]

He also admitted that he felt that "the arrival of the period of this convention brings with it a crisis, particularly in relation to the education of pious young men in the ministry, of the utmost moment. May the blessed Redeemer preside in the meeting, and direct to the adoption of such measures as shall promote the prosperity of Zion, and display of his own glory."[15]

The 1820 Triennial, "for the purpose of carrying into effect the benevolent intentions of our constituents . . . in one sacred effort," adopted measures to bring the national institution into reality. The education committee reported that a central position was most desirable and recommended that both literary and theological schools be included. The Convention passed resolutions:

Resolved, That the institution for the education of gospel ministers, be located at the city of Washington, or in its vicinity, in the District of Columbia . . .

Resolved, That this convention accept of the premises tendered to them for the site of an institution for the education of gospel ministers, and for a college, adjoining the city of Washington; and that the Board be directed to take measures, as soon as convenient, for obtaining a legal title to the same. And that the Board be further directed, to keep the institution, already in a state of progress, first in view, and not to incur expenses beyond the amount of funds which may be obtained for the establishment of either of the institutions.[16]

Article VI in the amended constitution stated that "special care shall be taken to keep and present, the accounts of contributions to missions, education and other funds particularly designated, sacredly and entirely distinct and separate." State conventions were to collect and forward funds to the General Convention, and students would be admitted without a classical background and allowed to take a divinity course in English. This last was evidently to accommodate the southerners.

It was no simple matter to secure a charter; in December of that year Rice advised his good friend General John Gano that "a bill for incorporation is now in Congress and by the aid of our excellent friend Colonel Johnson will probably pass. The chief opposer against it is Rufus King." He also apprised him that the building was "up and closed in, the inside work going on . . . All we want with the blessing of the Lord is money."[17]

Henry Clay, whose father and brother were Baptist ministers, also assisted in getting the charter passed the following February, after the Senate amended the bill to provide that persons of every (or no) religious persuasion should be eligible as students or trustees.

Amendment VI worried some, including members of the Board, as well as members of the constituency who lived in more remote areas. In a long letter of assurance to Rev. Daniel Merrill of Maine, Rice explained the involved procedure whereby the contributors from the education societies of the Baptist denomination were to "elect the Trustees out of nomination furnished by the Convention for that purpose." He averred to Merrill that "the whole concern [is] so arranged as to be effectively and completely within the control and management of the General Convention."[18] Rice added rather proudly (for he had resorted to persuasion to convince Staughton he should give up his successful Philadelphia pastorate), "We shall elect Dr. Staughton President of the College."[19]

In 1820 a building 117 by 47 feet and of five stories, including the basement and garret rooms which were dormered, was constructed. It included living facilities for one hundred students, recitation rooms, a small chapel, sixty fireplaces, and a well "which proved to be upon a never failing spring of fine water; a blessing which calls for sincere gratitude."[20]

Two houses, one for the president and one for the college steward, were also erected; all the buildings "range with the cardinal points of the compass, and exhibit the best possible view from every direction."[21]

Charles Wilson Peale of the famous Philadelphia family of painters was commissioned to design the seal, and the theological department was opened in the fall of 1821 with Professor Irah Chase coming to supervise instruction.

The school could hardly have had a more auspicious beginning. From President Monroe on, every President encouraged its founders and John Quincy Adams watched its progress with unusual interest, loaning it twenty thousand dollars and frequently visiting when he was President.

A medical department was begun in 1825, consisting of a two-year course of five months per year with Dr. Thomas Sewall as dean and assisted by President Staughton's son James, who had recently graduated from the medical school in Philadelphia. In 1826 a law department was added.

Everyone except Rice was astonished with the college's success. On this sub-zero January 9 in 1822, there were thirty-three students;

by October there were forty-six and by April of 1824, there were ninety-three, with twenty-one of the twenty-four states represented. The buildings were beginning to be crowded.

But even on this Wednesday in January, there was already a cloud over the proceedings due to the financial load which had been assumed. Rice, however—never one to trim his dreams to fit a budget—was not deterred, for he had come to feel that "the proper collegiate education of young ministers is, with me, the essential and paramount object of all my exertions."[22]

14. Rice and Judson

"Luther Rice was large-framed, impressive in presence, impatient of restraint. Adoniram Judson was delicately formed, slight in stature, modestly reserved. Rice was eloquent and magnetic; Judson was quiet and dignified . . . one was a raging torrent, the other was a master of methods. Rice won men by his enthusiasm, Judson by his everlasting persistence."[1]

Rice was an activist, Judson a thinker. Each personality complemented the other. Together they were a winning team and Judson perceived this more keenly than Rice, for he never wavered from the conviction that Rice was the best of all possible colaborers, even after conceding that Rice would never come out to Burma to pool their labors.

In any generation, Adoniram would be hailed as a precocious child—reading the Bible at three, fascinated by the world of languages, mathematics, and precise logic. His minister-father was as aware as any parent watching a firstborn and exerted every pressure toward excellence. This drive toward leadership and primary position in the family conspired to mold Adoniram into a rather rigid, perfectionist, and introvertive person. Yet there was something of the rebel and iconoclast in his makeup, a bit of the ascetic, and much of the scholar.

Luther, in contrast, was the last of six boys in the family, growing up in the more relaxed atmosphere of a younger child's place, his elders scarcely conscious of any giftedness he evinced. Though even as a child he sought the company of intelligent people, there was little intellectual self-consciousness about him. He was "a rare combination of deep-seated seriousness and an unconquerable love of fun."[2] Where Judson was often moody, Rice could never be sad for long, even when circumstances warranted it. Judson married three times and fathered twelve children. Rice tarried in many homes but never his own.

Judson was graduated from Andover before Rice came, but they were thrown together at the Brethren meetings, and Judson was often at Andover during the long months when they were waiting for the Board to act.

Their natural affinity was cemented during the harrowing eviction from Calcutta. Rice's energy and congeniality under duress were not lost on the Judsons.

"What happy days," recalled Adoniram, "we spent at Budgebudge and Fultah; what spiritual consolations and felicities we mutually imparted when chased about by the officers of the police. Have you ever seen happier?"[3]

When Rice bade a hurried good-bye to the Judsons, he promised to rejoin them in two years. They hoped Rebecca would return with him; in fact, that was a reason, as he wrote Marshman, for granting the leave. From the *Donna Maria* he lamented to the Judsons: "I had not separated from you two days, perhaps not a single day, before I earnestly wished myself back again."[4]

From Salem in a letter to Marshman, Rice wrote as he began his first southern tour: "Notwithstanding the war, it will be very practicable for me to return to India by the way of Brasil; perhaps by the way of the Cape of Good Hope,"[5] and included a letter to Judson which the Serampore group was to read and forward.

In September following the formation of the Convention, Rice wrote Adoniram and Ann from Vermont that he felt "greatly pained to find myself still at so great a distance from the dearest friends I have on earth," adding:

The Baptist Board of Foreign Missions instituted by the Convention, readily undertook your support and mine, but thought it necessary for me to continue my labours in this country for a time. Of this I am convinced in my judgment, though it is extremely painful to my heart to be thus detained here. I hope, however, in the course of five or six months to get the Baptists so well rallied, that the necessity of my remaining will no longer exist. And I certainly wish not to remain here a moment longer than my stay will more advance the mission, than my departure for the field again.[6]

That same month Rice rode down to Plymouth and spent the weekend with Adoniram's parents and sister Abigail. Adoniram had requested him to visit his father and explain their reasons for the seemingly impulsive entrance into the Baptist fold. The elder Judson had been chagrined, no doubt, upon hearing that his pride and namesake had defected to the Baptists. It was even whispered that something less, or more, than doctrinal persuasion prompted their change. Rice was the person to allay the elder Judson's fears. The father listened intently and the whole was reported to Adoniram Jr.:

Plymouth, I have not been able to visit till quite recently; . . . In your father's house, I felt as if among my own relations . . . your parents and sister were in usual health. Your father inquired respecting my change of sentiment and present views, but made not a single remark tending to the support of infant baptism.[7]

Adoniram Sr. journeyed to Philadelphia to attend a meeting of the Board, and in 1817 he and his wife and Abigail went to Boston and were immersed by Dr. Thomas Baldwin in the Second Baptist Church. Luther kept in touch with them and also with Adoniram's younger brother, Elnathan, who became a government surgeon and lived in Baltimore. Elnathan assisted in purchasing the lot for the college and contributed toward other items of Rice's soliciting, such as the money to frame a portrait of Adoniram which hung in the halls of the college.

On this same trip to New England, in the autumn of 1814, Rice visited Boston, Beverly, Salem, and the surrounding area. Rebecca was teaching somewhere near Boston. Certainly in the first two years while itinerating, he saw the Emersons and Rebecca, for he spoke at Beverly. Whether from his becoming a Baptist, or some other reservation which his change confirmed in her mind, Rebecca's answer remained negative. She never married, but taught school for several years, spending some winters in Charlestown, South Carolina, where she tutored a few pupils, and at least one year in Philadelphia, where she wrote a geography book on Pennsylvania for her pupils. She later became interested in the New England Female

Reform Society, serving as secretary, treasurer, and editress of its publication, *The Home Guardian,* also known as *The Friend of Virtue.* The Judsons could not know of the separation and were hoping that Rice would return and bring Rebecca with him.

At almost every meeting of the Board during these years, there was reference to Rice's return to the foreign field of labor. Board members were divided in their opinion as to where his maximum usefulness could be realized, but the discussion was always resolved by voting that their agent "continue his itinerant services in these United States for a reasonable time."[8]

Yet Rice was aware that there were those who thought he should return immediately. By the spring of 1815, a circular inquiry was mailed to all Board members, requesting their opinion on his field of labor. That spring he was writing Judge Tallmadge of his frustration in obtaining a suitable wife and unabashedly stating that he did not "expect to return to India without being provided for in this respect," quoting Rev. Robert B. Semple as saying, "It is probably an interference of Providence that you have not procured a wife as yet."[9] Staughton wrote Tallmadge that Rice "conceives the Mission his loveliest wife. To her I wish him affectionately wedded but I really wish, for the sake of peace, he would find one composed of flesh and blood . . ."[10]

Yet if marriage were the only deterrent, certainly there were women who were willing to go, even though Rebecca was not one of them. One of the Thurston girls of Haverhill sailed out to Bombay to marry the widowed Samuel Newell, and Mrs. Charlotte White, who had accompanied the George Houghs at her own expense, promptly married one of the English Baptist missionaries when she arrived in Serampore. Rice had long conversations with Mary Dunning at her brother's home in Savannah, and they discussed his joining Judson. Mary journeyed to New York and not only confessed her willingness to go as a missionary but assured Judge Tallmadge that her wealthy brother, who at first opposed the idea, had agreed to pay her salary and expenses.[11] Either Luther kept waiting for Rebecca to go, or he was not too seriously interested in marrying and returning to work with Judson.

At first he wrote that it would be a matter of months; then he was writing Judson in the fall of 1814 that it would be two years. The Judsons' anxiety about his return became increasingly evident in their letters.

In 1816, Judson wrote President Asa Messer of Brown, "I have been much encouraged and gratified by the kind reception that my companion Mr. Rice met with from the churches in America, and am anticipating his welcome return, accompanied I hope by others."[12]

About this time he reminded Rice, "You remember, that the furlough we gave you at the Isle of France, extended to two years only."[13] Perhaps Ann and Adoniram began to be apprehensive that he would never return, for at this time he continued:

Little did we then think, that three or four years would elapse, before we met again . . . I congratulate you on the success which has crowned your labours in America. It really surpasses my highest expectations. Still permit me to hope, that as you are spending the prime of your life in such valuable services, in America, for the heathen, you will give them your personal services in your old age; and that we shall yet unite our prayers and labours, and finally lay our bones together in an Eastern clime.

Since you left us, we have been called both to rejoice and to mourn over a dear little child. He died three months ago, at the age of eight months. So that we are now reduced to our former solitary situation. We are, however, daily expecting Bro. Hough and family. He has already sent round a press & expects to follow himself the first opportunity . . .[14]

Adoniram revealed to Luther that he had "been almost blind for four months past, afflicted at the same time with a nervous affection of the head, which has unfitted me for any exertion," and that he had completed a Burman grammar "which I hope, will be useful to you; also a tract, which I hope to get printed as soon as Mr. H. arrives."

Some had inquired of Adoniram how many converts he had won and what dividends they were reaping on their investment, to which he replied:

If any ask what success I meet with among the natives, tell them to look at Otaheite, where the missionaries laboured nearly twenty years and not meeting with the slightest success, began to be neglected by all the Christian world, and the very name of Otaheite began to be a shame to the cause of missions; and now the blessing begins to come. Tell them to look at Bengal also where Thomas had been labouring seventeen years, that is from 1783 to 1800, before the first convert, Kriskna, was baptized. When a few converts are once made, things move on. But it requires a much longer time than I have been here to make a first impression on a heathen people. If they ask again, what prospect of ultimate success is there? Tell them, as much as there is an Almighty and Faithful God will perform his promises, and no more. If this does not satisfy them, beg them to let me stay and try it, and to let you come, and to give us our bread; or if they are unwilling to risk their bread on such a forlorn hope, as has nothing but the word of God to sustain it beg of them at least not to prevent others from giving us bread. And if we live, some twenty or thirty years, they may hear from us again.[15]

He assured Rice that the "climate is good, better than any part of the East. But it is a most filthy wretched place" with no sign of creature comforts. But Judson vowed that if a ship were lying in the river and he could go any place he liked, "I would prefer dying to embarking." The last few words of this long letter were cut from the sentence before Rice allowed anyone else to read it, and the reason could only have been that they referred to Rebecca coming out with him. The long communication ended: "Nancy unites with me in affectionate remembrances; we both long to see you again, and welcome with Rice————."[16]

Recruits were being enlisted to augment the forces in Rangoon, sometimes with more zeal than discretion, and soon after the Houghs' arrival, Judson advised Luther to move with caution:

In encouraging other young men to come out as missionaries, do use the greatest caution. You have hit right in brother Hough; but one wrong headed, conscientiously obstinate fellow, would ruin us. Humble, quiet, persevering men; men of sound, sterling talents (though perhaps not brilliant) of decent accomplishments, and some natural aptitude to acquire a language; men of amiable, yielding temper, willing to take the lowest place, to be the least of all, and the servant of all; men who enjoy much closet religion, who live near to God, and are willing to suffer all things for Christ's sake, without being proud of it . . .[17]

Despite this warning, the Board failed singularly in their next appointees, the Edward Wheelocks and James Colmans who arrived in Rangoon, September, 1818. Both of the men, whom Rice never met, were young and tubercular, and their families and friends knew they had contracted this dread disease before they were appointed. Wheelock had hardly unpacked before he wrote his father back in Massachusetts that though the sea voyage was beneficial to his lung ailment, the exertions of arriving precipitated a show of blood again. But he assured his father that he was happy to die on heathen soil, having realized at least one of his lifelong ambitions.

Unfortunately, the Wheelocks were also deficient in ability to get along with other people; Eliza, especially, found it impossible to adjust to the schedule in the mission and to the demands wrought by several families living under one roof. She complained bitterly that Ann and Adoniram were highhanded and bossy, this hostility toward them developing into a paranoid tendency to feel that all were persecuting her and that the whole household was disposed to abuse herself and poor, dying Edward. The Colmans were congenial and adaptable, but his frail health was to limit their tenure to less than five years.

No wonder Judson longed for Rice. Cognizant of how much their labors were intertwined, he pled, "How much at times have we needed your congeniality of mind, the support of your tried attachment. When two faithful friends are united, how great is the mutual support."[18]

How did Rice withstand their repeated entreaty? Did he simply feel he was ill-fitted for the mission field, or that the work at home was a more rewarding field for his talents? In June, 1817, when he was becoming more and more engrossed in establishing the college, a paper, and home missions, he informed the Judsons that it would take a decade to finish his task in the States, and Adoniram answered:

Your mention of ten years has cut off the little hope I had remaining of uniting with you, as an assistant, in missionary labours. It seems that our paths have been diverging from the Isle of France, until they have terminated in scenes of labour the most remote and dissimilar possible; but I trust that we have both been guided aright, and that whatever local relation our bones may finally sustain in this world, our spirits will at last be united in the same celestial scene. . . . the plains of heaven. . . . the presence of the Lamb.

I feel disposed to pour out my regrets, but I suppose they would be unavailing. I really expect to see you no more in this world. It appears to me that the proposal of ten years is of the same use and benefit as a projecting crag in a precipice, which serves a little to break the force of the fall, but only bruises and mangles the poor wretch, who might as well go to the bottom at once. No! we shall meet no more in this world. I never said so before, but I think I may venture to say so now. We shall meet no more, unless some circumstances occur in America to induce you to change your mind very shortly.

When I think of our very pleasant intercours on board the Creole, and in our own hired house at Port Louis, I almost regret that I ever consented to your leaving me . . .[19]

Judson confided his fears concerning the feeble health of the new arrivals and mentioned that Hough was departing for Bengal from whence he might go "to Chittagong, and live there among the Muggs." Concluding that the departure of the Houghs and the imminent terminal illnesses of Wheelock and Colman would again leave him alone, he grew anxious.

Again he prodded Rice:

So you see that I am almost all alone again. Suppose you should think of coming out, after all. But no—perhaps it is not best; perhaps you should stay in America. I leave the matter wholly to your decision; circumstances qualify you to be the most capable judge, and I see how you will decide . . .

I see you, pale and thin, sitting in Rolt's little room, and writing out texts of scriptures . . . I see you playing the flute on board ship, while that queer Frenchman is taking you off, cap and all. I see you sitting on the side of Port Louis hill, looking away towards Madagascar and anon towards the East. I see you embarking in the American vessel, when circumstances prevented any other leave-taking than touching our hats. I see you seated in your wagon, posting through the states, now haranguing in an Atlantic seaport, and now penetrating an Indian forest. When shall I see you next? Who can tell what the receding mists of futurity will disclose? . . .[20]

Rice felt Judson was censuring him for not rejoining the mission and protested in his next letter. Judson was receiving other letters, some from Rice's critics, but defended his loyalty in his next to Rice:

If you could see all I have written about you *in connection with the letters to which I was replying,* you would be convinced, that I had *always* written as favorably to you as possible, and would not for a moment entertain the idea, that 'I was inclined to *censure* your not returning to India'. Perhaps some sentence, presented in its insulated state, might appear, especially to one who had not seen the letter to which I was replying, to convey such an idea. But I have never intentionally expressed my disapprobation of the course you have pursued, for on the whole, I have acquiesced in it, tho I have regretted my own loss occasioned thereby. I think you have done a vast deal of good in America . . .[21]

But Judson could not refrain from urging Rice, once more, to come out, informing him that the *zayat* was built, worship was begun, inquirers were beginning to attend, and a convert was to be baptized the next Sunday.

In view of these circumstances, will you come over and help us? You will be preaching to the natives in two years. Will it not be pleasant to instill truth into the minds of young converts from heathenism, to proclaim the gospel to all around, to stand before the king, and preach to the Burman court, in a word, to be a main instrument in introducing the Redeemer's Kingdom into this great empire?[22]

Judson admitted there was much in favor of Rice's staying in America and suggested that Dr. Staughton was best equipped, because of his central location and knowledge of both fields of work, to advise Rice, concluding: "If he says, Go, I think you ought to come out; but if he says stay, don't come. This is the sum of what I have to say."

Nevertheless he had quite a bit more to say, and reversed himself by giving Rice some partisan comments:

It is, however, at the present time, rather a question with me (a question which I do not presume to decide) whether you had not better come out. Members, in different parts of the country are expecting and wishing it. Your great work is mainly done. If you should close your American labours by actually embarking as a missionary, it would add great weight to all your past deeds, and be most suitable and worthy consummation. You would perhaps do more good in America, by such a measure, than your presence would effect. It would at least stamp a character of sincerity on the whole affair, which multitudes will otherwise question.[23]

Judson was correct in stating that there were those who questioned Rice's motives. Led by William White, William Rogers, Asa Messer, and Henry Holcombe, these said that Rice never, from the beginning, intended to return to help Judson. From the stance of another century, knowing the subsequent sad years of Luther's life, one wishes he had taken Judson's advice. Had he embarked and lived out his life in Burma, probably he would have been almost canonized as was Judson.

In this same letter Judson revealed his anxiety over Hough, who was still in Bengal. "What he went for, what he is doing, and when he will return, are questions that I must leave for him to answer." Then he divulged his deepest misgiving about Hough:

I am in distress about him. Perhaps I ought not to say a word that may hurt him. But as it may show you this necessity of your coming out, I will mention the secret to you. But let it not go beyond Dr.

Staughton. Brother Hough may come right at last. The truth is that he has got into a whirlpool of Swedenborgianism. He had almost given up the doctrines of grace before he left us. I lately received letters from him written several months after his departure, in which he does not say a word on the subject, and this confirms my fears, that he is settling down on the wrong side.[24]

Hough had little theological training, thus was vulnerable when exposed to a new and convincingly presented ideology. His wife was evidently not a believer since the Board once suggested that the appellation "Sister" be deleted from her name as it was "used by Christians to denominate a professor of Religion, which your committee understand Mrs. Hough is not."[25] Hough was also somewhat inept in arranging his own affairs. On his initial trip to Burma, he engaged and paid for passage on a ship out of Calcutta bound for Rangoon. After he and his family were aboard and several miles down the Hooghly, he found that the captain and crew drank heavily and fearing to proceed, he returned on a small boat to Calcutta though unable to take his printing press back. The owner refused to refund his passage, so the Board paid for two passages for himself and family. Burma's climate, both politically and physically, was fraught with peril, and his two young children's welfare may have influenced him to leave Rangoon.

At any rate, at the third Triennial Convention in 1820, the committee report on the Burman mission stated that "some circumstances attending this mission, at the same time, create painful regret. Mr. Hough has removed with his family, on his own responsibility, from Rangoon to Serampore. The Board hopes he has been influenced by higher motives than the fear of man or the love of ease; yet they cannot but consider his conduct as unwarrantable in its nature, and in its tendency injurious. The Board are of the opinion that he has virtually removed himself from under their patronage."[26] Following the Triennial Convention, the new Board met and voted "that relations with Hough were severed from the time he left for Serampore."[27]

When Judson heard that the Board had censured Hough, and not knowing the basis of their action, he jumped to the conclusion that Rice had disclosed the contents of his letter about Hough's leaning toward Swedenborgianism. This surmise was incorrect, since the Board's action had nothing to do with that, but he upbraided Rice in his next letter:

131

I once mentioned to you, that we had been examining the system of Swedenborg, and that Brother Hough was strongly inclined to adopt it. Since I have heard of the censure passed on him by the Board, I have thought it possible, that though I mentioned it to you in confidence, it may, in some indirect way, have operated to his disadvantage. I am anxious, therefore, to state what I have lately ascertained, that our examination of that system has terminated the same in both cases, or that we are both, I hope, more firmly established than ever, in the truth of the gospel.[28]

Judson had not even mentioned previously that he also was studying Emmanuel Swedenborg's teachings, but his very real concern for his colleague was further evident:

I feel much for Brother Hough. But I hardly know what to write relative to him, as I know not definitely what measures the Board has taken. I am just writing Staughton. . . . His leaving Rangoon has evidently assumed a different appearance, in consequence of his long stay in Bengal, from what it would have done had he succeeded in accomplishing the ends of his voyage. . . . His situation had, however, been extremely embarrassing, unforeseen difficulties have been thrown in his way, and for the last year, he has been within the deleterious influences of a person under whose lips is the poison of asps.[29]

The young widow, Eliza Wheelock, had gone to Calcutta and her acrimonious slandering of the Judsons continued; Judson was aware that Hough may have succumbed to some of her rumors. Also, Hough appears to have taken sides in the unfortunate Serampore controversy between the pioneer missionaries and the newer missionaries —the wrong side, since he went to Calcutta and there lived with the Lawsons. The Serampore missionaries were the side that was in constant correspondence with Dr. Staughton and other Board members in the Philadelphia Association. Yet Judson was anxious to clear Hough:

I do hope that on his wording a full explanation of his proceedings, his character will be greatly relieved and I am sure that in such a case, the Board will not give the immutable stamp of the Medes and Persians on their present decision concerning him. Mr. Hough appears to possess much of a Christian spirit, especially under present trial.[30]

Adoniram also asked for Luther's help about one of his own personal hurts. A letter of Dr. Samuel Worcester's stating that Adoniram had received a "formal and solemn reprimand" from

Dr. Samuel Spring at the meeting of the Board of Commissioners at Worcester in September, 1811, had been published in New England. Judson appealed to Rice: "You accompanied me at that session, and was frequently before the Board. If I received a formal reprimand, you must have known it. Will you be so good, as to tell me decidedly, whether Dr. Worcester's charge is correct or not? I want your testimony on this point immediately. Write this by the very first ship, care of Rev. Mr. Lawson, Calcutta, nobody else."[31]

If there were any person more persuasive and more ingenious in getting his way than Adoniram, it was Nancy, and so she returned to the subject they could not drop in a long, pathetic letter of appeal, July 5, 1819:

Little did we think at our sorrowful parting at the Isle of France, that almost seven years would elapse, and we should be still writing you. For the first two or three years after you left us, we hardly dared write a letter, thinking you would have left America before it would reach you; and even for the two or three last years, we have been hoping that unforseen events would transpire, which would clearly discover to your mind, that the path of duty led directly to Burmah. We have ever felt that though the breach which your absence has made in our little family, would be filled only by yourself, yet we ought to acquiesce, and quietly submit, if the advancement of the mission made it necessary. We have ever been convinced, that you being on the ground of operation, know better than we, what part or parts of the missionary machine needed to be kept in motion, and what means were to most necessary to excite that motion. Hence, we have till now, patiently submitted to the trial which your long absence has occasioned. But now, my dear brother Rice, we need missionaries on the ground more than any thing beside.[32]

Seeing the crying need of Burma, like so many missionaries before and since, the Judsons could not reconcile themselves to Rice's staying in America. So few on the field, so many at home, their hearts wrenched by the appalling spiritual needs of the Burmese, they voiced the age-old and unanswerable question: which is primary, to keep the home base strong or to extend the lifeline? Nancy tried to jar Rice into awareness of the lapse of time and the dearth of good men:

At the end of six years residence in this country, Mr. Judson finds himself *still alone* in missionary work. He wishes *now* to devote all his time to preaching the gospel to this people. But tracts are to be written; portions of scripture are to be translated, and many other necessary things must be done—but who will do them? . . . You my dear brother, are the person that we need just in this stage of the mission. Your age, judgment, and experience, qualify you in a peculiar manner to be of most essential service in those cases of difficulty and trial, to which we are so frequently subject in this country. Your correct ear and aptness for acquiring languages, together with the means and helps which Mr. J. has prepared, would enable you in *one year* from the time of your arrival, to *begin* to communicate religious truths to this perishing people.[33]

Is Luther worried about who will take his place in America? "No young man will feel the necessity of taking your place, till they see it vacated by your absence."

Is he hesitating about the climate, remembering his acute illness? "This is a delightful climate. The liver complaint is never known here."[34] Luther must have gulped at this dose of propaganda but she was not finished: "Europeans can bear the heat of the sun in the middle of the day, without feeling the least injurious effect. Instances of longevity among the natives are numerous; perhaps more so, than in any part of the world." She assured him that a missionary would probably live longer there than any other place on earth and added, "It is a good place to grow in grace, and prepare for heaven."[35]

But soon after this letter was posted, the Judsons' hopes were doused by receipt of a long letter from Dr. Staughton, citing reasons why Rice should remain stateside. Judson penned to Rice: "My last from Dr. Staughton has finally reconciled me entirely to your staying in America; but I cannot but wish you had replied yourself to my long entreaty . . . Go on, most dear brother; and may God prosper you abundantly in all your ways. I feel assured that though we labour apart on earth, we shall rest together in Heaven, in the embrace of everlasting love."[36]

A year later, Judson sent Rice's writing desk and papers to Boston, "notwithstanding your advice to the contrary," for Judson supposed them "to be letters and private writings which you would be unwilling to have exposed to any person whatever." He said, "If I should happen to die, I could not, you know, be answerable for their security. They might fall into the hands of some one, who would make a bad use of them."[37]

Judson accepted Rice's decision at last. For several years he reverted to his wish at times, but he tried to yield gracefully:

I frequently wish that I had seen Philadelphia and Washington and the scenes among which you are so much employed, that I might be able to form a more definite idea of your situation and movements. And I wish too, that you had once been in Rangoon, that you might sometimes look away and see the kyoung, which is my house; and zayat, which is my office. I am now writing in the zayat, at one of those little tables that you bought at the Isle of France. It is almost the only thing that remains of our common property. Time and worms have devastated trunks, and books etc.; and they will soon treat our bodies in the same manner—will they not my brother? But there is a world, where moth and rust corrupt not, and there I will introduce you to my precious little Burman church; and there they will meet their now unknown benefactor; of whom I sometimes tell them.[38]

Luther wrote to Adoniram through the years, laying bare the hopes and desires of his heart and just as candidly, his personal and denominational failures. As the cares of the college and the concomitant financial woes swamped him, something of his harassment was manifest to Judson, who responded:

I have received your two short, and almost illegible letters of last March, and it is hardly necessary for me to say, how fully I enter into all your views and wishes in regard to the new college, and whatever tends to raise the character of the Baptist denomination, and promote the cause of Christ at large, in the United States.[39]

To comfort Rice about the criticism he was receiving, Judson said, "Your labours will be ultimately appreciated, and the page of history will do you ample justice, notwithstanding the dissentient voice of the narrow-minded of the present day."[40]

Judson, though the younger, often became Rice's counselor in the later years of their friendship and advised: "Only be not elated by any success; walk softly before God." He added,

I wished that we might live and labor together; but I hope that, though separated, we are both doing important service for the same master, perhaps in ways best adapted to our respective capacities. I little thought when the boat rowed away from the ship in the harbour of Port Louis, and I left you standing on the deck, that I should see your face no more. Poor Nancy has gone on a pilgrimage for health and life, to the shrine of old England. Perhaps she will visit America . . .[41]

Nancy arrived in New England in September, 1822. After a few weeks of speaking, a constant flow of visitors, and the adulations of thousands—she had become a heroine—she went south to Baltimore to spend the winter with Adoniram's brother, Elnathan, the government surgeon. She spent the winter writing *An Account of the American Mission to the Burman Empire,* which was printed by the *Columbian Star* press in Washington.

Nancy became very fond of Elnathan during her furlough and wished he might accompany her back to Burma. What nicer surprise for Adoniram than the arrival of his only brother? But there were obstacles to this novel plan, for Elnathan was employed by the government and had no reason to expect a year's leave. Perhaps this could be remedied if Columbian College would appoint Elnathan a "nominal" professor.

Luther was the very person to arrange this. He had visited Nancy at Elnathan's boardinghouse, renewing their friendship. She appealed to him, but he was reluctant. Elnathan had never made any profession of religion, and recently the Board had refused Professor Irah Chase's request that he be their official representative on a trip to Germany in conjunction with his European tour.

Nancy thought Elnathan could bring back religious objects for the Missionary Museum at Columbian College. She was becoming accustomed to unusual considerations, and expressed pique with Luther that he did not gratify her wishes, in a letter from her home in Bradford before she sailed in June:

Brother is still with me, the *kindest* and most *attentive* and *affectionate* of brothers and I think *skillful physician.* He would have accompanied me to Calcutta, had you granted my request in giving him a *nominal professorship,* so that he could have assigned a plausible reason to Govt. for his long absence. He would have collected many things for your museum and have been at no expense to the Board. He would also have been firmly attached to the Southern Baptist interest and to the College which I fear is not now the case.[42]

She believed God "will one day open his eyes to behold spiritual things in a spiritual manner," and reflected, "I have not received a line from Dr. Staughton since I left Washington. I fear something occurred which has offended him."[43] Perhaps Dr. Staughton was averse to Elnathan's nominal professorship also.

Meanwhile, Adoniram was writing Luther that he hoped "Mrs. J. will return, accompanied by one or two good missionaries. I cannot help indulging a faint hope that you will come yourself."[44] Yet

Adoniram must have known this was a futile hope for in the same letter he noted, "You are evidently absorbed in the college. But it is a great and worthy object; and there is no truer maxim, that a man never does anything to purpose, unless his whole soul is in it."[45]

In subsequent years Adoniram and Luther continued to correspond, though perhaps in an intermittent fashion. In his last years Luther wrote asking Adoniram to recount the experiences revolving around their sailing in 1812, and Judson complied. Luther, in turn, continued to send Judson magazines and books, as he was able. In one of Judson's last letters, May 9, 1835, he wrote:

Your very interesting letters of April, last year, accompanying a file of the *Religious Herald,* reached me in December, on the return of brother and sister Wade. I am interested in all your efforts, and the success that crowns them. I doubt not that the Columbian College will be an honor to the country, and especially to the Baptist cause, an instrument in the hand of God, by which he will diffuse the glory and extend the reign of his Son. In your former connection with the board, and your subsequent devotion to the college, you, have doubtless committed some mistakes, and been betrayed into some sins; but the unjust reproaches with which you have been so liberally visited, are in my opinion disproportionate to the errors charged to your account.

I confidently expect that a reaction will take place; and . . . your name will be enrolled among the benefactors of our country, and of that denomination into which we are ingrafted together. The praise of man however, is not the boon for which we strive. Our mark is higher, our crown incorruptible. And let us have faith to believe that we shall assuredly obtain.[46]

That same summer Luther wrote Adoniram that in regard to his former differences with Irah Chase, Baron Stow, and J. D. Knowles, he had written each, asking for forgiveness, and a "perfectly cordial and happy reconciliation has taken place between us."[47]

As if he had a premonition, in one of his last letters to Judson, he said, "I have been lately meditating more and more on *keeping the heart with all diligence.* I am, I trust, more and more impressed, sweetly too, with the idea of *living for heaven,*" and as if in farewell:

And now, my ever dear brother, may the living God be your portion, your everlasting all. May the best of *heaven's* blessings rest on you and your dear, good wife . . . and may you see, even before the termination of the few years of your labours yet on earth, Burmah far more advanced in religious knowledge and in righteousness, than your beloved and highly favoured native country is at the present period![48]

Their friendship bridged the oceans and spanned the years. They were destined never to meet again and after hearing of Rice's going, Judson named his next son Luther. But the child was still-born, signifying perhaps an "aborted hope" about their united labors.

15. Baptist Circuit Rider

In all the upper reaches of the Ohio, bitterly cold weather gripped the country in a cycle of snow, ice, and thaw, followed by fresh snow. The winter's gnawing winds howled around the unsung frontier cabins and the inhabitants long remembered the year they dubbed "eighteen-hundred-and-froze-to-death." But Rice was inured to the cold and he spent the whole winter of 1815 to 1816 in Kentucky, making his headquarters with Dean Benjamin Stout in Lexington.

The tour began in late July when he bought wrapping paper and twine, sorted and bundled the *Annual Report,* packed the parcels on the floorboard of his wagon, lowered the tarpaulin sides and turned his horse west along the Schuylkill to the Falls.

On the first day out he made forty miles; four days later, the twenty-sixth, in a driving rain he traveled fifty-seven miles. The following day he "proceeded over the backbone of the United States"[1] and, descending the mountain, broke a wagon axle which caused a delay. Intent on reaching Madison County, Kentucky, by the first of August "so as to meet the North District Association,"[2] he had to abate his course until the wagon was repaired and thus failed to meet that appointment. At North Huntington he left "400 copies of the report of the Board of Missions with Dr. Shelton to be sent by boat to Cincinnati, to the Rev. Mr. Dennison."[3]

Rice was warmly welcomed on his first Kentucky tour; his routine was much the same in each circuit. He sent letters ahead notifying the leading ministers in the association of his coming, identifying himself, and expressing a desire to be heard and to present the missionary appeal as agent of the Board of Missions. Arriving at an associational meeting, he presented his credentials, letters of commendation, and usually was invited to a seat and requested to preach.

Henry Keeling wrote of Rice's first visit to the Chowan Association when it met at Sawyers Creek meetinghouse near Elizabeth City in North Carolina. "It was a beautiful day," he recalled, "and among the few who had assembled were the venerable Elder Martin Ross, and his faithful coadjutor and fellow-servant, Elder William Wright.

"As soon as the usual compliments had passed, Elder Ross says to Elder Wright, who was to preach the introductory sermon that morning, 'I understand Luther Rice is to be here today!'

" 'Luther Rice,' exclaimed the other. 'Is it possible? Then he must preach.' "[4]

Soon a tall, black-garbed figure appeared on the outskirts of the gathering, strode toward the two ministers, introduced himself, was asked to preach, and readily assented. "He had reached Norfolk the evening before in a boat from Baltimore and had ridden 60 miles that night; not in the cars, nor in a stage, but alone, on a strange bad road, sparsely settled; and had rested only for a short time at sister Bushnell's a mile or two from the church where he had taken breakfast."[5]

All his life Keeling could hear "the tones of his voice linger in our ears" as Rice sang, and the prayer "he offered was the most heavenly we had ever heard."[6]

After he preached on missions, he always took an offering. He also asked the association to appoint a person to correspond with the convention and to select someone to forward their proceedings to Dr. Staughton in Philadelphia and distribute the *Annual Report*. He usually recorded in his *Journal*: "Missionary business satisfactorily attended to."

During his itinerating, Rice saw many changes in transportation. When he was a lad in New England, turnpikes were beginning to be built, and the year he was born, neighbor Levi Pease began regular stage service between Boston and New York. The speed was four miles per hour, three pence per mile, and the trip spanned four days each way. But the mail was still delivered by courier on horseback, post riders covering thirty to fifty miles per day. He could remember when the first four-horse stage went through on the Post Road, attracting delegations from nearby towns. For local travel his family used a sleigh in winter and a two-wheeled wagon in summer; four-wheeled wagons came into use in New England about the turn of the century, but they were not common until after the War of 1812.

In later years, Rice often went by steamboat, the *Potomac* between Washington and Norfolk, the *Connecticut* from New York to Providence. Trains gained general acceptance during the latter years of his life but because of the nature of his itinerating, his schedule of appointments, and the frugality necessary during those years, horseback (the mode of his childhood) remained his most frequent transport.

Following the much-traveled roads of the sea coast on his first trip south in 1813, he had used public conveyances most of the way—a boat to Richmond and the stage through the Carolinas and Georgia. Sometimes he hired a chaise for side trips.

En route to Kentucky in the summer of '15, Rice had been told of the spiritual poverty in Indiana Territory and something of the Indians' plight in the territories. So after visiting Kentucky associational meetings and helping to organize four mission societies, he resolved to cross the Ohio into that area. In late November he found the country wild; "swimming the creeks" proved hazardous and long stretches of wilderness roads, some hardly more than trails, were often marked only by blazes on a tree.

In Indiana Territory he visited the McCoys and other area leaders including the Governor, securing an evaluation of the needs among the Indians from each person he met.

Some nights, as in Madison Township, were spent on the puncheon floor of an inn where in midwinter the house was "open, no light except by the fire, must camp down on the floor with little bedding . . . calmed my mind with reflection that it is good for me to experience inconveniences and hardships."[7] For this lodging he paid 50½ cents. He always paid his bill at the inns and offered to do so when staying in private homes, feeling as did McCoy that this left him at "liberty to talk on religious subjects without exposing myself to the censure of 'Wishing to live cheap by preaching.' "[8]

Rising before daybreak, Rice was on the road early, riding "to Mud Hole, 14 miles" where he breakfasted and baited his horse, all for 27 cents. The following night he tarried in the home of a Perry County couple, neither of whom, nor their children, could read. By the semi-light cast from the fireplace he "read to them two chapters and a part of a third, in the Bible and spoke a little while on the 'love of Christ constraineth us.' "[9]

Rice always invited those in the inn or household to join him in evening prayers and Bible reading, saying, "I make it a point to pray for every family where I tarry a night, or call in the day; for every person, individually, who makes a donation for any object for which I receive funds; for every one I converse with in the day; for every person I see during the day; . . ."[10]

And a friend in whose house he stayed said, "He prayed in my family, and that prayer I shall not forget. Every one in the house was named."[11]

In December of '15, he recrossed the Ohio at Louisville and was "requested to preach this evening and consented. Hand bills sent about the town to announce the service. Large assembly." He preached from that favorite text: "What is man, that thou art mindful of him?"[12]

At Frankfort on the fifteenth of that month, he preached in the statehouse on "Glory to God in the highest" and collected fifty dollars for the missionary society. He had no compunctions about preaching in the courthouses or statehouses; indeed, those were the only available buildings in many towns and served as pulpit and assembly for itinerating ministers of all denominations. In the Georgia Statehouse at Milledgeville or the Kentucky Statehouse at Frankfort, he took an offering, and he did so even when he preached in churches of other denominations.

Stopping overnight in North Huntington on this trip west, he preached in the Second Presbyterian Church, deciding after he arose to speak to take an offering, determining this "by seeing so many people approach."[13] The Presbyterians, either more wealthy or more generous, often outgave the Baptists. He often tarried overnight with Presbyterian and Methodist minister-friends.

When winter's harshness receded in February, he left Kentucky where on his first trip he had "found as much readiness here as in any other quarter to patronize the missionary cause and more liberality than in any other state"[14]—this true though money was a novelty in many a homestead. Riding southward through pennyrile country, he crossed the barrens to Nashville, thence to Abingdon, Virginia, northeastward to Roanoke and then south through North Carolina, north again to Richmond and then to the annual meeting in Philadelphia in May.

In those early days the nearest place he had to a home was the residence of the Staughtons when he was in Philadelphia. He was fond of each member of the family and they of him. Mrs. Staughton was a great helper in her husband's work, a "Goliath in intellect"; when Rice performed a marriage ceremony or received other fees he gave them to Mrs. Staughton. His days in Philadelphia were filled with visiting the pastors and societies, writing thirty to forty letters a day and assisting with the *Luminary,* the *Annual Report,* and other Board interests. He was a member of the Sansom Street Church and during the weeks before the Triennial met there in May of 1817 it was Rice, not Dr. Staughton, who visited Baptists about the city and raised the money to whitewash and refurnish the meetinghouse for the coming convention.

After the 1814 Convention, when he began distributing the *Annual Report,* he used a wagon to carry the copies. The vehicle would be bought in the East and sold for a profit in Kentucky or Tennessee, and he would ride horseback on his return to Philadelphia. Sometimes it was a gig (an early entry reads "swapped mare and gig for a horse and saddle"); but usually it was a dearborn wagon, a two-horse vehicle with canvas top and sides. On the 1815 trip he bought his dearborn in upper New York for forty-five dollars and sold it to Dean Stout in Lexington for one hundred dollars; in 1817, he sold his "dearborn and horse and harness to Colonel [Michael] Hall in Barren County, Kentucky, for $200 and the use of his horse to ride about 300 miles."[15] He often let his tired horse out to pasture at a friend's home, hiring or borrowing another steed to ride farther, then retrieving his own mount on his return.

He sometimes solicited other men's help in distributing the *Annual Report.* Meeting Peck in the summer of 1815, Rice enlisted him as well as James Welch, who was in Dr. Staughton's school, and Hough, who was awaiting passage to Burma. Rice set up regular distribution points for the report and paper and carried long subscription lists. He mailed or delivered a box of one hundred of these to someone in each place who promised to distribute them.

The lists and the homes where he called included many places and people. In Cincinnati, Rice stayed with General Jonathan Gano and Gano handled the reports. The General was son of the famous minister, John Gano, and brother of Stephen, pastor of the First Baptist Church in Providence. In New York, Rice tarried with Judge Tallmadge. When in the Charlottesville area, he stopped with farmer-preacher John Goss of Barbourville, who aided him in every endeavor, keeping exact lists of subscriptions to the *Luminary* and men who pledged to pay on Columbian College, carefully preserving these alongside such valuable items as a "receipt for cutworms."[16] Or he would stay with General William Madison, President Madison's brother, at Woodbury Forest in Madison County. In Lexington he always stayed with Dean Stout; he took great interest in the faculty of Transylvania College and in 1817, was offered its presidency. But he declined.

There was no Baptist church in Nashville until 1820, but Rice had homes and pocketbooks open to him—James Foster and Judge Trimble in Nashville, Colonel Cheatham in Springfield, Thomas Edwards in Lebanon, and mainly, south of Nashville in Williamson County, Elder Garner McConnico, founder of the Big Harpeth and other middle Tennessee churches.

Elder McConnico, an Elijah in appearance, was tall and commanding with a shock of black hair and piercing black eyes. A Virginian who migrated there, he enjoyed a wide reputation as a minister and owned a large mansion noted for its open hospitality. It was even rumored that Elder McConnico cast out devils. When a "jerker," the by-product of the excessiveness of the Kentucky revival, attended his service and began his motions, McConnico paused, saying sternly, "In the name of the Lord, I command all unclean spirits to leave this place." The contortionist quieted and the legend blossomed. McConnico also possessed a "forty-parson power to chant," for once when he arrived at the stream near Big Harpeth Church and found it rain-swollen beyond fording, he preached loudly enough that the congregation could hear across the stream.[17]

On each journey to middle Tennessee, Rice stayed with McConnico: "Get the minutes of the Cumberland Association and an account of the state of things in this quarter of Bro. McConnico."[18] Though McConnico later sided with the Primitives, much of the fruit of his service flowed into the Missionary Baptist fold.

Midsummer 1816 found Rice on the road to Virginia and the Carolinas again and in the autumn he retraced his route to Kentucky, going back south to Georgia in the winter. He stayed for sometime in Georgia which, in latter years, became his southern winter home. On November 29 of this year, he confided to his *Journal* that while in the Savannah home of the well-to-do Dunnings, he and Miss Mary Dunning engaged in a long talk "which has considerably quickened my desire for returning to dear Brother Judson in India."[19] Miss Dunning also quickened his purse with a generous check toward endowing the secretaryship of the Board.

Rice's correspondence and the homes where he tarried during these years reads like a roll call of the Baptist faithful—Valentine Sevier of Greeneville, Tennessee; Esquire Thomas Wilson of Worcester, Massachusetts; the Samuel Redds of "Cedar Vale," Carolina County, Virginia; Dr. Cullen Battle at Powelton, Georgia; Dr. Jesse Mercer of the same place; the Furmans in Charleston; Rev. Edward Baptist of Powhatan County, Virginia—the list was as endless as the roads he took on behalf of his denomination.

One of Rice's frequent entries in the early years ran that his evening's host had not received his report or paper, "it not having come to hand." So it was to save time and expense, as well as to avoid loss, that he assumed much of the Board's distributing. The government mail was slow, expensive, and erratic. Parcels posted in Philadelphia were shipped via New Orleans up the Mississippi and down the Ohio and Tennessee Rivers to the valley towns, taking many weeks or months in transit.

A regular stop on his circuit was the camp meeting such as Halifax camp meeting in Virginia. He was there in 1816—"several wagons with families have come to the association bringing provisions"[20]— and he was there in August of 1836, only a few weeks before his death. He loved the Virginians and they returned the affection; he claimed more homes there than in any other area and visited in every valley and town of the state.

One of his favorite spots was the area around the capitol— Caroline County, King and Queen County, and Richmond itself. Late in the day or evening there would be the yelping of dogs, the joyous cries of the children, the alighting of the black-clad figure from the high seat in the gig, bundles, deerskin trunk, and saddlebag carried into the house by the children. The saint in a sulky had arrived and if the hostess had been forewarned, dinner was waiting. After a hearty repast, talk would digress from local events to the Convention, the missionary accomplishments of Judson and his colleagues, the prospects for the new college, the Bible society and Sunday School movements, and what Baptists were doing in other states. Since Luther knew anecdote after anecdote, sang at the drop of a hat, played the flute skilfully, and possessed a "flaw" of humor, the children sat wide-eyed, listening. Adults might deplore his ready wit and amazing stories but never the children. Where else or from what other visitor could they hear accounts of an actual visit to India, Brazil, or the vast country west of the mountains? He could tell of sleeping on his saddlebag for fear of losing the collections and laugh about it, or enthral them with stories of wildcats, bear, deer, and Indians beyond the Alleghenies. If the evening were long, he had a special rendition of his trip to India which he told, which often merited a special offering.

One of the homes in King and Queen County where he often visited was that of Deacon John Bagby of the Mattaponi Church. The big brick house was on the outskirts of Stevensville, in sight of the Church, and the eleven children in the home sat around the big table in the dining room after the evening meal, listening to their father and Brother Rice speak of the denomination and its plans. Servants drew near, intent on all that was said. Deacon Bagby was interested in Rice's college where southern sons of the Baptists could attend; the Bagbys sent five sons to Columbian, three of them becoming ministers, and the Bagby family gave scores of its progeny to Baptist leadership. The eldest son in this home, Richard Hugh, was to name his son Luther Rice Bagby in the years ahead, recalling the delightful visitor who opened up vistas of an outside world when he spent the night at "Bunker's Hill."

Rice was often at other homes in the county—"Mordington," the home of Robert Semple, another man whose interest he kindled for education; the home of the John Pollards; a bit north, the home of the timid but able Rev. Andrew Broaddus; and in Caroline County, the home of the Charles Todds.

Sometimes in the long stretches of wilderness where the roads were hardly more than cart tracks, he lost his way, as he did in East Tennessee in September of 1819: "Set out with a view of getting to Blountsville to preach tonight but getting out of my way among the mountains, knobs, and creeks, fail of the object and find myself obliged to put up two miles before reaching."[21] Or the time in Rutherford County, North Carolina, when he lost his way after traveling fifty-one miles one day, about which he wrote Asaph:

Being obliged to ride in the night, on Friday night I got lost. The roads in this part of our country are none of them fenced, and are mostly through wood; I had to go in that night by roads, but little travelled—missed the way, got out of roads, at length, into mere paths, and ultimately, lost the path—found myself alone in a dreary wilderness, unable to discover the point of compass; totally ignorant which way to direct my course, to find any road or habitation of men. I stopped, and besought the Lord to lead me out—rose from my supplications, and attempted to advance. In less perhaps, than two minutes, certainly in less than five, fell into the road which conducted me to the place that I calculated to reach that night, at which I arrived about 1 o'clock. Have now just come from attending Sandy Creek Association, and am on my way to the Charleston . . . Frequently, after completing a day's ride, instead of indulging in the repose which nature solicits, it is necessary for me to employ my pen; however, fatigues too often overcome me, or perhaps I too easily yield to the inclination to rest.[22]

In May 1817, his report to the Board read:

Since the date of my letter of the 19th of June, 1816, I have travelled 6,600 miles—in populous and in dreary portions of country—through wildernesses and over rivers—across mountains and valleys—in heat and cold—by day and by night—in weariness, and painfulness, and fastings, and loneliness; but not a moment has been lost for want of health; no painful calamity has fallen to my lot; no peril has closed upon me; nor has fear been permitted to prey on my spirits; nor even inquietude to disturb my peace.[23]

Occasionally his life was endangered where the roads were inhabited by the worst sort of men by day and wild creatures by night, as the time in Wythe County, Virginia, when he "fell in company with two men who appeared to be entirely without any settled object ahead, or concern to get forward on their journey, and manifestly base men. They kept about me yesterday and today they seemed inclined not to get far from me, particularly so as I approached a lonesome long piece of woods through which I must pass to go to Grayson. My suspicions were so great that I thought proper to take another road."[24]

As he journeyed he took a kind of roving census of religious conditions in the country, asking how often divine worship was held, what denominations were to be found, and whether or not the inhabitants had Bibles in their homes. Results were reported to the various societies back East. In western Pennsylvania in September, 1818, he passed through Centreville, "then along a good turnpike but in an uneven and rugged country. Breakfast at the turnpike gate. New Milford is a handsome little valley. Find that there are some Baptists about the Great Bend . . . there are Episcopalians, Presbyterians, and Methodists in this place but cannot ascertain that there is a single Baptist here. A Bible Society is here and a Sunday School. Travel 50 miles."[25] On a branch of Sequatchie River in Bledso County, Tennessee, he found that even in this remote area there was "preaching in this neighborhood, by Baptists once a month—Methodists once a month, Schismatics once a month. Bibles possessed by most of the families."[26]

He was concerned about the local churches. Stopping in Lynn, Massachusetts, during the early years of his journeying and finding several Baptist families without a church, he persuaded them to begin meeting. Then he obtained Boston ministers to come out for midweek services until a church was constituted and a resident minister obtained.

In Alexandria on his way to the 1817 Triennial, he promised "br. Cone fifty dollars to the Baptist Church in this place if they will purchase a certain house for a meeting house."[27] In Philadelphia he would preach "at the African Church and take communion with them."

Hundreds of texts that he preached through the years are listed; on one trip alone he preached from thirty different texts. These varied, but favorites cropped up again and again, such as "We have seen his star in the east," "What is man?" "What manner of love is this?" "Earnestly contend for the faith," "What is a man profited?" and missionary sermons such as "Thy Kingdom come," and "Let the whole earth be filled with his glory."

Not immune to the beauties of nature, he noted the grandeur of the view in Sequatchie Valley, the misty blue line of the Blue Ridge in Virginia, sumac embroidering the Kingston Turnpike in a Tennessee autumn, the lace of dogwood in the spring—these soothed his spirit, as nature's tranquilizers have done for many a wayfarer.

But there were harrowing days, too, when the bone-chilling rain beat against his all-covering surtout and he became so stiff he could hardly walk when he dismounted. He would rise before day and ride ten to twenty miles before breakfast; many a hunter's moon found him pressing on to keep an appointment.

The health bequeathed by his hardy sires, his easy sanguine temperament, and his bubbling sense of humor were all allies for the peripatetic life he led. Conditions were still primitive in many places and conveniences unknown. Even a light was a luxury: "Arrive at Br. Sheltons just at the close of daylight and commencement of shadows by the moon. Not able to write any this evening for want of candles."[28] Often he copied minutes of the local association or missionary societies or framed a constitution for a new female society by the light of an open fire or a pine-knot "till midnight as usual."

His mount became a chronic worry. A good riding horse was difficult to find, and it was the rare one that could stand Rice's grueling pace. It appears from his *Journal* that he treasured his horses and spent more for baiting, shoeing, and such items as "oil for my horse's back" than he did for his own personal needs. He owned many horses through the years and wistfully gave them such names as "Step Lively"—which he didn't, or "Timely"—which he wasn't, or "Nonesuch"—perhaps as a retort to the sales pitch of the man from whom he purchased him. "Columbus," his most famous horse, was one of his last and a gig horse. "Columbus was almost as well known as his master; and whenever he appeared at the door of minister, merchant, or planter, it was understood that a donation was wanted for the College."[29]

In North Carolina, March, 1817, after trading for a horse with which he was elated, possibly a Tennessee quarterhorse, he exulted that though it was "small and very poor, has carried me five miles an hour . . . I have long wished to obtain a horse whose travelling gait would carry me faster than about 4 miles an hour . . . If my present horse continues to travel as he has done today it will save me 2 hours in every 40 miles . . . worth at least $240 a year and will render my service to the missionary cause worth at least an equal sum."[30] Ever the optimist, Rice found no mount who could maintain this pace for long. At four miles an hour his per-day mileage revealed something of the grueling nature of his tours. Day after day, the entries listed forty to fifty miles covered, plus speaking engagements, soliciting, letter writing, and conferring with local Baptists. In April, 1818, he wrote Dr. Staughton that he had "traveled 9,359 miles and received $5,443.57" that year.

Sometimes he would fall in with drovers going east to the markets and stay overnight in their inns. Oftener he journeyed short distances in company with the ubiquitous Yankee peddler, that itinerant merchant of the west with his thread, needles, clocks, wooden nutmegs, and basswood hams.

Rice's longest day's journey, besting Wesley's ninety miles in one day, came during a torturous week in the Carolina and Virginia area in the autumn of 1816. On the twenty-fifth of August he was at the New Globe meetinghouse on the Johns River in North Carolina, having just come from the Appomattox Association in Virginia and the County Line Association near Caswell, North Carolina. The Mountain Association was meeting with New Globe and Rice preached and recorded, "missionary business satisfactorily attended to."[31] The same day he departed and traveled forty-nine miles, retracing his route to Wilkesboro, and the next day he rode from Wilkesboro to Hamptonville, on to Huntsville and into Rockinham County, a distance of ninety-three miles. Tuesday, he traveled forty-nine miles and on Wednesday he left "Brother Eames" in Pittsylvania County, Virginia, and rode to Lynchburgh, a distance of sixty-three miles, where he saw someone who agreed to copy "the Strawberry Association for me."[32] By Saturday he was in Madison County and "proceeded to Culpepper meeting house, 13 miles; get my horse shod, then to Groundvine meeting house, thence to Battle Run meeting house near Gaines Crossroad, 8 miles find the Shiloh Association in session, missionary business attended to my satisfaction, invited to preach tomorrow . . . 29 miles today, 412 this week . . . three nights rode all night . . . one of them in much comfort . . . probably slept not more than 10 hours in 6 days and nights."[33] Then he added the reason for this prodigious exertion: "My coming to this association appears to have been important."[34]

It was during his last years of mendicancy for Columbian College that he acquired Columbus and traveled in a sulky, the descendant of the one-horse chaise. High and light, making for mobility, it was a one-seat vehicle invented by an English doctor who wished to avoid carrying passengers as he made his rounds; when imported to America and used mostly by the men, the women dubbed it the "selfish."

Edward Kingsford remembered:

Nothing but absolute necessity ever prevented him from accomplishing any purpose which he had formed in his mind, or from fulfilling an engagement he had previously made. In his numerous journeys in the South, he had frequently to cross deep and rapid streams, yet he appeared never to have been disconcerted by the threatened impediment, or deterred from making the passage, however dangerous. At one time, on approaching a stream, he perceived by the turbid state of the water, that it could not be forded without some danger, he left the horse and sulky on the bank, and plunged into the river. Just as the water reached his neck, he found himself approaching the opposite shore; he then returned and with his horse and carriage, dashed through the foaming flood. At another time, on a similar occasion, discovering that he could not keep his books, papers, and other baggage dry, if he swam his horse and sulky through the water, he disengaged his horse from the vehicle, and with portions of his book, crossed the stream thirteen times, and then, wet as he was, pursued his journey. Once, when he came to a very deep and rapid river on which stood a mill, he called to the miller to help him over. 'Help you over?' said the man, with astonishment, 'you will not be able to cross that river to-day.' 'Yes, I shall,' said Rice, 'if you will help me.' Immediately alighting, he commenced operations. He first took one wheel off the sulky and carried it through the mill; he took off the other, and transported it in the same way. Afterwards, by the aid of the miller, he carried the body of the sulky through. By a number of successive trips, he conveyed over the harness and the baggage, then mounting his horse he swam him through the river, and then went on his way to secure the object to which he had devoted his life. Upon another occasion, a friend sent him in a carriage to a place where he was to be met by another; but the latter failed to meet him, he pursued his journey carrying a small trunk. A part of his journey was pursued through a long and dreary swamp. Being asked by friends, sometime after, if he did not feel afraid while passing through the swamp on foot and alone; he replied, 'I thought of nothing except the object that was before me.'[35]

If Baptists had patron saints, Rice would surely be the one for state secretaries for, in a general sense, he was the first—visiting the associations, bringing the published reports of the Board, evaluating the census of spiritual conditions which he took in each region, encouraging the called ministers, and remaining indefatigable in his labors to seek out and train more competent ministers.

He often stayed for weeks at a time in one of his adopted homes— the Battles', Mercers', Thomases', or Turpins'. His tastes had always been simple. He liked plain food (he imagined "gout lurking in the dishes of a banquet table"), and most often he bought apples and cider at wayside shops along the road.

Almost dehydrated by his long hours on a dusty road, nothing refreshed him so quickly as a cup of hot tea or coffee. The ladies at Mrs. Bushnell's in Chowan Association once counted the number of cups of tea he consumed, incredulously reporting "sixteen or seventeen." (Henry Keeling deprecated the number by saying that "the teacups in those days were not much larger than acorn hulls").[36]

In every congregation there were kind ladies who looked after his wardrobe, keeping his clothes presentable. This was fortunate, especially during his last years of denial for the college, for as he grew older he tended to become careless in his dress. Leaving Philadelphia on his first western tour, Luther received "6 cravats and 2 large and elegant silk handkershiefs" from Spencer Cone's sisters, and Miss Eliza Staughton presented "from the young ladies, an elegant black vest."[37] That winter Mrs. Stout gave him a "shirt and two pairs of flannel drawers,"[38] and Mrs. James Barrow in Beulah, Georgia, often refurbished his whole attire with "knit stockings, a flannel wrapper," and other needed items.[39] But the people in the First Baptist Church, Richmond, and other Virginians outdid all others with such items as a vest coat, hat, or fifty dollars' worth of cloth for a surtout. Rice always listed personal gifts as he did free lodging and meals, fervently wishing that his "conduct might be answerable to such kindness."[40]

In the last year of his life he wrote Judson that his papers were in a room at Columbian College, the

. . . only spot having any thing of the nature of home on earth—except, indeed the affectionate kindness of many brethren and their families, where I am in the habit of calling, in different and distant parts of the country. These homes, as I frequently call them, are exceedingly dear to me. None but a pilgrim, literally 'sine dome' . . . can realize how sweetly precious they are.

One of these, where I frequently find rest and comfort, as did the prophet by the kindness of the good woman, who had a chamber built for him upon the top of her house, is the home of brother William H. Turpin, at Augusta, Georgia, which place is, as I sometimes say, my southern headquarters for the winter; and whose name has probably become somewhat familiar to you . . . Another is that of elder Jesse Mercer, Washington, Georgia, another, Archibald Thomas, Richmond, Virginia, and I might mention many more. I am now at Powelton, Georgia . . . at the house of Dr. Cullen Battle. . . . one of my homes.[41]

Like the wayfarer Paul before him, he was destined to spend much of his life traveling. Year after year, "in season and out of season," he took to the road that stretched away to the night with no beloved face awaiting his arrival—"on frequent journeys, in danger from rivers, danger from robbers . . . danger in the wilderness, danger at sea, danger from false brethren; in toil and hardship, through many a sleepless night, in hunger and thirst, often without food, in cold and exposure." He could also add with Paul, "Apart from other things, there is the daily pressure upon me of my anxiety for all the churches."[42]

16. Years of Trouble

From its inception there were differing opinions about the purpose, membership, and work of the Convention. Some men believed its sphere of commitment covered the support of Judson and Rice and any other foreign work the Convention should agree to enter but that it should never include domestic missions, education, or publications work, feeling that these were best fostered as local projects by local societies, either on an associational or regional level. Rice and others were convinced that they must develop a national consciousness as a denomination and that every facet of work should be channeled through the Triennial Convention. These men assumed that education, home missions, and publications were vital segments of such a unified plan.

Dr. Staughton and Rice were a marvelous team, seeing alike the task before the Board and straining every nerve toward the development of a comprehensive strategy. They were joined in those early years by Dr. Furman, president of the Convention, Dr. Baldwin, president of the Board, and other men who cooperated with the executive group residing in Philadelphia.

But from these first years there were some (some even officers in the Convention) who disagreed with the steps taken in 1817 that changed the Convention's constitution to include the western mission. When it was altered a second time to include education, they were positively alarmed.

One of the first critics was the three-hundred-pound pastor of the First Baptist Church in Philadelphia, Henry Holcombe, vice-president of the Executive Board. Soon he was joined by Daniel Dodge and Rev. William Rogers, a former pastor of Dr. Holcombe's church who was also an officer of the Board.

Some of Holcombe's antipathy toward Rice and the work of the Board stemmed from the friction between Staughton and himself. Dr. Staughton had preceded Holcombe as pastor of the First Baptist

Church before leaving with part of the flock to found the Sansom Street Church. In each place crowds of elite Philadelphians came to hear Dr. Staughton, and he was by far the most popular pulpiteer in the city at the time. Drs. Holcombe and Staughton took different sides on two associational votes, the first involving which of two First African Churches would be recognized by the association as the legitimate congregation, and the second concerning a charge of immoral conduct against Dr. White, pastor of the Second Baptist Church, Philadelphia. The latter charge brewed for many years, Dr. Staughton defending Dr. White and Dr. Holcombe condemning him, until White was finally dismissed by his congregation and left the city.

Dr. Holcombe was a man of prodigious energy with a decided preference for leading rather than following. Even before leaving Georgia, he had a reputation for sowing disharmony, and his Philadelphia pastorate was marked by constant friction, sometimes between his church and the association, sometimes between himself and members of his congregation, and often between Holcombe and other ministers within the Board.

In the summer of 1815, dissension was evident within the Board. In the spring it had voted to inform Rice that "the Board entertain a very high sense of the services he had rendered as their Agent in originating Auxiliary Mission Societies; and that as the way is now opened by the return of peace, for his resuming his missionary labours in India that he soon as possible prepare to embark for that purpose."[1] But a month later this action was reversed and they agreed "that brother Rice for some time longer continue his labours as an agent of the Board, subject however to such openings in Providence, and such success attendant upon his labour, as in the judgment of the Board may render his continuance in this country no longer requisite, and his removal and missionary station requisite and proper."[2] This action was to set a pattern.

That summer a circular written by Rev. White was sent to the absent members, requesting their opinion on the "detention of Mr. Rice a further time in this Country,"[3] and inquiring whether or not the term *missionary* was confined to one sex only. This last question referred to the status of Mrs. Charlotte White who was scheduled to accompany the Houghs to India. Replies to this letter favored Rice's staying and stated that the term *missionary* could apply to either sex.

153

In a Board meeting of early September a letter was read from Judge Tallmadge in which he proposed that "an Agent of talent ought to be employed by this Board, none so suitable as Mr. Rice." He suggested that Rice be retained until the following March and that he "be apprised of their resolve."[4] Holcombe read a protest to this and at the next meeting Dodge, Rogers, and he resigned together. They subsequently withdrew their resignations, to the anguish of other Board members, and from this time the lines of division were drawn.

Soon there appeared a series of letters addressed to Dr. Staughton. A tract entitled *Plain Truth* (published anonymously but often attributed to Dr. Holcombe) made violent charges against Dr. Staughton, stating that he maneuvered the proceedings of the 1814 Triennial and also the Board meetings. It also attacked Rice for not returning to India, saying that he was unwilling "to shoot the bourne from which no traveller returns in the midst of life, though he warmly recommended this course to others."[5]

William Rogers was writing derogatory letters to men throughout the country, and an almost scurrilous letter from Asa Messer to Rogers reveals that some were conniving at this early day to unseat Rice as agent of the Board. Messer was president of Brown University, and the opposition to Rice and the Convention's expansion was to center in Rhode Island, Massachusetts, and New York. To Rogers, Messer wrote:

It seems, then that Mr. Rice will not sail for India the ensuing season. What do people think of this business? Do they not begin to make into a sort of Prophecy a declaration which Dr. H. sometime ago made to the missionary board . . . Will the board be willing to convert their *Asiatic Preacher* into an *American Beggar?* Or, should they be willing to make contributions for his support? I feel for the honor of the denomination; and I hope that such steps may be taken as will keep it from pollution. I hope, at any rate, that the question will *soon* be decided, whether Mr. Rice should sail to India, the Board will retain him in their service? It is talked this way there must be a meeting of the Board in N. Y. that new arrangements must be made, that probably *some* members must be put *out* and some put *in* . . . I, at any rate, hope that you will attend all the meetings . . . Should there be a meeting in N. Y., Dr. Baldwin, I apprehend, will attend it, but whether he will draw with you, or with me, or with others, you can tell, perhaps better than I. You know, however, his great veneration for Dr. S. . . . Brother Gano seems decided, *either* that Mr. Rice shall go to India, or leave the mission . . .[6]

As this letter discloses, Rev. Stephen Gano of the First Baptist Church in Providence also sided with those who felt Rice had committed himself irrevocably to foreign work and that having put his hand to the plow, he should not "look back." Gano apprised Tallmadge that he could "never be reconciled to Mr. Rice's conduct, and the deception practiced with respect to his intentions of going to India fills my mind with disgust."[7]

It was to take ten years before they succeeded in their stratagems of getting some members *out* and others *in* on the Board and arranging a meeting where the majority attending would be from New York and New England. In the intervening years, circumstance and Rice's mistakes played into their hands.

In one of the Board's meetings when they were discussing Rice's future departure to Burma, Luther submitted a statement in which he gave as a reason for the delay that he had "not obtained a companion to go with him, useful to the Board." At another meeting a resolution stating that the "appointment of Rev. Luther Rice, a Missionary by this Board was an appointment for India and understood to have been accepted by him as such,"[8] was carried unanimously. Clearly, Rice's unwillingness to rejoin Judson, for whatever reason, marred his relationship with some of the Board.

And his remark about not obtaining a suitable wife was repeatedly used against him, hurtfully so. Rogers reported to Furman:

But tho we had determined, a few weeks before by unanimous vote, to send him off to the East Indies, he has evaded compliance with our desires. A considerable time has elapsed since he informed us, as it would seem, to prepare our minds for acquiesence in his continuance amongst us, that he had a "liver complaint" and was under the impression that he could not live three months in the East Indian climate. But then he lately put his objection negative on our united vote without adverting to any other ground of objection to the eastern hemisphere as the assigned field of his missionary object, he very grandly informed us, that he had used all lawful endeavors to obtain a wife without the least prospect of success, and that he could not think of returning to that country in a state of celibacy![9]

Rogers admitted that the Board reversed its former decision and continued Rice as a "domestic missionary, on the foreign mission funds, that, by dint of assiduity, he may, if possible change his deplorable state!"

In the Boston area, disagreement was already taking the form of talk about dismembering the infant Triennial Convention so that each sector could go its own way. James Manning Winchell of the First Baptist Church there wrote Rice as early as August, 1815:

My brethren here and brother Chase will testify that I have used my influence in your favor when a large number of my brethren have differed from me in opinion. The great cause is what I regard. And nothing but union will carry us forward. For Union therefore I have pleaded and averted the progress of those measures which I thought would widen the breaches among us.[10]

William Rogers constantly wrote criticisms to men over the country of the way the Board was handling its business. As soon as the first *Annual Report* came from the press, he remarked to Dr. Furman: "To say that it contains neither valuable information, evidence of genius, nor strokes of eloquence, would be doing it injustice." But his purpose in writing was to become personal—to deprecate Rice and impugn his motives:

The first intelligence which turned our thoughts toward it [missions] was, that Mssrs. Judson and Rice, a couple of highly respectable missionaries sent to the East Indies, by certain Pedobaptists, had renounced their principles and joined us. And soon afterwards it was proclaimed from Massachusetts to Georgia, that Mr. Rice had arrived, from those distant shores, to solicit our patronage, and should he receive it, to return, with the avails without the least unnecessary delay, to encourge the heart, and strengthen the hand of his br. Judson. These tidings extended their effects with the rapidity of lightning from the east to the west, and south, and, with the power of an electric shock, warmed all our hearts, and loosened our very *purse-strings*.
After all, we do not know, to this day, that Mr. Judson has ever joined us, tho we have, we think, prematurely, adopted him as one of our missionaries. It is well known that some, both men and women, of different Pedobaptist Orders, have been immersed, from time to time, but remained in their respective communions all their day.[11]

Rogers informed Furman that Rice brought no letter from the Lall Bazar Church in Calcutta and had only recently joined the Sansom Street Church. Rogers ignored the fact that Rice could not have known when he left India where he would be working.

For a time, even Judge Tallmadge succumbed to the opinions of Drs. Rogers and Holcombe, Rice protesting the "wound to friendship" which Judge Tallmadge's coolness inflicted and in turn the noticeable reserve in Dr. Furman's demeanor after Judge Tallmadge had discussed the situation with him. But these two men soon began to view the Philadelphia discord in its true light, for the South Carolinians and Georgians knew Dr. Holcombe. To Judge Tallmadge, Furman deplored Holcombe's conduct: "Some evil, I fear, has taken deep Root in his Mind, which spreads its baneful Influence through his whole Sphere of Actions,"[12] and Tallmadge lamented the content of the pamphlet *Plain Truth* and the attacks on Staughton and Rice.[13]

About the Philadelphia friction, Dr. Furman noted to Rev. Edmund Botsford that "there is a source of evil there, men working for the devil."[14]

Rev. Botsford's own thoughts were as follows:

To me it has an awful appearance to see those who ought to set the best example, setting the worst. I am very apprehensive Dr. H. is at the bottom of all this disturbance. I received a letter the other day from Dr. Staughton. He says the man from Georgia is trying to rend all that do not bow to him, or words to that import. We Baptists are like the Arabians, against every man, and every man against us, yea we exceed, we are against ourselves.[15]

Botsford wrote Rogers, upbraiding him for writing fractious letters and counseling him to sow peace. Holcombe was manipulated off the Board in 1817, but as long as Rogers and Holcombe lived, they fomented trouble within the Convention.

On his first western trip Rice received a welcome hand from the pastors and honor because of his office as representative of the Triennial Convention. A typical reaction during the first years was that of the Elkhorn Association: "The missionary Preacher Luther Rice, having arrived after election of preachers, elder Warden gave place to him. Rice preached from Matthew 6th and 10th 'Thy Kingdom Come.' From $150 to $200 was collected for missionary purposes."[16]

But soon disaffection set in, many feeling that the Board was an eastern body and that their money would be taken East where the men there would decide how it was to be spent. Isaac McCoy spoke ruefully of his fellow Kentuckians:

When the Board of Foreign Missions was first heard of, it occurred to Kentuckians that the Seat of this institution was in the eastern part of the United States, where it also originated, and we cannot consent that any should take the lead of us, in a thing that is clever. Let us therefore, instead of becoming auxiliary to them, have an institution of our own . . . some saw the Board as giving too much to the missionaries . . . imagined they saw horns springing up . . . and I sometimes think that a few had learned another lesson, to wit, that the Missionary cause was calculated to rob the purse.[17]

So the Kentucky Missionary Society wavered between becoming auxiliary to the Triennial and becoming wholly independent. They fostered the school for Indian children at Great Crossings, Kentucky, and though it was never large in size or effectiveness, they were reluctant to relinquish its supervision. The Board sent Rice on a special mission in 1818 to woo the Kentucky society back into the fold and, at the time of his visit, it did vote itself an "auxiliary to the Board and the Board engaged to appropriate its funds to such objects, only as the Society shall designate, and in every way to facilitate, to the utmost of their power a common design."[18]

Still there were ministers and factions who were openly opposed to missionary causes. One of the most contentious leaders of antimissionism was Daniel Parker, eccentric Georgia backwoodsman who was pastor of a Tennessee church in the early 1800s before moving to Illinois.

Diminutive in figure, ill-clad and uncultured, Daniel Parker compensated for his lack in size and commanding presence by spirited, though uncouth, speech. An astute debater and a tireless ranter of the fanatical variety, he rallied and led the antimissionary forces until their impact was felt throughout the transmontane region and even into Texas, whence he eventually immigrated.

He announced his opposition to missions in 1815 while still in Tennessee. As early as February, 1818, Rice was warned:

Elder Daniel Parker from Tennessee has lately settled on Wabash, Crawford County and I understand, is more opposed, if possible, to the Board than even Brother Devin, and altho there has been a little variance between them, yet I fully expect, like two men of old "they will be made friends" that their united efforts may oppose the ravages of this frightful monster, which they suppose was bred at Rome. But don't imagine dear Brother that our cause is sickening in the Country. Blessed by God, it is quite otherwise.[19]

Rice attended the Illinois Association in Crawford County the following autumn and his presence inflamed Parker still further.

The antimissionaries generally opposed a paid ministry, Sunday Schools, temperance societies, and theological training. Peck, McCoy,

Welch, and all other Board appointees who worked in the area, as well as Rice, felt the opposition's wrath in varying manifestations. Parker obstructed Peck's seminary at Rock Springs, voting against its charter during his term in the Illinois legislature. Peck countered anti-Sunday School forces by organizing Bible societies which no orthodoxy could oppose.

McCoy informed Rice a few months after his Illinois visit that though Parker was continuing his tactics, "truth has nothing to fear from investigation, and I am persuaded that opposition like pouring oil on fire will only serve to increase the flame."[20]

Despite McCoy's optimism on this score and his concurrence with Rice in a policy of peacemaking (never openly debating or fighting such men) Parker's movement grew; for notwithstanding his strange two-seed-in-the-Spirit predestinarian tenet, his doctrine was so interlaced with Baptist beliefs as to confuse and even confound the unwary or those unskilled in interpretation of the Scriptures. In the early 1820s, the Board's publications work became another of Parker's passionate hates, this latter emanating from the time when the *Columbian Star* rejected some articles he submitted.

A more formidable adversary of missions and theologically trained ministers was Alexander Campbell, brilliant erstwhile Presbyterian-turned-Baptist. Reared and educated in Ireland and Scotland where his father was embroiled in the Seceder and Covenanter controversies within the Presbyterian Church, he and his family migrated to western Pennsylvania and then to Virginia (now West Virginia) where they were repulsed in their efforts to affiliate with the Presbyterians. They formed a Baptist Church and united with the Redstone Baptist Association.

Campbell came into the Baptist churches in the guise of a Baptist, thereby gaining many an unsuspecting pulpit; and his doctrine of baptism for the remission of sins infiltrated many congregations before they became aware he was not a Baptist, nor simply a reformer—which he claimed—but the founder of a new denomination. Baptists had no concerted way to act against his onslaughts, for the district association was their only method of proceeding aside from the vote of a local church. Though they had experienced marked growth prior to his coming, for thirty years after he began touring the Ohio Valley in the second decade of the nineteenth century, he and his followers were a divisive force within the Baptist churches.

He made his first Kentucky tour in 1817, waging open warfare on all organized work: missionary societies, education societies, theological training, a paid ministry. The frontier yielded no peer for his magnetic personality and superior education; even some ministers, such as Barton Stone, and occasionally whole congregations, defected to his movement. In 1823 he began publishing *The Christian Baptist* to propagandize his movement and in its pages his clever invective attacked all of the work which Rice, as agent for the Board, was promoting.

His chief argument was that the education and missionary societies were antiscriptural because they were manmade organizations. Where Parker and the other hyperCalvinists felt missions were an impertinence because God had predestined to call and justify the elect, Campbell taught that every cent given to missions was a contribution toward reenslavement, an argument that struck a telling blow to the Kentuckians, most of whom were only one generation removed from Virginia and a state-supported church, and who bore a congenital suspicion toward organizations.

Campbell and his followers claimed the Bible as their sole guide, much as other evangelical groups before him had done, but he artfully pressed the claim that his interpretation was infallible: "I take the Bible for my sole guide. I cannot be wrong in any particular." He claimed exclusive truth, an absolutism harking back to the Roman Church, and his followers likewise were anxious to dispute, wholly sure of their leader's competency.

Campbell was a remorseless denouncer of theological training, seemingly embittered and hostile to the ministry. (This perhaps dated from boyhood memories of his father's difficulties with the church authorities). Living on a fine farm with slaves to cultivate it, of paid ministers he scoffed:

Upon the whole I do not think we will err very much, in making it a general rule, that every man who receives money for preaching the gospel, or for sermons by the day, month, or year, is a hireling . . . All that the clergy sell is breath, and that is one of the most common things among the living. It is as little expense to a man who can talk, to talk, as it is for the laity to hear. He sells you divinity which is supposed to be a heavenly commodity, and costs no money.[21]

Campbell, inconstant as most reformers, afterwards embraced some of the very things he opposed, but the havoc was wrought in the churches and the Baptists paid most dearly.

Campbell's attacks were against the goals which Rice had set for Baptists. His major debates were with other men, many of them Presbyterians, and Rice refrained from debate.

There were others, Baptists among them, who attacked Rice personally. One of these was John Taylor, an influential pioneer preacher in middle Kentucky who received Rice amiably on his first tour but soon disapproved of Rice's money-raising technique and published a tract, "Thoughts on Missions." He made a scathing attack upon Rice, calling him a "modern Tetzel, and that the Pope's old orator of that name was equally innocent with Luther Rice and his motive about the same." He added: "Tetzel's great eloquence, and success in getting money, alarmed first Martin Luther and afterwards, the chief of the States of Germany. Our Luther by his measures of cunning in the same art of Tetzel may alarm all the American Baptists."[22]

Some of the untrained ministers were skeptical of Rice, Peck, and others because they were educated easterners and the land speculators and hucksters had come from New England; the missionaries were equated with these shrewd types, especially if they collected money and were paid a salary. Rice's old friends, Samuel Mills, Jr., and classmate Schemmerhorn, had made a tour of the South just prior to Rice's trips, staying overnight with Taylor and divulging their procedures for raising money. Taylor was offended rather than won over by their confidences.

After voting against a resolution to allow a missionary to speak at the Sagamore Association, one backwoods antimissionary arose and with uncommon candor confessed: "Well, if you must know, brother Moderator, you know the big trees in the woods overshadow the little ones, and these missionaries will be all great men, and the people will go where they preach, and we shall all be put down. That's the objection."[23]

All of these impediments—Parker, Campbellism, Taylor, the suspicion toward easterners and organizations—meant a falling off of receipts to the Board. When Rice began taking subscriptions for the lot in "Washington City," the list grew rapidly, many pledging to contribute. But in 1819 the panic in the West and the subsequent depression which lasted well into the '20s sharply curtailed the collection of these subscriptions. During this time the buildings were rising at the college, and Rice was forced to remain longer and longer periods in the city to supervise the beginning of the college.

During these years when it would appear that Dr. Staughton, as president of the college, would perform the supervisory tasks, he was not even in Washington except occasionally. Both his church and the college trustees were concerned. He explained to his congregation in 1821 that he planned to remain president of Columbian College until the Triennial met again in 1823, adding: "It would be necessary for me to visit Washington, I suspect, only two or three times in a year, and that only for two, or at most for three weeks at a visit."[24] He later came for two or three days during the middle of some weeks but did not move there until two years after the college opened. And as his son-in-law admitted, "Pecuniary affairs were the least that ever occupied the mind of Dr. Staughton."[25]

Dr. Staughton's son James and Professor Alva Woods were sent to Europe to tour and to purchase a library and apparatus for the laboratories. That Dr. Staughton was cognizant of Rice's labors and his financial struggles on behalf of the college is seen in a letter to James in Europe: "Mr. Rice, in his late tour to the North, has very much relieved the affairs of the college. He has sold shares in a loan, to the amount of seven thousand dollars. His spirits are high. He says that he sees the shore and three or four thousand dollars more will land him safely."[26]

Yet Staughton was a Philadelphian with elegant tastes which he indulged after moving to Washington. Perhaps he relied too heavily on Rice's discretion and willingness to assume the financial responsibilities of the college, and certainly one of Rice's own stumblings involved belief that he and his fellow Baptists could accomplish any good objective envisioned. It may have been that Rice overly persuaded Staughton to leave Philadelphia and his successful pastorate there and therefore could not deny him any request in the next few years nor candidly reveal to him how precarious the financial situation was until the time was too late.

Still another factor in Rice's gathering troubles was the character of some of his friends. He had recommended each of the initial appointees to home missions: Peck, Welch, McCoy, Posey, Ranaldson. These men were a credit to the denomination, though Welch and Peck were rather summarily dismissed in 1820 and Ranaldson soon afterwards. However, the Convention was very interested in the Indian mission work, and more men, such as Lee Compere at the Withington Station, were appointed to work among them.

But the Board members were horrified as the accounts came in

162

from some of these men, especially McCoy and Posey, whose stations some years exceeded the cost of the Burman mission. A delegation was sent to view Posey's work at Valley Towns in the early 1820s and it reported that the money spent was not excessive nor extravagant. The subsequent removal of the Cherokees and the closing of the schools eased the strain from Posey's mission, but not so with McCoy's.

McCoy tended to view the Board as a golden goose, and he was never satisfied or able to live on his allotment. Though always regretful when remonstrated with, he never changed his ways. From Fort Wayne he wrote Rice, "I never considered that I was authorized to draw for more than $500 a year. But after leaving the settlement, and mingling with the Indians, I found it impossible to live on that sum. In removing to this place our expenses have been augmented beyond our calculation. We cannot live without Bread . . . therefore I have in turn to give drafts on the Board which they are not bound to honour."[27]

And Rice answered, "I can easily appreciate your difficulties in relation to funds and suggest the propriety of your estimating before hand as timely as possible and making application for funds, stating with as much particularity as the case will admit the object for which the said funds will at any time be wanted."[28]

Soon McCoy was involved in the political question over the removal of the Indians to reservations which, more than any other man, he promoted and abetted by every means at his disposal.

At first he worked through Rice and others in Washington. As early as 1820 he wrote Rice and Senator Richard Mentor Johnson, beseeching them to implore the Secretary of War for the Baptists' share of the ten thousand dollars which the Government annually allotted for the education of Indian children.

In the winter of '21-22, he made the first of those long horseback trips to Washington to solicit aid, and on January 10, accompanied by Rice, Chaplain Burgiss Allison, and Colonel Johnson, McCoy waited on John C. Calhoun, Secretary of War. Never paltry in his desires or demands, McCoy had plenty to request of Calhoun.

"I desired for myself the appointment of teacher, for bro. Jackson the office of blacksmith, for bro. John Sears the office of teacher for the Ottawas and begged permission to furnish the names of others whom government shall appoint to aid the Indians a while hence," he wrote.[29]

Secretary Calhoun's eyes must have nearly popped out of his head, but McCoy was not finished:

I petitioned for a miller for the Miamies, . . . I proposed removing the principal seat of the mission from Fort Wayne to the sections of land on which government shall place the teacher and smith for the Puttawatomies and to build a Mission house worth $1000 and begged the President to approve this location and to defray two thirds of the expense of erecting the same. I also desired that the proper share of the $10,000 appropriated for Indian Reform be allowed us annually.[30]

The Government granted most of McCoy's requests, but this in no way diminished his demands on the Board. Through the next years he badgered Congress, the Presidents, and cabinet to set aside lands for the removal of the Indian and at the same time he wrote and pled with the Board to approve all his expenses. So this dipping into public funds did not lessen the demands of the mission on Rice.

In direct contradiction to the Board's instructions "that all monies received by McCoy for the benefit of the establishment, from agents or individuals, be placed at the credit of the Board,"[31] McCoy continued to collect on his travels and use these collections for his work without forwarding them to the Board. Where Ranaldson, though in need of further assistance in Louisiana, forwarded his receipts to Philadelphia, McCoy sallied down to Logan County, Kentucky, and solicited funds; he begged offerings of the Bardstown Society which had struck out the phrase, "auxiliary to the Baptist Board of Foreign Missions," and he did the same toward other societies, particularly those in Ohio.

As Dr. Staughton assumed from Rice the official correspondence, he tried to guide McCoy; but McCoy was always changing stations, letting Christiana and assistants hold the fort while he rounded up more and more Indians to come and live at the school at Board expense, thus spiraling his costs. He informed Rice that he proposed to give "to parents or guardians of each child annually, a female Hog, and for every ten which shall regularly attend our school, a milch cow."[32]

McCoy visited Washington in the early spring of 1824, returning home via Philadelphia and New York where he spoke in the churches, collecting money for his work. Since he was far in arrears at his station and had overdrafted $1,700, Rice asked him to forward the money he collected to the Board.

Rice was anguished to learn that McCoy defied these suggestions and pocketed all the offerings he received en route home, leaving the Board, with Rice as the responsible agent, with the $1,700 overdrafts. In one of the sternest letters he ever penned, Rice said, "I regret that you did not pursue the course . . . which the Board of Managers directed, . . . there will not be the same pleasant state of things in relation to future drafts as otherwise there would have been. Still I will do all I can for the station, and for all other missions of the Board."[33]

McCoy defended his actions by saying that the New Yorkers preferred to give their money directly to him rather than through the Board. And it was true that such men as William Colgate, the soap magnate, forwarded money from the New York societies directly to McCoy—which fact revealed that there were men who were in collusion to circumvent the Board with their funds, channeling them through the various individuals and societies they preferred, rather than through the central agency.

At each meeting of the Triennial Convention, there were skirmishes between those who wanted home missions to be placed in control of societies or local groups and those who had secured its inclusion in the Triennial's work. At the 1823 Triennial in Washington, the committee on domestic missions strongly recommended that domestic missions be operated by the states.

From that time, home missions in large part reverted to its former status, with the Massachusetts Missionary Society assuming the support of Peck and the Mississippi Missionary Society, that of Ranaldson.

Rice compounded his troubles by poorly handling the opposition to the college. Education was a long-term commitment and many were reluctant about the convention's engaging in it. Still others felt that Rice was too hasty in his approach. Richard Furman, though anxious for a seminary, wrote Dr. Staughton lamenting their haste.[34] And Dr. Thomas Baldwin, as influential in the North as Furman was in the South, wrote Rice his opinion on November 22, 1819:

I have been apprised of Dr. Furman's dissatisfaction, with the proceeding relative to the Institution . . . It must be evident to Dr. F. and to every other person upon the slightest observation, that the Institution was not set in motion in conformity to the *principle* established by the Convention: viz: "When competent and distinct funds shall have been raised for that purpose,—the Board will proceed to insti-

165

tute a Classical and Theological Seminary"—and it will not be pretended that *competent* funds distinctly assigned for that object had been raised, . . . This hasty, unauthorized procedure is probably the ground of Dr. Furman's objections. For my own part, tho' I would not adopt the principle, that "the end sanctifies the means", yet if the institution can be supported, without resorting at all to the funds of the Society, I shall wish it success with all my heart. But there is extreme tenderness with respect to these funds manifested from all parts of the country. Indeed they ought, and must be held sacred, for the object for which they were given.[35]

Dr. Baldwin was correct in stating that the Convention's action had specified that the college should await the raising of "competent and distinct funds." Why Rice rushed into this is one of the enigmas of his character. When he came to the Baptists, there were some things he did not understand about them; he may not have understood that their democratic process depended upon a majority opinion which in turn frequently awaited a long, hard task of persuasion.

The Board minutes reveal the concern of the Philadelphia men during the period while the buildings were being erected and the College opened. At almost every meeting there was reference to the College. In September, 1820, the Board was "of the opinion that a regular committee ought to have been appointed as soon as the arrangements of the Convention place the aforesaid [college] under their charge";[36] and they appointed a committee of Rice, Brown, Reynolds, McLaughlin, and Staughton to oversee and be responsible to the Board which in turn was accountable to the Convention. At the same time, this Convention Board instructed the building committee that they should "in no case go beyond the funds in hand; whatever engagements be entered into beyond this, must be considered, as resting exclusively upon the brethren who originated the business."[37]

However, the Board did sanction the transfer of four thousand dollars set up for a professorship to the building, "giving security for returning the amount when the subscriptions for the building shall admit."[38]

Perhaps Rice thought there was enough pledged to the College to warrant its establishment, and these pledges failed to materialize due to the financial panic. Perhaps it was because so many of the men he admired—Staughton, Brown, Johnson, Mercer—were eager to see the College begun. Most probably it was his overwhelming conviction that education was the primary need among Baptists and basic to all others, an urgency brooking no delay. He did not move alone—others such as Obadiah B. Brown were as culpable—but he would suffer most from their precipitancy.

Dr. Baldwin also revealed his concern about the *Luminary*, stating that "the blending of this with the Missionary concern, you probably know has given much uneasiness to many of the friends of missions. (It is so different from what we had reason to expect, that we hardly knew how to account for it . . . .) Nothing in my opinion will do away this impression, but a complete statement to the next Convention of the receipts and disbursements of the Treasury for that object."[39]

Baldwin elucidated his feeling still more by saying that the *Luminary* should stand on its own merits but that if they used the "Baptist Board of Foreign Missions" name, it would have unqualified success. Then, any profits which might accrue could be turned over to the Board, but the Board should not underwrite any of its expense. This was contrary to the purpose and plan for its publication which Rice had intended. He had always supposed it would be a vehicle for the Board, publishing the *Annual Report* and thus be subsidized, at least partially, by the Convention funds. The Board subsequently voted that the "funds of the Convention shall not be responsible for the expenses of the Luminary."[40]

With Board approval, the *Luminary* and its printer, John Meehan, were moved to Washington and into one of the two houses at 925 "E" Street which Rice had purchased with the intention of giving them to the Convention. Obadiah B. Brown became the *Luminary* editor. In 1822 the *Columbian Star,* a weekly folio sheet, was begun in the same office. The *Star* was devoted principally to foreign missions and Columbian College; it was first edited by Meehan, later by J. D. Knowles, a student in the College, and in 1826 by Baron S. Stow, another student in the College.

Thus it became evident that there were grave doubts about the seminary and many who feared it might usurp the place of foreign missions in the giving and planning of many Baptists. They did not wish the Convention to have a denominational paper if being an official publication involved financial support by the denomination. They viewed the Board and the Convention only as instruments for foreign missions.

Rice's friend Jonathan Going, who was to stand and defend him in the 1826 Triennial meeting, warned him of the feeling about

167

borrowing from the foreign missionary funds for the education fund:

> You are aware that some excitement is felt in New England, and especially (and, indeed, I hope chiefly) in Boston and Providence, in relation to some steps of the Board, respecting a loan of certain Missionary Monies, to the Trustees of the College—I hope the utmost prudence has been and will be used in the Affairs. Unless the matter be adjusted to the satisfaction of our castever friends, you may depend they are resolved to "cut the knot";—to secede from the Convention; and declare for Independence. This is a thing which has long been brewing; and perhaps, it would be no breach of charity to say that there may be some who will gladly embrace this, or any other opportunity to give a color of justification to an open rupture. Now I think such an event, on every consideration, most sincerely to be deprecated. Union is almost everything: and scarcely any thing, of course, too great to be sacrificed to its attainment or preservation.[41]

Yet the Education Committee proceeded to request a loan "not to exceed $10,000" from the monies which were invested in United States stock, then much above par. The Board of Directors of the Boston Mission Society objected, and Rice and Dr. Staughton traveled to Boston to meet with them and try to allay their fears. The building was nearly completed and they offered to mortgage the land and its buildings, but the Boston men demurred at this because of the delicacy of prosecuting a sister institution should it default. Then Dr. Staughton and Rice suggested that individual security, consisting of the signature of twenty men for four hundred dollars each be given as collateral for the loan. This, as Rice wrote Obadiah Brown, the Bostonians intimated would be satisfactory, adding, "Mr. Bolles of Salem, our decided friend, urges this . . . and I am of the opinion the measure will prove satisfactory."[42]

Correspondence between Rice and Brown reveals that even by the summer of 1821 when this loan was requested and the College was not even opened, the debt on the buildings and premises was almost hopeless. The Board was having difficulty paying a little on each of nearly twenty notes each discount day. Rice spent several months in New York and New England, aided by Alva Woods, trying to raise funds. He borrowed one thousand dollars from William Colgate and a similar sum from Horatio G. Jones, but their plight was a day-to-day desperation at this stage and Rice confided to Brown:

> I suffer occasionally an agony of feeling in view of the pecuniary difficulties with which we are encompassed but still have a confidence

that the same kind hand of Divine Providence which has carried us thus far, will be our helper to the end . . . if only we get through the present season without disaster. I do hope in the last resort the banks will *renew* our paper rather than *protest* it.[43]

In 1822 a bequest of $5,000 to the college relieved the pressure only temporarily, and that winter Rice almost broke down under the strain and was confined to his room for several weeks. He made another gross mistake the following year when he failed to present an account of his collections because of his "incessant labors." This was grist for the rumor mills and the *American Baptist Magazine* pounced on it by correctly pointing out that the Convention met only once in three years and surely the "multiplicity of the Treasurer's labours preventing him from bringing a report" was an unreasonable excuse, because "bookkeeping is a simple business."[44]

By the time of this 1823 Triennial, it had become general knowledge that the College was heavily in debt and a committee was appointed to "investigate the concerns of Columbian College." They reported that the "trustees stated expenditure of $70,000 and debt of $30,000." The committee stated further (and only the sanguine Rice could have worded this appendage) that "all things coming to the college would liquidate the debt."[45]

In June of that year Ann Judson sailed for Burma, along with new appointees, and the second half of the ten-thousand-dollar loan was called for. Dr. Staughton wrote William Colgate:

Bro. Rice not anticipating such has gone on a six weeks tour of the South. In his absence I am seriously afraid little if anything can be done toward refunding the $5,000, the remaining loan to the college and yet without it or some other resound that the Providence of the Redeemer shall open I really know not what we shall do.

Bro. Baldwin has drawn for $5,000 and Bro. Stokes has not more than $3,000 at his command. Shall I beg of you, whose delight I am convinced is doing good, to wait on Bro. Stokes. Perhaps something can be devised with the blessing of the Lord . . . Were Bro. Rice in Washington, his genius, his laborious efforts and his resources, which his connections with the banks command, would make everything easy . . .

Do, my dear brother, in this affair all you can, and the Lord will recompense you and your brethren will help you.[46]

Rice was beginning to see that something must be done to assuage the just anxieties of the northerners, for this inability to repay the loan when called set off another round of recriminations. At last, he was obviously disturbed by the criticism and reported in the *Luminary*:

Unfortunately, during my excursion to North Carolina, in June, and sooner than had been expected, the opportunity occurred for Mrs. Judson's sailing for India, and there was a call for more cash than was actually in the Treasury. This appears to have created suspicions that all was not right, in relation to my settlement with the Treasury; but, in the course of the year, and in perfect harmony with the original arrangement, the whole of the College Stock has been redeemed, and probably the unpleasant impressions, produced by a temporary misapprehension, have been entirely effaced, or nearly so.[47]

Since the College had begun to demand so much of his time, an arrangement had been made in 1820 whereby he was to devote half of his time to collecting for the missionary fund and half for the College, but the patrons of missions, especially those in New England, felt they were not getting a just share of his endeavors. They were also critical of Staughton as corresponding secretary. The New Englanders appointed a committee to investigate means to revive the missionary spirit. Francis Wayland was chairman and brought a long report which stated:

In the spring of 1818, we actually had twenty-three thousand dollars in the treasury . . . the mission treasury has been exhausted, no one can tell us how. The receipts have been year to year diminishing . . . Scarcely any missionaries have, of late, been sent out, nor does any one feel the importance of sending them . . . We hear of the president of Columbian College, we hear of the college, we hear of the debts and embarrassments of the agent, but we hear nothing of missions.[48]

In analyzing the causes of the decline in missions they mentioned "the want of a suitable person as corresponding secretary," and added that Dr. Staughton was "freely accorded the praise of eloquence, learning, literature, unbounded hospitality, and affable good will." Asking the question whether or not he could discharge the duties of corresponding secretary while head of a college, they answered negatively, stating that "experience leaves no doubt on this point."[49]

This committee also noted the valuable qualities of Rice and admitted that they did "not hesitate to attribute the great success

170

of our missionary attempts to his high personal and moral endowment," but accused him of diverting the public mind from the missionary cause to the College.

On June 14, 1824, the Board of the Convention voted to instruct Rice to give the treasurer in New York all Convention funds which he held and that thereafter, all "funds for education, and all funds in any way appertaining to the Columbian College, or the Latter Day Luminary and Columbian Star, to be entered in a book entirely separate from the book in which the mission funds are entered."[50]

Trying to placate the New Englanders in the fall of 1824, the Board voted to place the Burman mission under Boston control, and the next month Rice moved that "considering the multiplied and onerous services of the beloved Corresponding Secretary . . . the Board, will, with pleasure, employ the aid of an Assistant Corresponding Secretary, in conducting aforesaid foreign correspondence, particularly in relation to the Burman and other Associated Missions, should such an arrangement meet his approbation."[51] The Board approved Rice's proposal; Lucius Bolles was chosen as Staughton's assistant; and an executive committee, residing in Boston and vicinity, was appointed to administer the missionary affairs.

Rice decided that he should make quarterly reports and that "my agency should be absolutely without charge to the mission fund."[52] Obviously these gestures were an attempt to alleviate some of the fears many had about his work.

In early 1824 another of Rice's dreams was fulfilled, though he was neither the originator nor the prime mover in its founding. While still in Philadelphia, some of the men, including students who regularly met and talked in Dr. Staughton's home, discussed the formation of a tract society. They knew of the American Tract Society's effectiveness and wished a similar one for Baptists. But the press of responsibilities upon each of the men prevented their giving attention to this until after the College was begun and the *Luminary* was moved to Washington.

There James Knowles, *Star* editor, and John S. Meehan, the Convention printer, and others were impelled to promote its formation. Knowles received a letter from a former classmate, Rev. Noah Davis, then living in Salisbury, Maryland, urging the immediate formation of a tract society. Samuel Cornelius, pastor in Norfolk and soon to move to Alexandria, also wrote about the same time making the same suggestion. Meehan approached George Wood and inquired if he would consent to become the society's agent should a society be formed. Meehan received Wood's assent, so Knowles and Baron Stow began to write editorials in the *Star* and a few who were interested announced an initial meeting to be held in the home of Mr. Wood.

His home was next door to the printing offices on "E" Street, and at 7 P.M., February 20, twenty-five Baptists (eighteen men and seven women) met and formed the "Baptist General Tract Society." Its constitution stated that the "sole object shall be to disseminate evangelical truth and to inculcate sound morals by the distribution of tracts."[53]

The Tract Society was an immediate success, publishing over eighty-five thousand tracts the first year and gaining the support and patronage of Baptists in every area. But it experienced transportation difficulties since postage was generally prohibitive and few vessels sailed from Washington to other ports. Almost half of its parcels had to be shipped to Philadelphia, where they were loaded on packets for Savannah, Charleston, New Orleans, and elsewhere.

By 1825 Noah Davis, who said the previous year that "no place is more suitable for such a society" than Washington, and George Wood, its agent, were agitating for removal of the Society's publishing office to Philadelphia. They were prevented in executing their plan only by Rice who, "with his lion-hearted courage and confidence in the greatness of his strength," as Wood expressed it, "would not consent to the removal."[54] Rice had kept his dream of making Washington a Baptist center of influence and talk of removal "was a sort of treason."

Yet events were hastening toward a worse disaster due to the slough into which the College finances had fallen. The Board and agent had been given warning by the 1823 Triennial, yet no retrenchment was inaugurated.

Private creditors such as William Colgate and Horatio G. Jones were pressing for payment on the long overdue notes, and Rice was writing letters of promise, asking that they wait a little longer. To Jones: "Yes, my dear brother, I do ask a little longer indulgence. The darkest time is just before day! I do dearly believe day will soon dawn. Be assured your claim shall not be overlooked when means come into hand to meet it."[55]

The trustees decided to appeal to Congress for relief by addressing a memorial to them asking for aid in the form of proceeds from

172

the sale of public lands in the District. James Barbour of Virginia presented the bill on April 19, 1824, and in speaking of the efforts of the founder he said, "One individual in particular (and it is but an act of justice that he should be named), the Rev. Luther Rice, with an unwearied industry and an unyielding perseverance which prompted him to traverse every part of the Union in aid of this beneficent object, contributed principally to that success."[56] The session ended before Congress acted upon the memorial, a turn of events that could only gratify the hearts of many true Baptists who believed in the traditional principle of church and state separation.

The first commencement occurred on the fifteenth of December, 1824, and elaborate ceremonies were held. President Monroe, Cabinet members, leading Congressmen and General Lafayette, then on his triumphal tour, were present and welcomed. Afterwards, the General and his suite, Secretary of State John Quincy Adams, Secretary of War John C. Calhoun, Speaker of the House Henry Clay, and other dignitaries were entertained in the mansion of President Staughton. A similar commencement was held in 1825.

Costly levees were held and the ultimate folly was committed in 1824 when it was announced that another "building of the same magnitude with the former" was begun. Whose madness was responsible for this puzzling blunder cannot be ascertained. Perhaps the College's success—the enrolment far exceeding even Rice's hopes —led the College Board to assume that the erection of another building would augment the income. Certainly Dr. Staughton, Dr. Brown, and other trustees who may not have been culpable in the precipitant founding of the College were equally responsible for this last sad step of indiscretion which catapulted the College affairs into an almost hopeless condition and Rice into being dismissed. For although these plans had to be scuttled, for many years the unfinished buildings stood as a public reminder of the state of financial affairs within the College.

Professor Irah Chase arrived back in Washington from his European tour in late November, 1824, and immediately evinced dissatisfaction with the school. He and Staughton evidently disagreed about the curriculum of the theological department. Also he began to feel that New England would better support a theological school; he differed with Rice and Staughton about the wisdom of a theological seminary as a part of a great university. Perhaps Chase was simply critical of Rice's handling of the financial affairs; he complained because all of the faculty salaries could not be paid.

Whatever his reasons, Chase went to Boston in the early summer and there talked to Francis Wayland, his friend since Andover student days. In the vestry of Wayland's church in May, 1825, Newton Seminary had its origin, and in the late summer Chase went to Newton, taking with him his following of students and patrons. This was a severe blow to Columbian College and especially to Rice.

Still a greater blow was to fall. At the meeting of the Convention Board in September, 1825, finances were at a low ebb and ways of replenishing the treasury were discussed. Samuel Lynd, Staughton's son-in-law, moved "that in the opinion of the Committee any measures that may be adopted for the resusitation of the funds of the Convention will be unavailing while Mr. Rice continues to be agent of the Convention and Treasurer of the Board of Trustees, and that therefore it is their deliberate judgment that he ought to resign both these offices immediately."[57] The remainder of the day and all the following day were given to discussion, but "the question being put, was decided in the negative, only Dr. Staughton and Mr. Lynd in favor of it."[58]

This meant that Staughton, Rice's closest colleague through all the years of the Convention's infancy, now thought that he was expendable. In the coming councils in New York, Staughton would be numbered among the delegates representing New England, though he had never lived there; and he would vote with those who would seek to discredit Rice.

17. Dismissal

As the time for the Triennial approached, the New Englanders and the New Yorkers laid their plans. There had been much grumbling because so many of the delegates of the 1823 Triennial Convention had been from Washington, Virginia, and the South, so the place of meeting for the 1826 Triennial had been changed from Washington to New York City. Lucius Bolles wrote David Benedict in February, urging him to attend the May meeting because he felt the state of things was such that if the Convention did not do something, "New England, and perhaps the whole denomination will desert it." He added, "I should deeply mourn if I found my brethren compelled to withdraw from it."[1]

The advocates of a strong general convention which would supervise and channel all Baptist work realized that the whole future course of Baptists was at stake. As Staughton wrote his son James: "I look for a great struggle in New York, but I have the good hope that righteousness and truth will prevail. Perhaps brighter days are before us."[2]

Among those aroused and fortified with arguments before the delegates convened in New York in May were the editors of the *Baptist Missionary Magazine*—Daniel Sharp, Thomas Baldwin, and Francis Wayland.

Wayland was the son of a Baptist minister. He had been studying medicine in the summer of 1816 when Rice stayed in his father's home in Troy, New York, and Francis had heard Rice preach. He always recalled the effect it produced on him. "I was constrained to believe that the sentiments of my heart were in harmony with the gospel; that I loved God and all that God loved; and that it would be a pleasure to me to devote all my life to his service."[3]

He forsook medicine, enrolled at Andover Seminary where he stayed a year, and then accepted a divided call to the First Baptist Church of Boston. There, despite an ineffective delivery, he soon became a favorite among the elder Boston clergymen, Drs. Baldwin and Sharpe particularly. Each of these men edited the *Baptist Missionary Magazine* and in 1823, Wayland became a coeditor.

In 1823-24 he wrote a series of articles in this magazine under the name of "Backus," discussing the basis of representation in the Triennial Convention—*i.e.,* whether the delegates should continue to be from missionary societies, as was the general practice then, or from associations or states. He also discussed the scope of the Convention's concern. His judgment was that education and missionary societies should be under the superintendency of the Triennial, that state conventions should be formed and these should send delegates to compose the Triennial Convention.

But soon Wayland reversed himself on this stand and was advocating the removal of the missionary board to Boston and advising that the Triennial confine its interests to missions. He came to the New York meeting with the prestige of his recently published sermon, "The Moral Dignity of the Missionary Enterprise," and it was an ironic twist in Rice's fate that this young man of thirty, whom he had inspired to enter the ministry, would sway the Convention toward a departure from Rice's hope of a strong and unified general Convention.

Rice had little time to devote to the impending struggle; for in the late winter he began a southern tour to collect funds for the College, which lasted until there was barely time for him to arrive in New York City. From each stop along his tour through Virginia, the Carolinas, and Georgia, he wrote Obadiah Brown, sending his collections and specifying how to apply them. From Alexandria, Fredericksburg, Richmond, Louisburg, Shocco, Robertsville, he daily remitted every cent he begged, as he told Brown from Coosahatchies, "I enclosed all I had, leaving not a cent in my possession to meet any casualty before collecting more."[4]

The Convention met in the Oliver Street Church, the first Baptist church in which Rice had spoken after returning to America in 1813. Many faces from the first Triennial in 1814 were missing. Richard Furman had died the past winter; John Williams, the pastor of Oliver Street, was gone; so were Dr. Henry Holcombe, Judge Tallmadge, William Rogers.

At eleven o'clock on Wednesday, April 26, the delegates met and reelected Robert Semple of Virginia as president. In the afternoon session Rice moved "that a committee be appointed to investigate the conduct of Luther Rice in what may be considered as belonging thereto on his own individual and personal responsibility, in what may be considered as belonging to his official relation to this body, and in what may be considered as belonging to his official relation to the Columbian College; and report to this body."[5] Lucius Bolles was appointed chairman of a committee of eleven.

Plans had been made not only to divest him of every Convention office but also of his trusteeship of the College. The first he could accept; but to take away his ties to the college was asking a parent to become a non-parent, and he would fight it. On Thursday afternoon, he asked that his name be added to the list of trustees of the College and "after some discussion" and prayer by Jonathan Going, the body adjourned.

The next morning "the motion of Mr. Rice that his name be added to the list of nominations for Trustees" was discussed again. After some hours' debate it was resolved:

That this discussion be for the present postponed. That this Convention take measures to ascertain immediately the financial condition of the Columbian College, with a view to relieve it from present embarrassment.

That the above resolutions be referred to a Committee. That Messrs. Semple, Going and Mercer be a committee to devise, if possible, and present at 3 o'clock, some plan of arrangement on the subject of placing Mr. Rice's name on the list of nominations for Trustees.[6]

At the 3 o'clock session that day the committee reported:

Mr. Rice having declared his determination to devote his time to the collection of funds for the college, and never again to perform any part of the service of disbursing monies on account of the college, unless especially directed to do so by a resolution of the Board of Trustees; and having also expressed a determination to retire from a seat in the Board of Trustees; provided he shall be found in the opinion of the Convention on the investigation which he had invited, unworthy of that office, it is the opinion of the committee that his name ought to be placed on the list of trustees.[7]

The committee and Rice signed this report and it was read and adopted.

Francis Wayland was appointed chairman of a committee on the *Star* and *Luminary* which was instructed "to inquire into the state of the property which at the last Convention the Agent estimated to be worth ten thousand dollars and which he then proposed to deed to the Convention without delay."[8] A committee composed of Howard Malcom, Daniel Hascall, Jonathan Bacheller, Abial Fisher, Heman Lincoln, and John Conant was appointed to examine the account of the agent. These records were called for the following Monday and Rice could not produce them, giving lack of time to prepare them so quickly as the reason.

On Wednesday, May 3, Wayland's committee report was read and accepted. This committee stated that "in consequence of not being furnished any documents upon the subject before them, are unable to report so fully as could be desired; they however by calling upon several persons who are, or have been connected with these establishments"[9] arrived at several facts.

Their findings pointed out that the buildings and equipment in which the Convention press was housed were bought by Rice with the announced intention of deeding them to the Convention, that they were heavily mortgaged, that there was a flaw in the deed by which Rice transferred them to the Convention, that Rice had juggled receipts and disbursements from one account to another in operating the *Star* and *Luminary,* that his bookkeeping was so poor it was almost impossible to assess the true financial situation, that it would require a competent bookkeeper several weeks to audit the "choirs" of ledger books dating back ten years, that, therefore, the whole business be referred to the Board of Managers, giving them the power to dispose of the property as they saw fit or to deed the property back to Rice if the debts appeared to exceed the property's worth. The committee concluded that "notwithstanding, the blameable want of discretion apparent in the conduct of the business, the committee had no evidence of any intentional wrong on the part of the agent or any design to injure the convention."[10]

Lucius Bolles and his committee, appointed to investigate the conduct of Rice regarding the college,

entered into a lengthy investigation of the conduct of Rev. Luther Rice, and what related thereto in regards to his private responsibility as a man, his conduct as agent of the convention and as agents of the board of trustees of the college, and treasurer of that board. They had a number of witnesses upon the various charges exhibited against him and gave him an opportunity of refuting them. After this tedious and unpleasant examination they were "happy to report that nothing affecting the moral character of Mr. Rice, has been proved against him, unless a want of punctuality in complying with his contracts be considered of that nature; and to that he pleads inability."[11]

At the first Missionary Jubilee in 1864 one of those present remembered that Rice rose after the seemingly irrefutable charges were made and began his defense with "by the Grace of God, I came into the world and by the Grace of God, I expect to go out of it," and in a one-and-a-half hour speech presented a defense that no one had expected possible.[12]

However, the committee stated that "many imprudences have been laid to his charge" and that he admitted some of them; they knew that the education committee was actually responsible to the Convention for the management of the College but said, "The injunction of the Convention not to increase the debt was so far disregarded as to go on with the business upon subscription instead of money in hand. As the subscriptions were not collected as fast as the money was wanted, a debt of fearful amount was contracted which has since accumulated."[13] Since the 1823 Triennial when a reckoning was held,

various transactions have been entered by Mr. Rice in conjunction with the board of trustees of said college, some of which appear to your convention to be exceedingly imprudent. In all these transaction Mr. Rice seems to have been the acting man, but not to have done anything without the final sanction of the Board.[14]

They designated two transactions as the grossest indiscretions: one, the purchase of two houses on Greenleaf's Point from Richard Mentor Johnson for fourteen thousand dollars and the other, the taking up of a claim of an Indian agent, Thomas McKenney, against the United States for eleven thousand dollars. The report read that "though all the Board of Trustees gave their sanctions to them yet since it was at the instance of Mr. Rice, he is, in our estimation, highly reprehensible."[15]

Regarding the buildings that housed the printing press the committee found nothing "worse than a want of candor in distinctly naming to the Convention that said houses were under a mortgage to a large amount."

The committee concluded:

In all these transactions, however, your committee can take pleasure in stating that they see nothing like corruption, or selfish designs; although he has fallen into imprudences of very distressing tendency, he does not seem to have any other object in view than the prosperity of the college.

The committee noted that Rice was subject to censure because he was "too loose in all his dealings"—not being governed "by the committee and board of education" and "following his own plans, counting upon an easy acquirement of their sanction and thus of using their high confidence in him."[16]

This was a sad day for Rice, but a worse was yet to come. On Saturday the Convention debated the future scope of the Triennial, the New Englanders speaking on behalf of severing all relations with bodies other than the foreign mission societies. Some spoke against them, one being Jonathan Going of Worcester, the man who would later become the first secretary of the Home Mission Society. Some were silent, among them John Mason Peck, who had resolved to say nothing. The discussion was long and heated. Then the sandy-haired and stooped Wayland, soon to go to Brown for a long and distinguished tenure as president of that college and destined to guide many a decision in future northern Baptist conclaves, stood and spoke and carried the day. He said that the education and missionary endeavors could never be successfully merged under one union and that therefore the Board should sever relations with all but the foreign missionary concern.

The Convention amended its constitution to limit itself, as in the 1814 constitution, to foreign missions. It voted to sever connection with the College and to instruct the Board of Trustees "to alter the ordinances of the College so as to place the power of nomination in some other body than this Convention, taking due care to preserve to the Baptist denomination the effective control of the Institution."[17]

Triumphantly, the *Baptist Missionary Magazine* reported:

It is now a simple body, with one undivided object, and that object, is the promulgation of the gospel amongst the heathen. The reason for the adoption of this admendment, it is unnecessary here to offer. They were such as to satisfy almost every member of the Convention . . .[18]

As an old man, Wayland proudly remembered his stand and felt it was the wise one. There were others who made their homeward journey from New York that May of 1826 with heavy hearts, feeling that the action taken was a regressive step, limiting the Convention to foreign missions. These felt that such a step relegated the chief business of the church to societies composed of a small group in the church and sometimes even to one sex within the church, and that it also opened the door for a general union made up of organizations that were not wholly church-controlled.

So Rice was not only stripped of his offices but, more seriously, of his dream to unite all Baptists as a national body channeling every facet of work through a central organization. And in the overzealous pursuit of his highest hope, he had inadvertently forfeited the others.

It was a strange fact that he became the scapegoat for all that had gone wrong and that not one of the men involved in the Columbian College dealings received any reflected obloquy from his dismissal. This was true both of trustees and administrative faculty.

Evidently the investigators felt that Rice often acted beyond the Board's authorization and that that body was unaccountable for his actions. Obadiah Brown, often ascribed as a cofounder of the College and long-time president of the Board of Trustees, was not called to give any accounting of his part in the affairs of the College.

In light of Staughton's own involvement with the College, his treatment by the Convention—in such contrast to that accorded Rice—can only be explained by his stand. He sided with Professors John Conant, Alexis Caswell, and William Ruggles against Rice and other College trustees, and in the New York councils he stood with those who effected Rice's dismissal.

Distrust had developed between them, stemming from Rice's belief that Staughton was too extravagant at the College and Staughton's unhappiness with Rice's inability to keep the financial funds flowing into the treasury. Staughton and Rice had sincerely loved and trusted each other; more than any other person Staughton had been the one who influenced Rice during the years of indecision to remain in America. Together they had planned a great future for American Baptists. Therefore, Staughton's disenchantment must have come from the financial debacles of the college. He felt Rice responsible and thought the only way to rid the College of its problems was to oust him. Not even Staughton foresaw that the College would not be freed of his help and concern, even by dismissal.

Peck, on his way to New York, had stopped in Washington a few days. He spoke with both Staughton and Rice and described the long and painful conversations with Rice, deploring "the separation of those who had been warm friends, by coldness, distrust, and jealousy."[19]

When the new Board of the Triennial Convention met, Staughton was elected president of it and Dr. Baldwin was elected secretary at a paid salary, a fact which seems to have met full approval from those who had criticized the salary of eight dollars per week which Rice had drawn as agent.

Demoted, censured, rebuffed, Rice turned unremitting toil toward his last great dream, a national Baptist university.

18. The Shadowed Years

Before the delegates departed from New York, some of the men who were anxious that the College be saved met and discussed ways to restore confidence in and financial security to it. All agreed that funds must be raised immediately to stave off foreclosure by the creditors, yet contributors would be reluctant to pay anything unless they were sure the institution would survive. It was decided that a minimum of fifty thousand dollars would be required to salvage the previous investment, and they resolved to raise this amount by appointing agents to secure pledges. These agents were to seek out other strategically placed men who would in turn raise one or two thousand dollars from persons in their area. It was hoped that the northern states would raise twenty thousand dollars and the southern, thirty thousand dollars.

Soon General Green, government printer, had handbills stating:

Whereas, it is well known that the funds of Columbian College in the District of Columbia are in a depressed condition; and, whereas, at a meeting of a responsible number of the friends of the College in the City of New York, May 9th, 1826, it was unanimously resolved: That measures be adopted, for the benefit of the said College: We, therefore, whose names are underwritten promise to pay to the Treasury of said College the sums annexed to our names, responsible within sixty days after the completion of the subscriptions on condition that the sum of Fifty Thousand Dollars shall be subscribed within two years of the above day and on farther condition, that it shall be certified by a Committee appointed by said meeting for that purpose, consisting of Rev. Messrs. Semple of Virginia, Bolles of Massachusetts, Elon Galusha of New York, Brantly of Philadelphia and the Hon. Alexander Thompson, Pennsylvania, that the state of the financial concern of said College warrants the payment of the money.[1]

No one was to commit himself beyond a pledge until it was ascertained whether or not the total could be raised and doing so would redeem the College.

Rice took no time to brood over the events in New York. Fifteen days after the Convention's conclusion, he wrote Obadiah Brown, president of the Board, from Richmond: "I have got upon my books $6,400 towards the $50,000."[2] He was concerned about appointing other agents and urged Brown to write the middle and northern states and enlist the services of several men for two or three months: "If Benedict, and Going, and Galusha, and Maclay, and Yates, could be induced to take hold of the case in earnest, I do think $20,000 might be subscribed in those states in three months."[3]

Rice kept up a steady stream of letters to Brown, advising him of things that needed to be done at the College. While in North Carolina, subscribing the pledges on the fifty thousand dollars, he received copies of the *Star* containing derogatory editorials by Baron Stow; Stow said that it was the unanimous opinion of the Board that Rice had defaulted on his obligations to the Convention. Stow had edited the *Star* since January of '26 and had sided with Chase, Ruggles, Caswell, and Conant. He not only used the very paper Rice founded to attack him, but was also using the supplies which Rice had purchased. Rice protested to Brown, "You ought certainly to call on Stow to pay for the paper that was in the office when he took it, which was purchased on my credit, and for which the paper makers want their pay; . . . surely he can have no claim on our indulgence in this matter while pursuing the miserable course he has adopted."[4] He inquired of Brown: "Is not Mr. Stow a member of your church? And is it consistent that he should be suffered to publish known falsehood without any attention on the part of the church?"[5]

Rice cautioned Brown to be sure that the interest on John Quincy Adams' 20,000-dollar loan was paid on time, for "I do think it of great importance that Mr. Adams be paid, in time to allow of recommending the College in his Message."[6]

In this summer of '26, Rice's letter to Brown was filled with concern lest the members of the Board of Trustees should become predominantly non-Baptist, for he felt those who were not Baptist "will attempt some alteration of the Charter by the aid of Congress next session."[7]

Rice had asked the committee appointed by the Convention to give him several months to present accounts of his collections over the past twelve years, but he left his books and papers with a Mr.

Smoot in Washington and within two months of the Convention, in July, the committee reported that there were deficits and Rice had defaulted on his commitments. Rice said to Brown, "As to my being a defaulter as reported by the Committee you know it cannot be so . . . In time I shall be able to make out a statement; but at present we must *pump ship* for life."[8] And to his friend John Goss, Rice conceded that the report was "a mortal stab on my reputation."[9]

Stow continued his tactics, printing injurious statements purported to have the "unanimous approbation" of the Board and Rice cried out to Brown: "The most immediately galling point at present is that Stow should have the managing of the *Star,* publishing whatever he pleases to my injury. While no word of explanation or reply can be got into that paper. Do, as soon as possible, take the whole concern, *Star* and all, out of his hands if possible."[10] And later: "I am not made of iron or brass, and although from the habits of enduring may be able to bear as much of abuse, perhaps, as most persons, yet there are limits beyond which bearing is impossible."[11]

All autumn and winter Rice ranged the southern states begging subscriptions, but in early 1827 he was back in Washington to give a report to the Board of Trustees and to make a long statement relative to the charges in the published report of the committee. The Board voted to retain Rice as agent and announced that though the "pecuniary concerns are embarassing they are not hopeless."

In a letter to Enoch Reynolds that spring, Rice gave his most comprehensive public statement about how he viewed the debts and something of the reason for them:

The question is sometimes asked me, *How can the college be so much in debt after all that that has been collected for it?* To this I give in substance, the following answer, viz: The debt, exclusive of certain government transactions, is $95,000. The amount actually received in donations, about $40,000; leaving $45,000 of debt, above the amount received. But, more than $20,000 paid in interest on loans, discounts on uncurrent bills and etc., at least $20,000 in expenses of the Institution, above its income, including the support of beneficiaries and unpaid bills of the students . . . and more than $10,000 in expenses of Agents, and trips of three Professors to Europe; will make a sum equal to the amount received by donations, $40,000 so that the existing debt ought to be equal to the original cost of the property; and this is the fact . . .[12]

Rice published in the *National Intelligencer* a rebuttal to Stow's charges but immediately was repentant, writing Brown, "I am heartily sorry that I published those remarks."[13] Dr. Brown's church, the First Baptist, did review the conduct of Stow and Rice, both members of the congregation, but Stow departed about the same time, easing the strain in relations; William Brantly assumed editorship of the *Star,* subsequently moving it to Philadelphia and naming it the *Star and Christian Index.*

During most of the next years, Rice stayed away from Washington. He seemed to feel that it were better for the College for him to be in the background. He did not believe in nurturing hurts or grievances and he wrote Brown to treat the offenders with graciousness, suggesting that Brown write friends of the College as he himself had done through the years:

Cultivate intimacy and good feeling with the Faculty, particularly the two Professors in the College, and don't be discouraged . . . Write to Galusha, to Going, to Benedict, to Bolles, to Sharp, to Knowles, to Babcock, to Maclay, to Brantly, to Dagg, to Brown of Scotch Plains, to Rathbone, to Ball, to Clopton, to Semple, to Ryland, Wilson of Society Hill, to Mercer, to Sherwood, and to as many others as you can think of. Make it a point to write two or three letters at least every day. *Our enemies have done much by private letters* and it is your business to correct the mischief by the same means. Write to Wayland, also, and to Rowen of Providence . . Don't be discouraged, either. The College *can* be saved with the blessing of God. But you *must set your pen to work!*[14]

But Brown was not the man to assume the voluminous correspondence which Rice had maintained through the years, for he had a growing pastorate, a job as post office clerk, and now the heavy demands of running the College and trying to untangle its finances.

In the spring of '27, President Staughton and Samuel Waite, a student, went South to raise money for the College, and Staughton tasted something of Rice's daily toil on the long and lonely roads. The two were in Charleston when Staughton received a letter from his son James stating that Judge McLean and five other trustees had resigned in a body and "passionately urging him to abandon his office."[15] Staughton returned to Washington in haste and on April 27, he and Professors Ruggles, Caswell, and Conant resigned, thus forcing the College to close.

Rice was in the Richmond and Fredericksburg area of Virginia when he heard of the resignations and knew that the College was closed. He had had an attack of fever the previous fall and was at a church in Caroline County when a second attack occurred. He went to "Cedar Vale," the home of the Samuel Redds.

He was too sick to drive home in his sulky, Emily Redd gave up her seat in her father's carriage to him, and she mounted his high "old sulky" and drove home some five or six miles. He was very sick then, for a week or ten days. When his clothes were brought in by the washwoman they were examined and put in order, a thing very much needed. He spent little on himself. All that could be saved must go to the college. There was among the clothes a cravat so worn out it was past mending, which Emily Redd thought no robbery to appropriate and put another in its place . . . new, and as much alike as could be, even to the small "L. R" embroidered on it.[16]

As soon as he was able he wrote Brown, "Since writing you from Fredericksburg ten days ago have been mostly confined by a fever, under the operation of medicine. I am now well again and have taken up the line of March. I am on my way to bro. Semple's neighborhood, and expect, if the Lord will, to meet with him and Ball tomorrow at Upper King and Queen meetinghouse. My object there is to make sure, if possible, his going to Washington and bro. Ball with him."[17]

They wanted Semple to assume the duties of agent and treasurer for the College and hoped Eli Ball would travel to collect funds.

Rice had decided that he—his property and his life—were expendable. His reputation was almost gone, and therefore he felt it would be better for him to receive the onus for all that was done. Of the remaining property which was his at the printing offices, he wrote Brown to "make the best possible disposition of the other Office Property, without any regard to me. I have no *private* property, while the College owes one cent, or any person is bound to pay any thing for it."[18] And of the debts he wrote, "Leave me and the debts yoked together."[19] Finally he sent in his resignation as a trustee, feeling that some might do more for the College if he were no longer on the Board. With his resignation he wrote Brown, "Let me perish, if thereby the College can be saved!"[20] And again: "As for myself personally, that is much the smallest portion of the concern! I have even prayed that the Lord will take me away, if that should be needful in order to the saving of the College."[21]

His resignation was accepted and published in the *Star* and Rice was again concerned that the institution might slip out of Baptist control: "Let me earnestly entreat you to see to it that you keep a sufficient number of true Baptists in the acting Board and don't put in too many that are not Baptists . . . to insure *Baptists'* support, we must have Baptist Trustees, at least a majority in the acting Board."[22]

A faculty and president had to be obtained with haste or the College could not be reopened. All that summer of '27, Rice was writing Brown suggestions: "As to a president of the College, if you can possibly get Brantly, I believe it will unquestionably be best to so do."[23] But they had a difficult time. In August Daniel H. Barnes was elected president but the trustees could not meet his conditions of acceptance, so the College could not reopen in the fall. It was the following June before Stephen Chapin, one of Rice's suggestions, was obtained.

Brown wrote him that they planned to pay the new president fifteen hundred dollars a year and Rice remonstrated, "Don't think of it! Save every cent, in every way that is possible, till we get out of debt. Begin small, and grow gradually, and regularly, and surely. How much better if we had begun in that way at first."[24] He reminded Brown that

our misfortunes have been owing not less to the undue multiplication of Faculty, and unreasonable expense thereby incurred, and vain glorious parade in that particular, than to any other single item of improvidence or bad judgment. There is no evidence that the *parade and display* which we made of *faculty,* at all increased the number of students. Certainly they did not increase in proportion to that parade and display . . . the fact of a College there in operation will bring students. The reality of good management and instruction, without ostentation, will increase them . . . Do, brother Brown, bestir yourself, and get the College started again next term. It *can* be done. It is all important that it should be. It is ours to labor and suffer; but in due season we shall reap *if we faint not!*[25]

At "Mordington," Semple's Virginia home, Rice had long conversations about the situation in Washington, especially the inner workings of the Board. Semple revealed that before Staughton's resignation there had been discussion of his drinking, and that Dr. Thomas Sewall had mentioned Brown's also. Rice advised Brown:

Possibly you have heard the vile slander which had been started of your drinking! I believe brother Semple begins to have his eyes opened

187

as to Dr. Sewall! Perhaps it might be prudent for I don't think your health would suffer by it, to discontinue the use of spirits. At any rate, feel thankful to the Lord that *I have been led to do so.*[26]

Temperance societies were beginning to be formed all over the country to counter the excessive drinking practices prevalent, and strong feeling was developing against Baptist leaders who drank or took a toddy, even for "health" reasons.

In August of 1827, Rice wrote Brown that he had left his sub-scription book with Semple and that it listed "$45,150 . . . so that when Galusha shall have made up the additional $5,000 in New England the whole will be completed."[27] Until the total was subscribed, the payments would not be coming in to alleviate their situation. As Rice lamented, "Every thing seems taking a turn to render the final salvation of the concern as difficult and tardy as possible."[28] Realizing that little was done beyond his own efforts, Rice wrote:

I have seen Ball and Clopton, and they have concluded to go forth to the work, Ball to South Carolina and Clopton to Georgia to fill the quotas of those two states towards the $50,000. This will insure the completion of the amount; and I am now disposed to believe it prac-ticable to save the College without New England, and even without New York, even after all the injuries the North has inflicted upon the concern.[29]

Soon Clopton was reporting, "I have just completed the sum of $5,000 besides the $1,000 obtained before we crossed the Georgia line."[30]

Rice heard that the Board of Trustees was thinking of reemploying Alexis Caswell and William Ruggles, two of the professors who had forced the closing of the school the previous year. This seemed expedient to satisfy prospective patrons who otherwise refused to support the school. The news was disquieting to Rice, who at first felt he could not bear their return, but in a few days he wrote Brown about Caswell that "notwithstanding the perfidious manner in which he assisted in breaking up the Institution it may be a serious question if it would not be best and invite him to return. Semple seems to be of this opinion." And of Ruggles, he said to bring him back also.

Of General Green's position, which had been printed in the *Na-tional Telegraph,* Rice said,

His opposition appears to me an entirely unprincipled opposition . . . as far as I can judge his effort is directed to the *injury of the institution for the sake of carrying a point relative to Ruggles!* This appears to me to have been the *very principle* of the course pursued by Smith, Staughton, Ruggles, Caswell and Stow, in breaking up the Institution a year ago; and I did hope that none on our side of the matter would ever be guilty of adopting so bad a principle as the ground of their conduct touching this concern . . . it would be better if he deported himself like a Baptist having the honor of the Lord Jesus and his cause at heart.[31]

And to Brown he said, "I hope you will avoid doing anything whatsoever that might possibly be considered wilful or retaliatory."[32]

Brown was to be replaced as chairman of the Board by Semple, and Rice advised forbearance.

Whatever may be the measure of reproach, affliction, or humiliation, which the Lord may see best should come upon us, let us patiently bear, and patiently toil and patiently wait, with much prayer and great searchings of heart of the Lord himself . . . Personal interest with me is nothing, till the College shall be absolutely free of debt.

He also advised Brown: "Semple must work with the Administration men and General Green with the Jackson men; and Dr. Sewall with both. Let Semple be introduced to Mr. Clay. He wishes it and you can introduce him any time."[33]

Chapin accepted the presidency in June of 1828, coming from Waterville College, and with the return of Caswell and Ruggles, the college was opened for the fall semester.

Brown wrote that Semple wanted Rice to go to Kentucky, and Rice replied to Brown: "I had no objection to a trip to Kentucky, though I make no great calculations upon its results . . . he had only to signify that he thought it best, or wishes me to go there . . . I expect, if the Lord wills, to be at Washington the 10th on my way to Kentucky. Whether there is now danger from the Marshal or constables, I don't know, but think you had better not mention the fact of my intended visit there to *any one*."[34]

Rice evidently thought he might be apprehended by the officers about some of the contracts. Semple had published accounts of the College's indebtedness, stating that a tremendous debt was due to two unwise contracts, which the investigating committee had cited earlier. The first was the purchase for the college of two houses on Greenleaf's Point. Bought from Richard Mentor Johnson for $14,000, this price was far above their true value in Semple's estimation.

It cannot be ascertained what induced Rice to buy these houses; perhaps he was taking them in lieu of some debt to Johnson and the transaction was forced upon him. Perhaps it was, as many thought, that Rice speculated on them. He and Senator Johnson roomed together for a while at the Browns when Rice first moved to Washington. Johnson was a well-known Washington figure, popularly supposed to have killed Tecumseh in the Battle of the Thames; he was one of the satellites revolving around Andrew Jackson, and his scandalous commonlaw marriage to a mulatto seems not to have been general knowledge in Washington. But it might be asked where his integrity was in the contract about the houses, for he was a trustee of the College and would, it would seem, be responsible to protect the College's interest as well as his own.

The other great indiscretion which Semple attributed to Rice involved a contract with McKenney. "He made a contract to the government by which he again bound the college for nearly $12,000 and took in exchange Thomas L. McKenney's notes due to the government and a small sum in cash paid him by Col. McKenney."[35] Again it is not possible to discern Rice's motive in this seemingly ruinous and obviously unwise contract, but correspondence between him and Brown reveals that he did not act alone in entering the contract. His good friend Semple, who became head of the Board, never knew this. And it was Rice's own choice, for when the Government was pressing its claim in the summer of 1826 and the matter was about to go before a jury, Rice wrote Brown that since McKenney had defaulted on his contract, it should properly fall to him. "However, if nothing else will relieve the case from going to jury before the exchange of obligations with the Government perhaps you had better disavow the arrangement altogether, and insist that I acted without authority!"[36]

Brown was happy to do this; it removed any taint of blame from himself and other Board members. Brown maintained his standing and prestige throughout all the accusations and insinuations, and Rice bore the brunt of the abuse and the near annihilation of his reputation. It is a singular fact that Brown died a well-to-do minister[37] with no touch of suspicion on his name.

Rice made the tour to Kentucky and though he collected little for Columbian College, while there he preached such a stirring sermon at Mount Pleasant on the value of Christian education that a group of men was led to found Georgetown College, securing a charter the following January.

From the South that winter Rice was starved for news from the College and implored Brown in every letter to "let me know how many students there are . . . how Dr. Chapin comes on[38] . . . I should be glad, also, if you would state a little how affairs are getting on . . . how many students and the prospects of things concerning the College."[39]

It is assumed that Brown welcomed Rice's remittances of money to operate the College; but he answered infrequently, Rice bemoaning, "It is not customary for you to write to me . . . till I have made request after request and complaint after complaint . . . and while I have to acknowledge that this state of things is not gratifying to me, there is no reason to presume it will be altered!"[40] And in another letter: "It is peculiarly mortifying and painful to me that I can so seldom obtain an answer from you, even when I send on money."[41]

In a statement to the Board of Trustees, May, 1829, Rice said that he had paid in $5,313.48,

which is several hundred dollars more than I have collected on College subscriptions during that period. This has been accomplished by my having collected a considerable sum on account of printing a Hymnbook at the Columbian Office while under my control and from the sale of certain books, pamphlets printed at the same office; the proceeds of which, as indeed of every thing in my power, you are aware, have been anxiously turned to the purpose of extricating the College from embarrassment . . . It is, also well known to you, that toiling as I have done for the Institution without any compensation and even providing for my personal expenses of late by special means, I am without home and utterly destitute of property. However, after having labored for the benefit of this College nearly ten years it is a source of no small consolation to me that it has now the prospect of realizing complete relief, ultimate enlargement.[42]

With this report he sent in his resignation, since recently those in Philadelphia had spoken ill of the Board for retaining him as agent. He continued to work for the College and was eventually reappointed though always without salary.

Things were gradually improving at the College under the guiding hand of Semple. Private creditors were induced to settle for a discount, John Quincy Adams for thirteen thousand dollars of his twenty-thousand-dollar note, and others similarly. The Government passed "a law that provided that these contracts, so ruinous to the college might be rescinded and that we might be allowed to reconvey the houses and other properties received by them and cancel our bonds given for them."[43] By 1830 Semple could announce that when "our present subscriptions shall have been collected we shall have reduced the debt to less than $25,000."[44]

Rice's spirits began to rise and, ever dreaming, he wrote Brown in 1830:

The plan of pursuit before me to which I have found my mind steadily tending for a considerable time is this, viz: to be located on College Hill, get to be postmaster there: and make frequent excursions in different directions to collect college funds: *First,* to pay off the debts; or as nearly as shall be thought best before entering upon the next thing, which may be: *Second* to raise $15,000 for the permanent support of an instructor for young ministers: and *Third,* to raise scholarships of $2,000 each for the support of young ministers while pursuing a course of improvement in education.

If I should live long enough to raise the fund for the support of an instructor for young ministers, and to get one scholarship, with the blessing of God, I should think that my life had not been spent in vain.[45]

And he reported by fall that he was "getting along tolerably well with the president's $15,000 fund,"[46] and added, "I now enclose $220 which with a little balance that I suppose you have on hand of former funds will enable you to meet the payment of Dr. Chapin the 23rd of this month. I hope you will not fail to meet his salary promptly whatever else may be neglected."[47] It was Rice who continued to meet the payments at the College through these years.

Rice was provoked that Semple spent so much of his time at "Mordington," drawing $750 a year as chairman of the Board, while Rice himself barely subsisted. "Where is Br. Semple all this time," he demanded of Brown. "Has he accomplished his journey by land yet to Washington? I presume he must have been there by this time to get his salary!"[48] Rice even talked to Semple about working without salary and finally obtained Semple's assurance that he would do so if board could be arranged. Rice, never daunted, wrote Brown: "If you think proper to give him his Board and accomodations, I will engage to collect as much as would be the proper charge for it."[49] Rice sought to work in harmony with Semple:

"I am unwilling to do anything unless with the approbation of Dr. Semple . . . I am greatly anxious that we should all act in concern, and strain every nerve and accomplish the momentous object. So try and see if we can't hit upon some plan by which Semple and Green shall act together."[50]

Beginning in January of 1830, a new note entered Rice's thought and petitions to Brown. He was thinking of establishing his own home after all these years and wished to have the post office at College Hill so that he could continue to devote time to the College with free franking service for all his correspondence. Sometime during the past year he had begun courting a wealthy widow in King and Queen County, a "Mrs. G.," and he wrote Brown:

> It is my intention to marry, and I must needs have a home. But I shall not want the House, probably, for this purpose sooner than the first of January next—possibly not so soon even as that; but I wish to be provided for an anticipated event; and indeed this may possibly have some bearing on the result. Should I marry Mrs. G. there will be this farther advantage to the College. One, two, or three students added to the number.[51]

Mrs. G. had three grown sons, and Rice wished to occupy one of the two houses at the College which George Wood was then occupying, rent free. Rice noted, "Surely he ought not to have the use of it without paying any thing when the Board can rent it . . . for $900 a year."[52]

Rice was serious and entreated Brown: "I beg you will not neglect this matter, and let me know the result as soon as convenient, as it may be of some importance to me in the negotiation which I am actually carrying on relative to marriage."[53]

But Rice was again luckless in love, and tradition has it that the rich widow was fearful her inheritance would find its way into the treasury of Columbian College, her love of the College being considerably less than Rice's.

During these years, Rice continually harkened back to his hope for an educated ministry; in the summer of '31 he so longed "for a college where 70 to 100 or 200 ministers are training . . . because they are so needed and there is no probability of a supply of the right sort but in this way."[54]

Semple suffered a stroke that fall and died on Christmas Day. In July of '32 Congress granted the College $25,000 in city lots, a like grant to the Jesuits' college in Georgetown. In 1832 Abner Clopton became the General Agent, and that year Rice was offered the presidency of Georgetown College in Kentucky, but he declined.

He resumed his attendance at the meetings of the Triennial and was in New York in May of 1831 for the meeting of the missionary convention. Isaac McCoy noted in his *Journal* that the report on Indian work did not go as he wished, Francis Wayland opposing it, but that Rice was among those speaking in favor of the report and "appeared to good advantage."[55]

In 1831, Asaph wrote Luther that their mother had died in her eighty-eighth year in his home in Northborough; Amos, the father, had died four years before so that now only Asaph and Sarah remained in Northborough.

While in Providence, Rhode Island, in 1832, he suffered a mild stroke and after the manner of the day, he was asked if he were prepared to die, to which he replied, "Yes, though I should like to bring up the college first."[56]

There were rewards mingled with the shadows of these years. The foreign mission expansion under the Triennial was heartening; at the 1832 meeting, the number of missionaries had increased to seventy-two. At that same meeting Jonathan Going and John Mason Peck led in founding the American Baptist Home Mission Society which resumed the type of work in the West that had been begun in 1817 and then discontinued.

As he traveled, Rice invariably crossed the path of men whom he had influenced and helped. In New Bern, North Carolina, Samuel Waite was prodding the people of that state into an organized state convention with a paper and an academy, the forerunner of Wake Forest College. Jesse Mercer was the leader in his state, having acquired the *Star and Christian Index* and moved it to Georgia as *The Christian Index.* He also had begun a manual labor school which was to become Mercer University. Isaac McCoy had become agent for Indian affairs and was resettling the tribes of the upper Mississippi in Indian Territory.

Rice continued to carry the load of concern about President Chapin's salary and that of the faculty, writing every patron.[57] He pleaded for funds to keep William Ruggles as math teacher at Columbian when he had been offered a larger salary elsewhere— this to one of the men who had forced the 1827 closing of the college!

194

Rice's old friend William Staughton had married Anna Peale of the famous family of painters, and accepted the presidency of Georgetown College. But Staughton died en route there in 1829. His son-in-law wrote a *Memoir* in the usual panegyric vein of that day. Even so Rice protested to one of the Baptist papers that it was not as worthy of the man as it should have been.

He felt that something had gone out of his life when he resorted to retaliation against Stow and refuted his statements in the papers, and now he came to feel he must rid his heart of all malice. Costly as it was, he wrote each of the young men with whom he had differed, "confessing pride and haughtiness of spirit" and asking their forgiveness.

Each of the three answered, Knowles first:

You may be assured, that my feelings toward you have always been of the most cordial good will. Whatever I may have thought or said at moments of excitement, respecting your official conduct, I have never ceased to regard you with sincere respect for your talents, with gratitude for your public services, and for your personal kindness to me, and with affection for your many virtues, I have often taken occasion to defend you. I have desired, and predicted that you would one day fully reinstate yourself in the confidence and affections of your brethren . . .

And so, my dear brother, you perceive how unnecessary it was to ask my forgiveness. I never felt myself injured, and there never has been a time when I could not cordially take you by the hand. Yet at moments of excitement, I may have done or said something to injure your feelings. If so, I am sincerely sorry, and ask your forgiveness. May our gracious Savior forgive us all, and make us henceforward more fit to serve him.[58]

Six days later, Chase penned:

The reference which you make to the period of my residence on College Hill, and the sentiments which you express, have awakened emotions which I shall not attempt to describe. Rest assured, my dear brother, that not a particle of hardness toward you is cherished in my bosom. I have remembered you with fraternal feeling in my prayers, and have thus found a sweet relief amidst the pangs occasioned by the change in our relations . . . God grant that during the remnant of our sojourn on earth, we may "keep the unity of the spirit" in the bond of peace.[59]

And last came a letter from the one who had injured most, Baron Stow:

I wrote you seven years ago, under the influence of feelings and convictions, such as seem to have dictated yours. I deeply felt at the time and have so felt ever since, that in the unpleasant differences which occurred between us, I had unnecessarily injured you, and I then felt, and still feel, that I ought to acknowledge the wrong and solicit forgiveness.

I freely forgive you, my dear brother, and feel as cordial towards you as at any period since our first acquaintance. I shall be happy again to meet you, and to say many things that I cannot write. I feel under obligations to you for many acts of kindness; I should be glad to have it in my power to reciprocate them.[60]

During the 1830's, Rice also began to dream of settling in Washington in a pastorate. Frequently he wrote friends about his distress that there was no Baptist church in the Georgetown area. Now that the salvation of the College was in sight, he yearned to aid in forming "a Baptist church or two at Washington—probably I may be able to do more for the college itself in a short time, in that connection, than in my present sphere of labour . . . I know not what may be in the future of Divine Providence, but wish simply to move on in the line of duty . . ."[61] But in this too, Rice was to experience the "sickness of hope deferred," for he was never quite able to secure the College to the point where he could relinquish his life as a wayfarer.

19. The Last Journey

Rice attended his last Triennial Convention in the First Baptist Church of Richmond in May of 1835. The delegates from 19 states heard many gratifying reports. The denomination had grown remarkably in the 21 years since that first meeting in Philadelphia. Baptist churches now numbered more than 8,000 with over 600,000 members. The Convention supported 25 mission stations, employing 112 missionaries, and the call went forth for an annual budget of $100,000 for the next year. Fifteen institutions of higher learning enrolled more than 400 men in ministerial education.

There were problems of policy still, and sectional differences about slavery already clouded public discussions and were the topic of many private conversations. Churches in the North were pressing their southern brethren to take a stand against slavery. Some thought fellowship should be withdrawn from those churches whose members held slaves and that no slave-holding missionary should be appointed.

To this meeting the Baptist Union of Great Britain sent Revs. F. A. Cox and J. Hoby bearing a fraternal letter and instructions to pursue a judicious course in pointing out to the Americans their unchristian practices about slavery.

Cox and Hoby spoke at the Convention, were much moved by the "vast assembly, composed of three classes of hearers, the white population occupying one side, the black the other, and ministers of the gospel from distant parts crowding the centre"[1]; but they made no public pronouncement against slavery, having been informed that "the laws of the State prohibit all such public discussions in Virginia . . . consequently the convention would have been dissolved by the magistrates had it been attempted."[2] For failing to make a public utterance, they were highly censured upon their return to England, and the English Baptists sought to bring increasing pressure on the American brethren in their next letter to the Convention.

Hoby and Cox met privately with some of the leaders and when confronted about slavery, most of the men apologized or excused themselves on the basis of the manumission laws, but William Bullein Johnson "came out squarely in support of Slavery."[3]

Rice had always felt it was a most detestable practice and frequently lamented in his *Journal,* "How afflicting to hear men professing republicanism, advocating slavery."[4]

Rice was not well and his ill health was impeding his usual travels as he wrote President Chapin following the Convention: "I did not get started so soon as I expected from Richmond, owing to the rain Friday and Saturday. I succeeded in stopping the chill and fever operation that had commenced upon me but still I am not well. However, through mercy I am able to travel, and I shall proceed as fast as possible, if the Lord wills, to the southeast."[5]

The discerning among the groups he visited noted his marked pallor, his quietness, and his thoughtfulness of each person he met. Near the last he wrote to a friend that the "incessant and injurious levity, foolish talking and jesting, in which I so long and so criminally indulged, has been, I hope, by the special mercy of the Lord, somewhat effectually done away."[6] Among his friends there were those who said that Rice's only flaw was wit, and one of them, James Furman of South Carolina, spoke to him about his use of humor. The purging of this "flaw" had been a lifelong task, and there were many among his friends who felt it a sign that he was "ripening for heaven."

Perhaps Rice sensed that his task was nearly ended, whether completed or not, for in a letter written in September, 1835, he began talking of employing another agent to procure funds. Though unwell and spent, he was able to continue soliciting through the year and in February of 1836 wrote Dr. Chapin, "Let us patiently labor on . . . the blessing will surely come, if we faint not."[7] President Chapin, unlike Staughton, assumed that he was responsible for the administrative and financial business of the College and had proved a joy to Rice's heart, a steady and responsive correspondent.

While in the South that winter, Rice talked to Adiel Sherwood, whom he had long known, about aiding the College. Early in '36 Sherwood was elected "Professor of Learned Languages and of Biblical Literature" at Columbian College, and General Agent of the institution. He came to Washington in June and "after an examination of the indebtedness of the college, with Mr. Luther Rice, I was induced to accept."[8]

In his last letter to Judson, Rice wrote in June, 1836:

My health became much reduced last fall and winter, but is now, through divine mercy, quite restored. My strength is not, however, what it was fifteen or twenty years ago. I am now past fifty-three years of age, and feel the effects of time and toil, in the diminution of energy and vigour; but I hope that my powers will not quite decay, till I shall have the happiness of seeing the prosperity of the Columbian College—till from that institution some laborers shall have gone forth into some part of the heathen world, to preach among the gentiles the unsearchable riches of Christ.

Should my life and health be preserved, I expect to continue constantly travelling, as heretofore, for about two years to come. After that, I hope the Lord will provide for my becoming somewhat stationary, and allow me to rest a little, before I go hence, and be no more on earth. But in reference to this, as in all things else, I wish ever to be able to devoutly to say, the will of the Lord be done![9]

Every midsummer, Rice turned Columbus and sulky southward to the camp meetings in Virginia and the Carolinas and the associational and state conventions convening in late summer and early autumn. His presence was expected and brought a welcome benediction—the boon of a great man—to their annual deliberations.

August 13, 1836, found him on this usual circuit, posting: "Greeted with a hearty welcome at the camp-meeting at the Cross Roads this evening. Some twenty or thirty, or more, came as by one impulse to the margin of the camp ground, to salute me."[10]

In late August he traversed North Carolina and was on the Newberry-to-Augusta road when on Friday night, September 1, the pain in his side became so intense that he changed his course and went to the home of Brother Andrew Jackson Coleman, a friend in Edgefield County, South Carolina. On Saturday, Dr. J. C. Ready, minister and physician, doctored him, freely bleeding, after which "he fainted, not so much from the quantity of blood taken, as from a nervous dread he had always had of the lancet."[11]

Dr. R. G. Mays came to visit him also, and on Sunday morning Mrs. Mays rode over and pressed an invitation to come to their house. Sunday afternoon Rice rose, dressed, and drove in his sulky, alone, the two miles to the Mays' home. Alighting in front of the big, white, two-storied home, he did not appear overly fatigued to the Mays. They were unaware that Brother Rice had taken his last journey save one; he was more than tired, he was mortally ill.

Soon his painful symptoms returned—the nausea and pain in the side, which was "mitigated by frequent cupping" and blisters applied to the tender area. The two physicians, Drs. Ready and Mays, consulted and diagnosed his illness as appendicitis or "abscess of the liver,"[12] for which therapy was limited and remedies not available.

During the first week of September, he reminisced about the secret society, recounting with great lucidity the details surrounding the formation of the Brethren, and in his last thinking moments he reverted again and again to memories of the men. There was Mills, long dead at sea on a return scouting voyage to Africa. And Judson, whom he loved as a brother, he could see lifting his hand in salute at Port Louis as his boat receded from the shore. And there was Hall, quietly competent, "the beloved," laboring seven years in Bombay to win his first convert and then dying a stranger's death of cholera in a pagan temple with no friend near. And he could never forget the slight Newell as he was at Port Louis, brokenhearted over Harriet.

But there were other memories that flooded his mind and to Mrs. Mays he rejoiced that "the Lord raised up such a man as Kincaid to take his place in the mission field," saying, "He is a man so much better qualified than myself for the missionary work."[13]

"Every evening during his sickness he insisted that Doctor Mays should have family worship in his room; and whether the doctor or others prayed, he usually asked that they would pray 'if it be the will of God he might recover.' This request was always made with evident and calm submission to the will of God."[14] He always gave them a few lines of a favorite hymn to sing and on his last Sunday requested that they sing the hymn beginning, "Another six days' work is done, Another sabbath is begun," though his favorite was "When I can read my title clear."

He also remarked, "It is a matter of entire indifference to me where I should die, whenever the Lord chooses to call me, I am ready to go."[15]

Gradually he became weaker, his debility probably hastened by the bloodlettings. About the middle of the third week in September, he was unable to rise to shave and care for his personal needs. Thursday, the twenty-third, he had a chill followed by fainting and was unconscious for a while. Rallying, he inquired of the doctor, "Is my condition dangerous?"

Dr. Ready replied, "Some of the symptoms in your case, I cannot explain. Is there any request you'd like to make about your affairs?"

"Yes, send my sulky and horse and baggage to brother Brooks with directions to send them to brother Sherwood, and say that they all belong to the college."[16]

Entreated about the place of his burial, he said, "The Pine Pleasant churchyard, the most peaceful spot on earth."

Saturday, the twenty-fifth of September, dawned a golden autumn day, becoming hot in midday, the air still. It was the day of Rice's most adventurous journey. There had been many ridings into the unknown, many lost trails, many twilight arrivals. Countless times he had sat around the ever-changing family circles, lifted his voice and sung, "When I can read my title clear."

He was unable to rise from his bed, was feverish and insatiably thirsty. Ice was long gone from the icehouses and there was little that could be done to alleviate his distress. "He bears his suffering with more lamblike submission than I ever knew," Mrs. Mays remarked, afterwards adding, "I never heard him moan."[17]

He requested that they fetch Brother Todd, who lived fifteen miles away, the Mays surmising he wished to give some final instructions about the College. Toward evening and before Brother Todd arrived, he slept, once rousing to remark to Dr. Mays that he felt rather well, drifting again into sleep, lying on his right side. He expired quietly, Dr. Ready believing he "did not feel death as other men generally do."[18]

He died in another man's home, far from any member of his family, close friends, or the beloved College. A sad and pathetic picture? Not for one who "watched for the morning." As Asaph said, "Luther always expected that tomorrow would not only be a fair day, but a little fairer than today."[19]

And it was so.

20. Afterwards

Rice's death brought forth a steam of eulogies. In Washington, the faculty met and passed resolutions, stating that the College had "lost its most distinguished founder," and that "no discouragement could ever damp his zeal, no opposition allay his ardor for its prosperity." At the memorial service, Dr. Chapin said, "There was something extraordinary in his life—extraordinary in reference to the day in which he lived, and to the objects which he aimed to accomplish."

Next to Washington, his going was felt most keenly in Virginia and especially in Richmond where the churches met and Jeremiah Jeter preached the sermon. At the next annual meeting of Virginia Baptists their report stated that "here, he always found a hearty welcome. We loved him for truth's sake—we loved him for his works' sake."

His death was lamented in Georgia and South Carolina, and at their annual meeting South Carolina Baptists appointed William Bullein Johnson, Ivison L. Brooks, and Basil Manly, Sr., to receive funds and erect a monument over his grave. A marble slab was placed over the grave, the Rev. Mr. Brooks writing the inscription.

Baptist periodicals carried editorials and accounts, and for several years thereafter readers wrote to the papers, giving anecdotes or expressing appreciation for his life, many mentioning his frailties and noting that they loved him despite them. Henry Keeling recalled his tea drinking, arduous traveling, humility in prayer, beautiful singing, the fact that he was an open communionist, and that he had empathy with his audience. Mercer recalled that

Mr. Rice's self-denial was equal to his devotion to every good cause. Like his blessed Master, he went about doing good. He looked over the world, and found it full of human miseries, and forthwith he laboured with all his might for their removal. Thus labouring, not unfrequently, was he exposed to heat, to cold, and to the colder treatment of those whose good he sought to promote. For even Luther Rice had his enemies, may we not say his persecutors? With talents of the very first order, and an education that would have secured to him the smiles and favours of those who are deservedly called wise and good, he travelled up and down in the earth for the benefit of others. Oft-times, clad in tattered garments, to a stranger he would appear to resemble more a poor beggar than a great and good man.

William F. Broaddus recalled his scriptural preaching which magnified the sovereignty of God and asked, "O, brother Sands, where shall we go to find such a man as Luther Rice? . . . Is there any one brother Sands who can write a biography of this interesting man? It would, perhaps, be a difficult undertaking . . . But *half a biography* of such a man would be welcomed."

At the behest of Columbian College, James Barnett Taylor, librarian at the University of Virginia and soon to go to Richmond as the first secretary of the Southern Baptist Foreign Mission Board, was commissioned to write the biography and it was published in 1841, the proceeds going to the College.

Adiel Sherwood went on to Washington and he and others continued the work of freeing the College of debt. On March 5, 1842, five and one-half years after Rice's death, the College became free of debt. Its fortunes varied throughout the nineteenth century, falling again into dire days during the Civil War. Its name was changed to George Washington University, and in 1904 it passed out of Baptist control.

In reply to a request to delineate Rice's character, Judson said that he was not the best person to do that since they had been so long separated, but then staunchly affirmed: "I would only add, that I have ever considered him to be a faithful warm-hearted friend, and a most devoted Christian. Notwithstanding the various reports which have been circulated about him, I have never entertained the slightest doubt of his moral integrity."

His brother Asaph aided Taylor in writing his story and lived on in Northborough, an ardent abolitionist and prominent in town affairs until 1856. Asaph's son Anson also resided in Northborough and Sarah, the spinster-sister, lived until 1860. Rebecca Eaton lived in Boston until her death in 1857, and it was doubtless due to the fact that she was still living that Taylor did not identify her in his biography.

Alexis Caswell, President of Brown University, rose at the Missionary Jubilee in Philadelphia in 1864 and stated:

I knew Luther Rice, and owe it to him to speak a word for him. I was with him every day when at Washington. I was his successor as treasurer of the College. It was my duty to go over the books and examine all the receipts and disbursements. He has been aspersed. He has been accused of peculation. But he was never guilty of peculation. It is a grateful task to me to do such justice to my excellent friend. In powers of mind he was wholly unsurpassed. He was a marked man everywhere. He was beyond the charge of dishonesty. He never appropriated a dollar to his own use. He wanted simple food and raiment, and gave all the rest to open channels for a preached gospel. He preached like an angel. He had great weaknesses. One was excessive hopefulness . . .

For a century thereafter Rice was almost a forgotten man except for a few memorials—a dormitory at Southern Baptist Theological Seminary in Louisville, Kentucky, a plaque in the Lall Bazar Church in Calcutta, a slab of marble over his grave in the Pine Pleasant graveyard, a church in Washington, and that intangible and most lasting of memorials, the desire of some to redeem his life by living out the ideals and dreams he cherished.

Notes

Chapter 2

1. Andrew Henshaw Ward, *A Genealogical History of the Rice Family* (Boston, 1858), p. 13. Edmund married twice, and two of these children were by the second marriage to Mercie Brigham.

2. Charles Elmer Rice, *By the Name of Rice* (Alliance, Ohio, 1911), pp. 21-25.

3. Joseph Allen, *Historical Sketch of Northborough* (Worcester, Mass., 1861), p. 41.

4. *Ibid.*, p. 5.

5. *Massachusetts Soldiers and Sailors of the Revolutionary War*, CXIII (Boston, 1905), 143. Amos was a sergeant in Captain Samuel Wood's company, General Ward's regiment at Boston, 1775. He was second lieutenant in Captain Timothy Brigham's company, commissioned April 15, 1776, and again in 1777 in Lieutenant Seth Rice's company, Colonel Job Cushing's regiment, and in 1778 in Captain Nathan Fisher's company, Colonel Nathaniel Wade's regiment.

6. Ward, *op. cit.*, p. 103. Luther's siblings: Amos, Jr. 4/7/67; Asaph 11/11/68; Curtis 9/10/70; Sarah 10/17/72; Elizabeth 2/31/74, d. '79; John 8/30/76; Jacob 8/10/78, d. '80; Jacob 2/7/81; Hannah 11/1/85.

7. Peter Whitney, *The History of the County of Worcester* (Worcester, 1793), pp. 275-80.

8. *Massachusetts Gazette*, February 20, 1783.

9. *Vital Records of Shrewsbury*. Luther's mother's parents were Samuel and Abial Graves, and her sister Catherine was born in 1741. The family lived in Sudbury, but the father died when the girls were young, and the mother married Josiah Bennet of Shrewsbury by whom she had John, Dorcas, and Elizabeth, who married Luther Rice. This Luther Rice lived in Northborough for several years and then moved to East Andover, Maine, where he and his wife lived to an old age. Sarah Rice's sister Catherine never married but taught school and lived in Boylston, where she owned property.

10. *Northborough Church Record*, p. 132. (MSS in possession of the Unitarian Church of Northborough). He was baptized May 4, 1783.

11. Charles Stanley Pease, *Luther Rice, Missionary and Educational Pioneer* (MSS in the American Baptist Historical Society, Rochester). The house was built in 1768 and torn down in 1900, having been long unoccupied.

12. Ebenezer Parkman, *The Story of the Rice Boys* (Westborough Historical Society, 1906).

13. *Massachusetts Gazette,* February 17, 1773. Also told in Parkman, Forbes, Kent and other local histories.

14. Harriette Merrified Forbes, *The Hundredth Town* (Boston, 1889), p. 64.

15. Josiah Coleman Kent, *Northborough History* (Newton, 1921), p. 448. Nahum Fay's mother was Rebecca Rice, older sister of Amos, Luther's father.

16. Luther Rice, *Journal, February 25, 1803—April 8, 1807,* American Baptist Historical Society (ABHS hereafter).

17. Whitney, *op. cit.,* p. 272.

18. Northborough Historical Society, *History of the Northborough Free Library* (Northborough, 1908), pp. 3-4,8.

19. Ebenezer Parkman, *The Diary of Rev. Ebenezer Parkman,* ed. Harriette M. Forbes (Westboro Historical Society, 1899), p. 151.

20. Kent, *op. cit.,* p. 19.

21. Elizabeth Ward, *Old Times in Shrewsbury* (New York, 1892). p. 81.

22. Kent, *op. cit.,* p. 282; Forbes, *op. cit.,* pp. 111-19.

23. Forbes, *op. cit.,* pp. 173-80.

24. *Ibid.,* pp. 138-45.

25. William Houghton, *History of Town of Berlin* (Worcester, 1895), p. 361.

26. Leander Cogswell, *History of Town of Henniker* (Concord, 1880), p. 30 f.

27. Ward, *op. cit.,* p. 177.

28. Kent, *op. cit.,* p. 174.

29. *Vital Records of Northborough,* ed. Franklin P. Rice (Worcester, 1901). Simply states: "Pliny Billings, son of _____ and Sarah Rice, born July 2, 1792." Baptism from *Northboro Church Record.*

30. James Barnett Taylor, *Memoir of Rev. Luther Rice* (Baltimore, 1841), p. 15.

31. *Ibid.,* 17-18.

32. *Ibid.,* p. 18.

33. *Ibid.*

Chapter 3

1. *Northboro Church Record,* March 14, 1803. L. T. Gibson, "Luther Rice's Contribution to Baptist History," (Th.D. thesis, Temple University, September, 1944. Copy in American Baptist Historical Society, Rochester). Rice's diary and testimony confirm Dr. Gibson's dating of the time when Rice found peace, that is, more than two years after his admittance into church membership.

2. Rice, *Journal,* February 25, 1803 (ABHS).

3. *Ibid.*

4. *Ibid.,* p. 4.   5. *Ibid.*   6. *Ibid.,* p. 3.

7. *Ibid.,* p. 57.
8. *Ibid.*
9. *Ibid.,* p. 3.
10. *Ibid.*
11. *Ibid.,* p. 7.
12. *Ibid.,* p. 39.
13. *Ibid.,* p. 49.
14. *Ibid.,* p. 40.
15. *Ibid.,* p. 42.
16. *Ibid.,* p. 43.
17. *Ibid.*
18. *Ibid.,* p. 45.
19. *Ibid.,* p. 46.
20. *Ibid.,* p. 48.
21. *Ibid.*
22. *Ibid.*
23. *Ibid.,* p. 49.
24. *Ibid.,* p. 54.
25. *Ibid.*
26. *Ibid.,* p. 70.
27. *Ibid.,* p. 56, *Worcester Registry of Deeds,* Book 160, pp. 163-64. The deed was not recorded until 1805, Amos probably not going to Worcester until then. Luther stated that his father "gave me a deed of forty acres of land, in consideration of 30 dollars, which sum, as I take it, he considers my summer's work to be worth . . ." Surely he does not mean the value of the land was only $30, for he sold it to Asaph, February 27, 1807, for $900. It appears to be a coming-of-age gift, Amos having given each son a like gift.
28. Rice, *Journal,* March 25, 1805 (ABHS).
29. *Ibid.,* p. 53.
30. *Ibid.,* October 23, 1805.
31. *Ibid.,* December 3, 1805.
32. *Ibid.,* p. 52.
33. *Ibid.,* September 15, 1805.
34. *Ibid.*

Chapter 4

1. Taylor, *op. cit.,* p. 28.
2. Rice, *Journal,* November 27, 1805 (ABHS).
3. *Ibid.,* February 14, 1806.
4. William W. Rice, *The Centenary of Leicester Academy* (Worcester, 1884), p. 17.
5. *Ibid.,* pp. 14-16. This Aaron Lopez was one of two Jews who requested and were denied naturalization by the Rhode Island colony in 1768.
6. *Ibid.,* p. 26.
7. *Ibid.,* p. 30.
8. Rice, *Journal,* May 29, 1806 (ABHS).

9. Through the latter part of 1805 and of 1806, there are many entries about the conferences—at brother Asaph's, at a neighbor's, or at "Aunt Graves," his spinster-aunt, Catherine, who lived eight or nine miles away on the Berlin-to-Boylston road. Warren Fay, J. B. (Jonah Ball), and a Quaker are mentioned as other participants.

10. *Records of the Evangelical Church in Northborough,* 1836 (MSS in the Northborough Historical Society, Northborough). Attributed to Rev. Samuel Austin Fay, son of Warren Fay, Luther's colleague in beginning the prayer meetings in the old seminary building, which they fitted up for the purpose. "They met with much favor, and soon opposition became so strong that the door of the building was nailed, to prevent their admission." Notes "D" and "E" tell of these meetings.

11. Taylor, *op. cit.,* p. 36.

12. Rice, *Journal,* September 2, 1806 (ABHS).

13. *Vital Records of Belfast.*

14. William W. Rice, *op. cit.,* p. 33.

15. *Registry of Probate, Book 168,* Worcester, February 27, 1807.

16. Thomas C. Richards, *Samuel J. Mills, Missionary Pathfinder, Pioneer and Promoter* (Boston, 1907), p. 29. Leverett Wilson Spring, *A History of Williams College* (Boston, 1917), p. 79. Also the account of Byram Green, written in 1854 when he was the last survivor of the haystack prayer meeting (MSS in Williams College Library).

17. Richards, *op. cit.,* p. 26.

18. Taylor, *op. cit.,* p. 81.

19. *Ibid.,* pp. 53-54.

20. *Ibid.,* p. 56.

21. Richards, *op. cit.,* p. 35.

22. *Ibid.,* p. 35. Article II stated: "The object of this Society shall be to effect in the persons of its members a mission, or missions, to the heathen."

23. Article V: "The utmost care shall be exercised in admitting members. All the information shall be acquired of the character and situation of a candidate which is practicable. No person shall be admitted to see this constitution until from personal acquaintance it is fully believed by at least two members that he is a suitable person to be admitted, and that he will sign it, and until he is laid under the following affirmation: 'You solemnly promise to keep inviolably secret the existence of this society.'"

24. Richards, *op. cit.,* p. 38.

25. *Ibid.,* p. 39.

26. Horatio Bardwell, *Memoir of Rev. Gordon Hall* (New York, 1834), p. 249.

27. Rice was one of the members who rebelled, along with three others who became ministers and four who became judges, namely: Justin Edwards, S. M. Emerson, John Seward, J. H. Hallock, Daniel Kellogg, Darius Lynn, William H. Maynard.

28. Taylor, *op. cit.,* p. 61. There are thirty-eight conveyances of

property listed in the Worcester Registry of Probate with Amos Rice as grantor, showing that he sold most of his land during his lifetime; five of the deeds are to son Asaph.

29. Samuel Mills to John Seward, letter dated Andover, March 20, 1810 (copy in *Missionary Letters,* XVII, 44, Williams College Library).

30. *Ibid.*

31. *Ibid.* "I know not where Br. Rice is at present nor indeed where he has been for some time past. I am surprised that we do not hear from him as he perhaps knows that some of the Brethren are residing in the college." *General Catalogue of the Andover Newton Theological Seminary, 1808-1908* (Boston, 1909), lists Luther Rice's entrance for the regular course of study as July, 1810.

Chapter 5

1. Claude M. Fuess, *An Old New England School* (Boston, 1917), pp. 148-51.

2. James King Morse, *Jedidiah Morse* (New York, 1939), 109.

3. Henry K. Rowe, *History of Andover Theological Seminary* (Newton, 1933), p. 53.

4. Sarah Stuart Robbins, *Old Andover Days* (Cambridge, 1908), p. 17.

5. Rowe, *op. cit.,* p. 34.

6. Luther Rice, *Notes and Account Book, 1810,* n.d. (Luther Rice Papers, Special Collections Division, Gelman Library, George Washington University [GWL hereafter]).

7. Timothy Woodbridge, *The Autobiography of a Blind Minister* (Boston, 1856), p. 80. Woodbridge, grandson of Jonathan Edwards, in a letter to his brother, April 10, 1810, told of visiting Dr. Spring at Newburyport: "I told him many things about some of our students, who have bold missionary spirit, quite in advance of the age. The doctor is very susceptible to such things, and he kindled with missionary fire. We shall soon, I think, have some prominent missionary movement, looking at the conversion of the world."

8. Richards, *op. cit.,* p. 70. A letter to Gordon Hall from Mills, December 20, 1809: "Shall he [Obookiah] be sent back and supported to attempt to reclaim his countrymen? Shall we not rather consider these South Sea Islands a proper place for establishment of a mission?"

9. John Brown Myers, *The Centenary Volume of the Baptist Missionary Society, 1792-1892* (London, 1892), p. 8.

10. Woodbridge, *op. cit.,* p. 78.

11. Adoniram Judson, *A Letter to the Rev. Adoniram Judson, Sen., Relative to the Formal and Solemn Reprimand to which is added a Letter to the Third Church in Plymouth, Massachusetts, on the Subject of Baptism* (Boston, 1820), p. 7.

12. E. C. Tracy, *Memoir of the Life of Jeremiah Evarts, Esq.* (Boston, 1820), p. 7.

13. Woodbridge, *op. cit.,* p. 84. "Professor Stuart, who talked with me freely and confidentially, told me that they were very much pleased with the humility, earnestness, and decision of the young men. They

had thought over this subject, collected all the missionary information they could and prayed over it a great while."

14. Samuel M. Worcester, *The Life and Labors of Rev. Samuel Worcester*, II (Boston, 1852), 60.

15. Richard, *op. cit.*, p. 72.

16. William E. Strong, *The Story of the American Board* (Boston, 1910), p. 6. There were nine commissioners, five from Massachusetts and four from Connecticut.

17. Rice, *Account Book*, pp. 43, 44, 156 (GWL).

18. Richards, *op.cit.*, p. 52. Rice, president; Giddings, vice-president; Fairfield, secretary.

Chapter 6

1. Richards, *op. cit.*, p. 62.

2. First officers elected were all Brethren: president, Samuel Nott; vice-president, Mills; secretary, Robbins; treasurer, Richards; Prudential Committee, Mills, Rice, Richards. All these men except Nott were Williams men. Judson, often credited as a founder, had graduated, though he was often at Andover and attended Brethren meetings. He was not an originator of either the Brethren or the Society of Inquiry.

3. Taylor, *op. cit.*, p. 71.

4. Rice, *Journal*, March 2, 1805 (ABHS).

5. Ralph Emerson, *The Life of Rev. Joseph Emerson* (Boston, 1834), p. 142. Cf. footnote which describes the Ebenezer Eaton home.

6. *Ibid.*, p. 342.

7. *The Friend of Virtue*, V, No. 18 (September 15, 1842), 276. "My Grandfather," written by one of Rebecca's nieces.

8. Emerson, op. cit., p. 77.

9. Joseph Emerson, *Memoirs of Mrs. Eleanor Emerson* (Boston, 1809). Emerson's first wife, Nancy Eaton, Rebecca's older sister, lived only eight months after their marriage in 1803. His second wife was Eleanor Read, friend of his first wife, Nancy, whom he married, 1805; she died in 1808. Then he married Rebecca Hasseltine of Bradford, sister of Ann Hasseltine Judson.

10. Richards, *op. cit.*, p. 70.

11. *Ibid.*, p. 70. Mills wrote to Hall: "What! O shame! If Brother Judson is prepared, I would fain press him forward with the arm of an Hercules, if I had the strength, but I do not like this dependence on another nation, especially when they have already done so much and we nothing. I trust that each of the brethren will stand at their several posts, determined God helping them, to show themselves *men*. Perhaps the fathers will soon arise and take the business of missions into their own hands. But should they hesitate, let us be prepared to *go forward* . . . trusting to that God for assistance who said, 'Lo I am with you always, even to the end of the world.' "

12. Judson, *op. cit.*, p. 6. "They considered the proposal for a concert of measures, as impracticable and visionary."

13. *General Catalogue of Andover, op. cit.*

14. Joseph Tracey, *History of the American Board of Commissioners* (New York, 1842), p. 31.

15. Letter of Samuel Mills, in *Missionary Letters, op. cit.*, p. 10. Mills wrote of Hall: "I have no doubt that he is a more fit person for the work we contemplate than I am or perhaps ever shall be."

16. Richards, *op. cit.*, p. 78.

17. Taylor, *op. cit.*, p. 95.

18. E. D. G. Prime, *Forty Years in the Turkish Empire* (Boston, 1891), p. 43 f. Later volunteers' fiancées backed out also; see amusing account of last-minute recruiting of replacements by the Brethren. Prime also has been used for background of Michener's *Hawaii*.

19. Taylor, *op. cit.*, pp. 96-97.

20. William Bentley, *The Diary of William Bentley*, D.D., IV (Salem, 1907), 13. Bentley believed the Norris family gossip that "Hopkins, Emerson, Worcester, and Spring attended the deathbed" of Widow Norris, and persuaded her to bequeath her money to the seminary and missions.

Chapter 7

1. Prime, *op. cit.*, p. 43. Goodell was to serve forty-three years in Turkey as a missionary, and Cummings became editor of the *Christian Mirror*.

2. Tracey, *op. cit.*, p. 34.

3. James L. Hill, *The Immortal Seven* (Philadelphia, 1913), pp. 4, 114. This hymn, published by C. C. Carpenter, 1810, and also known as "Sovereign of Worlds," includes the following lines:

Yes : . . Christian heroes! . . . go . . . proclaim
Salvation through Immanuel's name;
To India's clime the tidings bear,
And plant the Rose of Sharon there.

4. Leonard Woods, *A Sermon Delivered at the Tabernacle in Salem, February 6, 1812, on the Occasion of the Ordination* (Boston, 1812), p. 32.

5. *Ibid.*, p. 37.

6. Prime, *op. cit.*, p. 43.

7. Hill, *op. cit.*, p. 4.

8. Bardwell, *op. cit.*, p. 251.

9. *Memoirs of Philotechnian Society and the Mills Theological Society*, p. 29. (MSS in Williams College).

10. Bardwell, *op. cit.*, p. 249.

11. Luther Rice, *Journal, February 6—November 25, 1812*, February 6, 1812 (ABHS).

12. *The Life and Writings of Mrs. Harriet Newell*, ed. American Sunday School Union (Philadelphia, 1831), p. 153.

13. *Ibid.*, p. 156.

14. Prime, *op. cit.*, p. 46.

Chapter 8

1. *Maritime Records, Arrivals and Clearances*, Outward, Sec. III,

Vol. IV, 1811-1816 (in Pennsylvania Historical Society, Philadelphia). Lists *Harmony*, Captain Michael Brown, bound for Calcutta, clearing the fourteenth.

2. Rice, *Journal*, February 23, 1812 (ABHS).

3. *Ibid.*, February 17, 1812.

4. *Ibid.*, February 22, 1812.

5. Letter, Dr. W. Johns to Mr. Ward, June 10, 1812, from Boston. E. S. Wenger, *Missionary Biographies*, I, 232-33.

6. *Ibid.*, p. 234. Printed from *Serampore Circular Letter*, July 1812, p. 133.

7. Rice, *Journal*, February 24, 1812 (ABHS).

8. *Records of the Evangelical Congregational Church in Northborough, op. cit.*, "Note D."

9. *Ibid.*, "Note E."

10. T. W. Valentine, *A Historical Discourse delivered before the First Baptist Church of Northborough* (Brooklyn, 1877). Rice, *Journal*, November 1, 1804 (ABHS): "I called at the shop of Mr. Grout . . . had some very interesting and pleasing conversation with him, since when, I have felt better." Other evenings he mentions having been to the shop of Grout.

11. William Johns, *Extracts from a Journal kept during a voyage from Philadelphia to Calcutta, by way of the Isle of France, on board the ship Harmony, Capt. Michael Brown, in the year 1812* (Serampore, 1812), p. 6.

12. Rice, *Journal*, March 15, 1812 (ABHS).

13. Taylor, *op. cit.*, p. 14.

14. Rice, *Journal*, April 7, 1812 (ABHS).

15. Johns, *op. cit.*, p. 8.

16. *Ibid.*, p. 33.

17. Rice, *Journal*, March 24, 1812 (ABHS).

18. *Ibid.*, March 25, 1812.

19. *Ibid.*

20. *Ibid.*, March 1, 1812.

21. *Ibid.*, April 23, 1812.

22. *Ibid.*, April 4, 1812.

23. Harriet Newell, *op. cit.*, p. 194.

24. *Ibid.*, p. 194.

25. Rice, *Journal*, May 2, 1812 (ABHS). The *Harmony* crossed the Atlantic to the Canary vicinity but then went off Trinidad far to the west, went south from there, skirting the South American coast, then followed the Brazil current across to the Trista da Cunha Islands, then east to Cape of Good Hope. Many a ship stopped at the Trista da Cunha for fresh water in later days, but the island was not settled until 1814, so the *Harmony* passengers would have been stranded had they beached on its shores in 1812.

26. *Ibid.*

27. *Ibid.*, May 17, 1812.

28. *Ibid.*, May 9, 1812.

29. *Ibid.*, May 10, 1812.

30. *Ibid.*

31. John Brown Myers (ed.), *The Centenary Volume of the Baptist Missionary Society* (London, 1829), p. 43.

32. *Ibid.*, p. 66, quoted from Sydney in the *Edinburgh Review.*

33. Rice, *Journal,* June 20, 1812 (ABHS).

34. *Ibid.*, July 2, 1812.

35. *Ibid.*, August 10, 1812.

36. Harriet Newell, *op. cit.*

37. Johns, *op. cit.*, pp. 46-47.

Chapter 9

1. S. Pearce Carey, *William Carey* (London, 1923), p. 135, quoted from Sir J. W. Kaye.

2. Myers, *op. cit.*, p. 61.

3. Ann Hasseltine Judson, letter to her sister, mid-June, 1812, from Serampore, *American Baptist Magazine.*

4. Harriet Newell, *op. cit.*, p. 194.

5. Rice, *Journal,* August 15, 1812 (ABHS).

6. *Ibid.*

7. *Reports of the American Board* (Boston, 1814), p. 28. "To the Honorable the Governor General, in Council. We the Undersigned, passengers lately arrived on board the American ship Harmony, having received an order to depart out of the country on the same ship, beg leave to state, that agreeably to our intention, stated at the police on our arrival of leaving the Company's dominions, we request liberty to depart, by the earliest opportunity, for the Isle of France; and therefore that the Harmony may not be refused a clearance on our account."

LUTHER RICE
GORDON HALL
SAMUEL NOTT

Calcutta, August 21, 1812.

8. Adoniram Judson, *op. cit.*, p. 6.

9. *Ibid.*

10. James D. Knowles, *Memoir of Mrs. Ann H. Judson, Late Missionary to Burmah* (Boston, 1829).

11. Carey, *op. cit.*, p. 320, quoted from a letter to Andrew Fuller.

12. *Ibid.*, quoted from a letter, Felix Carey to his father.

13. Bardwell, *op. cit.*, p. 251, from a letter to his cousin, John Hall, written from Bombay, October 13, 1813.

14. Taylor, *op. cit.*, p. 110.

15. Judson, *op. cit.*, p. 3.

16. Rice, *Journal,* September 27, 1812 (ABHS).

17. Taylor, *op. cit.*, p. 110.

18. Rice, *Journal,* October 8, 1812 (ABHS).

19. *Ibid.*, p. 64.

20. *Massachusetts Baptist Missionary Magazine, III,* No. 11, 322.

21. Taylor, *op. cit.*, pp. 105-6.

22. *Ibid.*, p. 65.

23. *Ibid.*, p. 66.
24. Taylor, *op. cit.*, p. 116.
25. Rice, *Journal*, October 25, 1812 (ABHS).
26. Taylor, *op. cit.*, p. 112.

Chapter 10

1. Rice, *Journal*, November 18, 1812 (ABHS).
2. Taylor, *op. cit.*, p. 126.
3. *Ibid.*, p. 127.
4. Rice, *Journal*, November 22, 1812.
5. *Ibid.*
6. Ann Hasseltine Judson, letter to Mrs. Jonathan Carleton, Calcutta, October 21, 1812 (copy now in the Library of the American Baptist Historical Society [ABHS hereafter], Rochester, New York).
7. Luther Rice, letter to Rev. Joseph Emerson, Calcutta, October 22, 1812 (now in the American Clergy Collection, Library of Congress).
8. *Ibid.* In this very long letter seeking aid of Emerson, Rice chose a likely advocate; for not only would he be sympathetic because of the connection with the Judsons, but Emerson's biographer, (Emerson, *op. cit.*, p. 292) states that Rev. Emerson often heard Rev. Samuel Stillman preach while a student at Harvard and "thought of becoming a Baptist . . . but could not accept closed communion." Rice used the old-fashioned spelling of "Rebekak", though she often spelled her name "Rebecca."
9. Luther Rice, letter to Joshua Marshman, Port Louis, March 11, 1813.
10. Taylor, *op. cit.*, p. 133.
11. *Ibid.*, p. 135.

Chapter 11

1. Pease, *op. cit.*, p. 34.
2. Taylor, *op cit.*, p. 138.
3. *Ibid.*, p. 138.
4. *American Board, op. cit.*
5. Taylor, *op. cit.*, p. 144.
6. Judson, *op. cit.*, p. 7.
7. T. W. Valentine, *A Historical Discourse delivered before the First Baptist Church of Northborough* (Brooklyn, 1877).
8. Francis Wayland and H. L. Wayland, *A Memoir of the Life and Labors* of Francis Wayland, I (New York, 1868), 54.
9. William Crane in *The Missionary Jubilee, an Account of the Fiftieth Anniversary Baptist Foreign Mission Society* (New York, 1863), p. 18.
10. Luther Rice, letter to Richard Furman, Savannah, December 13, 1813 (now in the Furman Collection of the South Carolina Baptist Historical Library [SCBHL hereafter], Furman University). "I . . . arrived without difficulty at the Vernon Church in time to meet 'The Savannah River Baptist Association.' "

11. William Cathcart, *The Baptist Encyclopedia* (Philadelphia, 1881), pp. 779-80.

12. Spright Dowell, "Jesse Mercer," *Encyclopedia of Southern Baptists* (Nashville, 1958), p. 849.

13. Taylor, *op. cit.*, p. 148.

14. Rice to Furman, December 13, 1813 (SCBHL).

15. Richard Furman, letter to Enoch Reynolds, dated 1814 (SCBHL).

16. Luther Rice, letter to Matthias Tallmadge, Raleigh, February 8, 1814 (in the Simon Gratz Collection, Pennsylvania Historical Society Library [PHS hereafter], Philadelphia).

17. Robert B. Semple, letter to Rice, February 24, 1814, King and Queen County (now in the Ferdinand J. Dreer Collection, PHS).

18. Richard Furman, letter to Edmund Botsford, April 1, 1814 (now in Botsford Collection, SCBHL).

19 Edmund Botsford to William Bullein Johnson, Georgetown, April 16, 1814, (Botsford Collection, SCBHL).

20. English—Jacob Grigg, Thomas Hewett, Richard Proudfoot, William Staughton, Thomas Brooke, Matthew Randall; Welsh—Edward Probyn, John Williams, Lewis Richards; Nova Scotian—Daniel Dodge; Scottish—James Ranaldson.

21. Josiah Randall in *The Missionary Jubilee, op. cit.*, p. 21.

22. H. A. Tupper, *Two Centuries of the First Baptist Church of South Carolina* (Baltimore, 1889), p. 147.

23. Furman's "Address," *Massachusetts Baptist Missionary Magazine*, IV, No. 3, 70. Also, *Proceedings of the Baptist Convention for Missionary Purposes* (Philadelphia, 1814), p. 42.

24. *Ibid.*

25. Taylor, *op. cit.*, p. 146.

26. *Proceedings of the Baptist Convention, op. cit.*, p. 3.

27. *Ibid.*, p. 5.

28. *Ibid.*, p. 9.

29. *Massachusetts Baptist Missionary Magazine, op. cit.*, p. 68.

30. *Minutes of Triennial Convention*, American Baptist Board of Foreign Missions, Valley Forge, Pennsylvania, 1814.

31. *Ibid.*

32. *Ibid.*

33. Proceedings of the Baptist Convention, op. cit., p. 32.

34. *The Missionary Jubilee, op. cit.*, p. 96.

35. *Baptist Magazine*, VI, 476.

Chapter 12

1. Rufus Weaver, address delivered at the First Baptist Church, Washington, D. C., March 6, 1932 (copy in Dargan-Carver Library, Nashville).

2. Rufus Babcock, *Memoir of John Mason Peck*, I (Philadelphia, 1864), 42.

3. W. S. Stewart, *Early Baptist Missionaries and Pioneers* (Philadelphia, 1925), p. 236.

4. *Ibid.*, pp. 236-37.
5. Babcock, *op. cit.*, pp. 49-51, letter, Rice to Peck, Knox County, Indiana Territory, November 30, 1815.
6. *Ibid.*, p. 44, quoted from Peck's diary.
7. *Ibid.*, p. 49.
8. *Ibid.*, p. 51.
9. *Second Annual Report* (Philadelphia, 1816), p. 67.
10. *Third Annual Report* (Philadelphia, 1817), p. 67.
11. Rice, *Journal*, December 2, 1815 (ABHS).
12. Isaac McCoy, "Autobiographical Statement to the year 1816, addressed to William Polke" (MSS in Kansas State Historical Library [KSHL hereafter], Topeka), p. 14.
13. McCoy, *Journal*, February 27, 1829 (KSHL).
14. *Ibid.*, May 21, 1821.
15. *Ibid.*, June, 1816.
16. *Ibid.*
17. *Ibid.*, January, 1821: "At Camp, 20 miles from Ft. Harrison."
18. McCoy, "Autobiographical Statement," *op. cit.*, p. 24.
19. McCoy, *Journal*, June 25, 1821.
20. Luther Rice to Isaac McCoy, Richmond, April 2, 1817 (KSHL).
21. McCoy, draft of letter to Luther Rice, May 6, 1817 (KSHL).
22. *Ibid.*
23. *Third Annual Report* (Philadelphia, 1817), p. 139.
24. *Ibid.*, p. 141.
25. *Ibid.*, p. 175.
26. Babcock, *op. cit.*, p. 69, quoted from Peck's diary.
27. *Fourth Annual Report* (Philadelphia, 1818), p. 200.
28. *Ibid.*, p. 182.
29. *Ibid.*, p. 202.
30. McCoy, *Journal*, November 6, 1817 (KSHL).
31. *Ibid.*, February, 1818.
32. Randolph Orville Yeager, *Indian Enterprises of Isaac McCoy, 1817-1846*, p. 6, (KSHL).
33. William Staughton, letter to Isaac McCoy, Philadelphia, July 2, 1821 (KSHL).
34. Babcock, *op. cit.*, p. 166.
35. Luther Rice, letter to John Mason Peck, Washington, February 16, 1820 (PHS).
36. McCoy, *Journal*, March 12, 1821 (KSHL).
37. Babcock, *op. cit.*, p. 151.
38. *Fourth Annual Report*, p. 202, states that Ranaldson's letter "communicating very important information about Louisiana, and soliciting additional missionary aid," transmitted at the same time $500 from the Mississippi Missionary Society.
39. Luther Rice, letter to Judge Matthias Tallmadge, Wilmington, Vermont, October 17, 1814 (PHS).
40. *Fourth Annual Report*, p. 199.
41. *Ibid.*

42. *Ibid.*, p. 200.

43. *Fourth Annual Report*, p. 200.

44. *Fifth Annual Report*, p. 377.

45. *Second Annual Report*, p. 74.

46. *Fifth Annual Report*, p. 401, letter from William Crane.

47. *Ibid.*, p. 403.

48. *Ibid.*, p. 384.

Chapter 13

1. Henry Keeling, "Reminiscences," *Religious Herald*, January 20, 1848.

2. *Ibid.*

3. *National Intelligencer*, January 15, 1822.

4. S. W. Lynd, *Memoir of the Rev. William Staughton* (Boston, 1834), p. 260.

5. General Address, Minutes of Convention, 1814.

6. Hortense Woodson, *Giant In the Land* (Nashville, 1850), p. 38.

7. Babcock, *op. cit.*, p. 109.

8. Article XIV, Constitution.

9. Matthias Tallmadge, letter to Richard Furman, New York, May 20, 1817 (SCBHL).

10. Minutes of Board, May 2, 1818.

11. *Fourth Annual Report*, p. 203.

12. Irah Chase, *Baptist Memorial and Monthly Chronicle*, April 15, 1842.

13. Rice, *Journal*, October 13, 15, 1819 (GWL).

14. Second Triennial Convention Report, p. 119. (Also, *Latter Day Luminary*, 1820, pp. 291-92).

15. *Ibid.*, p. 120.

16. *Ibid.*, p. 128.

17. Luther Rice, letter to Gen. John S. Gano, Washington, December 27, 1820, in Gano Papers, II (Historical and Philosophical Society of Ohio, University of Cincinnati).

18. Luther Rice, letter to Rev. Daniel Merrill, Washington, March 22, 1821 (in George Washington University Library [GWL hereafter]).

19. *Seventh Annual Report*, pp. 378-79.

20. Broadside, 1820 (in John Goss Family Papers, Alderman Library, University of Virginia).

21. *Ibid.*

22. Taylor, *op. cit.*, p. 204.

Chapter 14

1. Austen Kennedy DeBlois, *Fighters for Freedom* (Philadelphia, 1929), p. 319.

2. Pollard, *op. cit.*

3. Adoniram Judson, letter to Luther Rice, Rangoon, October 23, 1818.

4. Taylor, *op. cit.*, p. 131.

5. Luther Rice, letter to Joshua Marshman, Salem, September 27, 1813 (PHS).

6. Taylor, *op. cit.*, p. 153.

7. *Ibid.*, p. 154.

8. *Massachusetts Baptist Magazine*, IV, No. 3, 68.

9. Luther Rice, letter to Matthias B. Tallmadge, Philadelphia, July 8, 1815 (PHS).

10. William Staughton, letter to Matthias Tallmadge, Philadelphia, July 18, 1815 (PHS).

11. Matthias Tallmadge, letter to Richard Furman, New York, July 8, 1815 (SCBHL). Judge Tallmadge wrote Furman of Miss Dunning's willingness to go and that she would pay her expenses; it was the previous November that Rice noted having long conversations with her when he was in Savannah.

12. Adoniram Judson, letter to Asa Messer, Rangoon, January 16, 1816, (in Brown University Library).

13. Adoniram Judson, letter to Rice, August 3, 1816, now in Archives, Southern Baptist Foreign Mission Board [SBFMB hereafter], Richmond, Virginia.

14. *Ibid.*

15. *Ibid.*

16. *Ibid.*

17. *Third Annual Report*, p. 164, letter from Judson to Rice, Rangoon, November 14, 1816.

18. Taylor, *op. cit.*, p. 174.

19. *Ibid*, pp. 173-74.

20. *Ibid.*, pp. 175-76.

21. Adoniram Judson, letter to Rice, Rangoon, June 24, 1819 (SBFMB).

22. *Ibid.*

23. *Ibid.*

24. *Ibid.*

25. *Minutes of Board*, June 20, 1816.

26. *Address to the Convention from 1820 Triennial*, p. 115.

27. *Sixth Annual Report*, p. 132.

28. Adoniram Judson, letter to Luther Rice, Rangoon, September 7, 1820 (SBFMB).

29. *Ibid.*

30. *Ibid.*

31. *Ibid.*

32. Taylor, *op. cit.*, p. 177.

33. *Ibid.*, pp. 177-78.

34. *Ibid.*, p. 179.

35. *Ibid.*, pp. 179-80.

36. Adoniram Judson, *op. cit.*, September 7, 1820.

37. Judson, letter to Rice, Rangoon, January 9, 1821 (SBFMB).

38. Taylor, *op. cit.*, pp. 194-95.

39. *Ibid.*, p. 195.

40. *Ibid.*

41. *Ibid.*, p. 196.

42. Ann Hasseltine Judson, letter to Rice, Bradford, June, 1823 (SBFMB).

43. *Ibid.*

44. Taylor, *op. cit.*, p. 197.

45. *Ibid.*, p. 196.

46. *Ibid.*, pp. 294-95.

47. *Ibid.*, pp. 219-20.

48. *Ibid.*, p. 236.

Chapter 15

1. Rice, *Journal,* July 27, 1815 (GWL).

2. *Ibid.*

3. *Ibid.*

4. Keeling, *op. cit.,* December 30, 1947.

5. *Ibid.*

6. *Ibid.*

7. Rice, *Journal,* December 6, 1815 (ABHS).

8. McCoy, *Diary, op. cit.,* February 5, 1818.

9. Rice, *Journal,* December 7, 1815 (ABHS).

10. *Ibid.*, January 1, 1836, quoted in Taylor, *op. cit.*

11. Taylor, *op. cit.*, p. 314.

12. Rice, *Journal,* December 12, 1815 (ABHS).

13. *Ibid.*, August 1, 1815.

14. Luther Rice, letter to Jedidiah Morse, Lexington, Kentucky, November 21, 1815 (PHS).

15. Rice, *Journal,* July 29, 1817 (ABHS).

16. John Goss Family Papers (Alderman Library, University of Virginia).

17. *Baptist Encyclopedia,* comps. James Brewer and Lynn E. May (Nashville, 1958), p. 840.

18. Rice, *Journal,* February 26, 1816 (ABHS).

19. *Ibid.*, November 29, 1816.

20. *Ibid.*, August 17, 1816.

21. Rice, *Journal,* September 12, 1819, Virginia Baptist Historical Society (VBHS hereafter).

22. Taylor, *op. cit.*, pp. 170-71.

23. *Fourth Annual Report,* p. 145.

24. Rice, *Journal,* March 16, 1816 (ABHS).

25. *Ibid.*, September 5, 1818.

26. *Ibid.*, March 4, 1816.

27. *Ibid.*, April 11, 1817.

28. *Ibid.*, March 1, 1816.

29. Pollard, *op. cit.*

30. Rice, *Journal,* March 13, 1817 (ABHS).

31. *Ibid.*, August 24, 1816.

32. *Ibid.*, August 28, 1816.

33. *Ibid.*, August 31, 1816.

34. *Ibid.*
35. Edward Kingsford, *The Baptist Banner and Pioneer,* February 16, 1841.
36. Keeling, *op. cit.,* January 6, 1848.
37. Rice, *Journal,* July 15, 1816 (GWL).
38. *Ibid.,* January 3, 1816.
39. *Ibid.,* December 19-20, 1817: "Besides all the kindness of Mrs. Barrow in regard to my clothing and the half Eagle by his little son . . . br. Barrow has kept my mare about six weeks, and furnished me with a horse to ride . . ."
40. *Ibid.,* April 10, 1817. On his way to Philadelphia for the 1817 Triennial, Rice came through Virginia where the "Richmond Female Baptist Missionary Society" gave him a hat; George Greenhow presented him a coat; George Sedwick at Dumfries supplied cloth for a surtout; the ladies of Fredericksburg, "a black vest, cravats, pocket handkerchiefs."
41. Taylor, *op. cit.,* pp. 218-19.
42. 2 Cor. 11:26-28, RSV.

Chapter 16

1. Minutes of Board, March 6, 1815.
2. *Ibid.,* April 11, 1815.
3. *Ibid.,* July 5, 1815.
4. *Ibid.,* September 12, 1815.
5. *Plain Truth,* Letter V.
6. Asa Messer, letter to Rev. William Rogers, April 13, 1816 (in Brown University Library, Providence).
7. Stephen Gano, letter to Matthias Tallmadge, Providence, July 25, 1816 (PHS).
8. *Ibid.,* June 21, 1816.
9. William Rogers, letter to Richard Furman, Philadelphia, June 15, 1815 (SCBHL).
10. James Manning Winchell, letter to Luther Rice, Boston, August 21, 1818 (PHS).
11. William Rogers, letter to Richard Furman, Philadelphia, June 15, 1815 (SCBHL).
12. Richard Furman, letter to Matthias Tallmadge, July 17, 1816 (PHS).
13. Matthias Tallmadge, letter to Richard Furman, New York, September 28, 1818 (SCBHL).
14. Richard Furman, letter to Edmund Botsford, January 24, 1817 (SCBHL).
15. Edmund Botsford, letter to J. M. Roberts, December 29, 1818 (SCBHL).
16. *Minutes of Elkhorn Association,* I, 100.
17. McCoy, *Journal, op. cit.,* p. 41.
18. *Fifth Annual Report.*
19. Isaac McCoy, draft of letter to Rice, February, 1818 (KSHL).

20. Isaac McCoy, draft of letter to Rice, October 1, 1818 (KSHL).

21. *The Christian Baptist,* III, 238.

22. John Taylor, *Thoughts on Missions* (n. p., 1820), p. 9. Taylor also mentioned Rice's "prodigious appetite" and his tea drinking.

23. Babcock, *op. cit.,* p. 111.

24. Lynd, *op. cit.,* p. 255.

25. *Ibid.,* pp. 263-64.

26. *Ibid.,* p. 264.

27. Isaac McCoy, draft of letter to Rice, August 12, 1820 (KSHL).

28. Luther Rice, letter to McCoy, Philadelphia, October 10, 1820 (KSHL).

29. McCoy, *Diary, op. cit.,* January 10, 1822.

30. *Ibid.*

31. *Seventh Annual Report,* p. 387.

32. Isaac McCoy, letter to Rice, February, 1818 (KSHL).

33. Luther Rice, letter to McCoy, College Hill, May 11, 1824 (KSHL).

34. Richard Furman, letter to Matthias Tallmadge, Charlestown, June 20, 1818 (PHS).

35. Thomas Baldwin, letter to Rice, Boston, November 22, 1819 (now in the New York Historical Society, New York City).

36. Minutes of Board, October 20, 1820.

37. Minutes of Board, October 21, 1820.

38. *Ibid.*

39. Thomas Baldwin, *op. cit.*

40. *Second Triennial Convention Report,* p. 129.

41. Jonathan Going, letter to Luther Rice, Worcester, June, 1821 (PHS).

42. Luther Rice, letter to Obadiah B. Brown, from the steamboat *Connecticut,* Long Island Sound, August 27, 1821 (GWL).

43. Luther Rice, letter to Brown, New York, October 21, 1821 (GWL).

44. *American Baptist Magazine,* 1823.

45. *Ibid.,* p. 140.

46. William Staughton, letter to William Colgate, Philadelphia, June 18, 1823 (ABHL).

47. *Fourth Triennial Convention,* p. 420.

48. Wayland, *op. cit.,* p. 178.

49. *Ibid.,* p. 179.

50. Minutes of Board, June 21, 1824.

51. Minutes of Board, October 21, 1824.

52. *Fourth Triennial, op. cit.,* p. 421.

53. Lemuel Call Barnes, *Pioneers of Light* (Philadelphia, n.d.), p. 18.

54. *Ibid.,* p. 27.

55. Luther Rice, letter to Horatio G. Jones, November 10, 1825 (ABHS).

56. James C. Willian, *Brief Chronicles of the Columbian College.*

57. Minutes of Board, September 12, 1825.

58. *Ibid.,* September 13, 1825.

Chapter 17

1. Lucius Bolles, letter to David Benedict, Salem, February 20, 1826 (PHS).

2. Lynd, *op. cit.*

3. Wayland, *op. cit.*, p. 54.

4. Luther Rice, letter to Obadiah Brown, Lawton, March 6, 1826 (GWL).

5. Minutes of General Convention, April 26, 1826.

6. Material from the *American Baptist Magazine,* published by the Baptist Missionary Society of Massachusetts, containing the proceedings and missionary intelligence of the Board of Missions of the Baptist General Convention," VI, Series U, (Boston, 1826), 14f.

7. *Ibid.*

8. *American Baptist Magazine,* "Report of the Fifth Triennial, 1826," p. 23.

9. *Ibid.*

10. *Ibid.*, p. 28.

11. *Ibid.*, p. 29.

12. The speech of Josiah Randall. *The Missionary Jubilee, op. cit.,* p. 23.

13. *Ibid.*, p. 24.

14. *Ibid.*, p. 25.

15. *Ibid.*, p. 26.

16. *Ibid.*

17. *Ibid.*

18. *Baptist Missionary Magazine,* 1823.

19. Babcock, *op. cit.*, p. 216.

Chapter 18

1. *Columbian College Circular* (Washington, 1826).

2. Luther Rice, letter to Obadiah Brown, Richmond, May 24, 1826 (GWL).

3. *Ibid.*

4. Rice, letter to Brown, Murfreesboro, North Carolina, June 5, 1826 (GWL).

5. *Ibid.*

6. Rice, letter to Brown, Generette, South Carolina, June 22, 1826 (GWL).

7. Rice, letter to Brown, Mount Ed, Virginia, August 21, 1826 (GWL). "Smith, I am satisfied, will not be easy till he gets the College out of the hands of the baptists and he will have the full concurrences of Ruggles and Stow."

8. *Ibid.*

9. Luther Rice, note to John Goss on a Columbian Circular (in the John Goss Family Papers, Alderman Library, University of Virginia).

10. Rice, letter to Brown, August 21, 1826, *op. cit.*

11. Rice, letter to Brown, Hopewell, Virginia, August 24, 1826 (GWL).

12. Luther Rice, letter to Enoch Reynolds, Norfolk, Virginia, April 20, 1826 (GWL).

13. Rice, letter to Brown, Norfolk, May 28, 1827 (GWL).

14. Rice, letter to Brown, Richmond, April 6, 1827 (GWL).

15. Henry Allen Tupper, *Two Centuries of the First Baptist Church of South Carolina* (Baltimore, 1829), p. 220. Messrs. S. H. Smith, J. McLean, C. Worthington, R. C. Weightman, Reuben Post, and Baron Stow all resigned in a body. All except Stow were non-Baptists.

16. B. T. Goulding, letter to Dr. W. H. Whitsitt (now in the Virginia Baptist Historical Library, University of Richmond).

17. Rice, letter to Brown, dated May 19, 1827, "near" Bowling Green, Virginia (GWL).

18. Rice, letter to Brown, Louisburg, North Carolina, May 5, 1827 (GWL).

19. Rice, letter to Brown, May 19, 1827, *op. cit.* "Leave me and the debts yoked together. I am thoroughly persuaded it will be practicable for me to pay them in five or six years, if only the Trustees can set the College going . . ."

20. Rice, letter to Brown, May 28, 1827, *op. cit.*

21. Rice, letter to Brown, Fredericksburg, June 9, 1827 (GWL).

22. Rice, letter to Brown, Fredericksburg, June 26, 1827 (GWL).

23. Rice, letter to Brown, May 19, 1827, *op. cit.*

24. Rice, letter to Brown, "Mordington," July 12, 1827 (GWL).

25. Rice, letter to Brown, Hennico County, Virginia, July 10, 1827 (GWL).

26. Rice, letter to Brown, July 12, 1827, *op. cit.*

27. Rice, letter to Brown, Dumfries, Virginia, August 28, 1827 (GWL).

28. *Ibid.*

29. Rice, letter to Brown, Richmond, October 1, 1827 (GWL).

30. Jeremiah B. Jeter, *A Memoir of Abner W. Clopton* (Richmond, 1837), p. 200.

31. Rice, letter to Brown, Edenton, North Carolina, May 12, 1828 (GWL).

32. Rice, letter to Brown, Petersburg, July 14, 1827 (GWL).

33. Rice, letter to Brown, "Todd's," Caroline County, Virginia, October 23, 1827 (GWL).

34. Rice, letter to Brown, "Gregor's," Virginia, July 8, 1828 (GWL).

35. Robert H. Semple, *The Columbian Star.*

36. Rice, letter to Brown, "Steamboat Potomac," June 1, 1826 (GWL).

37. Rice, letter to Brown, Raleigh, July 28, 1827 (GWL). In this letter Rice refers to Brown's writing Thornton about "making an arrangement whereby to secure your property from the college creditors."

38. Rice, letter to Brown, Norfolk, November 5, 1828 (GWL).

39. Rice, letter to Brown, Richmond, January 10, 1829 (GWL).

40. Rice, letter to Brown, Fayetteville, North Carolina, October 6, 1830 (GWL).

41. Rice, letter to Brown, Richmond, January 26, 1829 (GWL).

42. Luther Rice, "Statement to the President of the Board of Trustees,"

College Hill, May 20, 1829, enclosed in a letter to Brown, from Balls, Virginia (GWL).

43. Semple, *op. cit.*

44. *Ibid.*

45. Rice, letter to Brown, Poplar Row, Virginia, February 2, 1830 (GWL).

46. Rice, letter to Brown, Fayetteville, October 6, 1830 (GWL).

47. Rice, letter to Brown, Augusta, December 3, 1830 (GWL).

48. Rice, letter to Brown, Lexington, South Carolina, March 9, 1830 (GWL).

49. Rice, letter to Brown, Richmond, August 31, 1830 (GWL).

50. *Ibid.*

51. Rice, letter to Brown, Robertville, South Carolina, December 14, 1830 (GWL).

52. *Ibid.*

53. *Ibid.*

54. Rice, letter to Brown, Raleigh, North Carolina, October 10, 1831.

55. McCoy, *Diary, op. cit.*, May 6, 1831.

56. Taylor, *op. cit.*, p. 311.

57. Luther Rice, letter to General Stephen van Rensselaer, College Hill, June 5, 1832 (PHS). Rice mourns over the possible loss of Ruggles who has been offered $2,000 and is only receiving $800 per annum. He hopes to raise enough to entice him to stay at Columbian.

58. Taylor, *op. cit.*, pp. 221-22.

59. *Ibid.*, pp. 222-23.

60. *Ibid.*, p. 220.

61. *Ibid.*, p. 226.

Chapter 19

1. F. A. Cox and J. Hoby, *The Baptists in America; a Narrative of the Deputation from the Baptist Union in England to the United States and Canada* (London, 1836), p. 32.

2. *Ibid.*, p. 68.

3. Jeremiah B. Jeter, *Recollections of a Long Life* (Richmond, 1891), p. 186.

4. Rice, *Journal,* September 20, 1817 (ABHS).

5. Luther Rice, letter to Stephen Chapin, Charlotte Court House, May 15, 1834 (GWL).

6. Taylor, *op. cit.*, p. 235.

7. Rice, letter to Chapin, February, 1836 (GWL).

8. Julia L. Sherwood, *Memoir of Adiel Sherwood* (Philadelphia, 1884).

9. Taylor, *op. cit.*, pp. 324-25.

10. Rice, *Journal,* August 13, 1836 (VBHS).

11. Taylor, *op. cit.*, p. 247.

12. Taylor's account is taken from the letter which James Welch wrote to Thomas Meredith, ed. *Biblical Recorder,* after visiting in the area and residing in the home of the Mays in the fall of 1837. Mr.

Motte J. Yarbrough, an attorney in Saluda, South Carolina, who has done research in the neighborhood of the Mays home, states that local tradition attributes Rice's death to appendicitis.

13. Taylor, *op. cit.*, p. 248. Rice received a letter from Kincaid just prior to his death, revealing that Rice's preaching was the primary influence in Kincaid's decision to go to Burma. See also, pp. 295-98.

14. *Ibid.*, p. 248.

15. *Ibid.*

16. *Ibid.*, pp. 249-50.

17. *Ibid.*, p. 248.

18. *Ibid.*, p. 250.

19. Taylor, *op. cit.*, p. 312.

Acknowledgments

Anyone doing research on Luther Rice soon finds that he must become almost as peripatetic as his subject was, for the material is found in many libraries. I am indebted to the following:

The Chattanooga Public Library and especially Miss Eloise Fisher; the New York Public Library and especially Mr. Robert W. Hill, Keeper of Manuscripts; the Boston Public Library; Northborough Free Library and Miss Elizabeth Hilliard, who not only wrote me many times about Rice background but also accompanied me on visits to Rice's home, church, and school; the American Antiquarian Society, the Congregational Library of Boston; the Library of Congress; the library of the American Baptist Historical Society, Rochester, and especially Mr. Edward C. Starr, Curator; the library of the Historical and Philosophical Society of Ohio; Alderman Library of the University of Virginia; the library of the South Carolina Historical Society at Furman University and especially Mrs. Ollin Owens; the library of George Washington University and especially Dr. Elmer Louis Kayser, University Historian; the manuscript division of the Kansas State Historical Society Library; the library of Andover Newton Theological Seminary; Virginia Baptist Historical Society at the University of Richmond; the Archives of the Southern Baptist Foreign Mission

Board and especially Dr. Jesse Fletcher; Dargan-Carver Library in Nashville, which has much of the Rice material on microfilm, and especially Dr. Davis C. Woolley and Dr. Lynn E. May.

I must give thanks to Mr. John A. Bigelow of Marlborough, Massachusetts, genealogist, historian, and past president of the Rice Family Association, who has given generous assistance on Northborough and Rice background; and to his daughter, Mrs. Parmenter, for her aid in securing copies of deeds from the Registry of Probate, Worcester. Also, to others who have assisted in various ways: Mr. B. Hoff Knight, Mr. Gordon Langley Hall, Rev. Gordon M. Torgersen, Miss Frances Hudgins, Dr. Malcolm H. Harris, Miss Blanche S. White, Mr. Arthur R. Eglit, Miss Katherine S. Diehl, Mr. Mouzon Peters, the Honorable Brooks Hays, Mr. Motte J. Yarbrough, Rev. Myron D. Dillew, and Jimmy Brownsey.

And, most of all, to the real Luther in my life who kept encouraging me and along with our sons, Mark and Kent, planned several vacations to areas where I could scout for Riceana. Begun as a hobby, my work has been fun.

I have cited sources where I thought they would be helpful, for I hope some serious scholar will be able to use this third biography of Rice and proceed farther on him and the men who joined him in charting a fairer day for Baptists.

Rice Manuscript Sources

American Baptist Historical Society (ABHS): *Journal, February 25, 1803—April 8, 1807; Journal, February 6—November 25, 1812; Journal and Account Book, November 23, 1815—May, 1816, November, 1816—September, 1817.*

Luther Rice Papers, Special Collections Division, Gelman Library, George Washington University (GWL): *Journal, March 19, 1815—November 15, 1815; Journal, May, 1816—October, 1816; Journal, September, 1818—February, 1819; Notes and Account Book, 1810.*

Virginia Baptist Historical Society (VBHS): *Journal, August 9, 1819—April 24, 1820.*

Letters of Rice are in many places. Gelman Library, George Washington University, has over two hundred. Others are in Pennsylvania Historical Society, American Baptist Historical Society, Kansas State Historical Society, Dargan-Carver Library, The Southern Baptist Theological Seminary Library, and several other libraries in fewer numbers.

Bibliography

Allen, Joseph. *Historical Sketch of Northborough.* Worcester, 1861.
Armitage, Thomas. *A History of the Baptists.* New York, 1886.
Babcock, Rufus. *Memoir of John Mason Peck.* Philadelphia, 1864.
Baptist General Convention. (U Series, VI). Boston, 1826.
Baptist Missionary Magazine, 1812-1837.
Bardwell, Horatio. *Memoir of Rev. Gordon Hall.* New York, 1834.
Barnes, Lemuel Call. *Pioneers of Light.* (Philadelphia, n.d.).
Bentley, William. *The Diary of William Bentley.* Vols. II-IV. Salem, 1907-1914.
Burnett, J. J. *Sketches of Tennessee's Pioneer Baptist Preachers.*
Cathcart, William. *The Baptist Encyclopedia.* Philadelphia, 1881.
Carey, S. Pearce. *William Carey.* London, 1923.
Carleton, William A. *The Dreamer Cometh.* Atlanta, 1960.
Chapin, Stephen, *Divine economy in raising up great men. A sermon delivered in the First Baptist Church, before the Board of Trustees of the Columbian College, D. C.* Washington, 1837.
Christian, John T. *A History of the Baptists* Vols. I-II. Nashville, 1922, 1926.
Cogswell, Leander. *History of Town of Henniker.* Concord, 1880.
Cox, F. A. and J. Hoby. *The Baptists in America; a Narrative of the Deputation from the Baptist Union in England to the United States and Canada.* London, 1836.
Durfee, Calvin. *Williams Biographical Annals.* Boston, 1871.
Emerson, Joseph. *Memoirs of Mrs. Eleanor Emerson.* Boston, 1809.
Emerson, Ralph. *The Life of Rev. Joseph Emerson.* Boston, 1834.
Fleming, Robert. *Sketch of the Life of Elder Humphrey Posey.* Philadelphia, 1852.
Forbes, Harriette Merrifield. *The Hundredth Town.* Boston, 1889.
Fuess, Claude M. *An Old New England School.* Boston, 1917.
Gammell, William. *History of American Baptist Missions.* Boston, 1849.
Gibson, L. T. *"Luther Rice's Contribution to Baptist History."* Unpublished thesis, copy in the American Baptist Historical Society, Rochester.
Hallock, William A. *Light and Love, A Sketch of the Life and Labors of Rev. Justin Edwards.* Boston, 1855.
Hervey, G. Winfred. *The Story of Baptist Missions.* St. Louis, 1884.
Hill, James Langdon. *The Immortal Seven.* Philadelphia, 1913.

226

Houghton, William. *History of Town of Berlin.* Worcester, 1895.

Jeter, Jeremiah B. *The Recollections of a Long Life.* Richmond, 1891.

Johns, William. *Extracts from a Journal kept during a voyage from Philadelphia to Calcutta, by way of the Isle of France, on board the ship Harmony, Capt. Michael Brown, in the year 1812.* Serampore, 1812.

Judson, Adoniram, Jr. *A Letter to the Rev. Adoniram Judson, Sen., Relative to the Formal and Solemn Reprimand to which is added a Letter to the Third Church in Plymouth, Massachusetts, on the Subject of Baptism.* Boston, 1820.

————. *A Sermon.* Boston, 1817.

DeBlois, Austen Kennedy. *Fighters for Freedom.* Philadelphia, 1929.

Kent, Josiah Coleman. *Northborough History.* Newton, 1921.

Knowles, James. *Memoir of Mrs. Ann H. Judson, Late Missionary to Burmah.* Boston, 1829.

Lynd, S. W. *Memoir of the Rev. William Staughton.* Boston, 1834.

Mallory, C. D. *Memoirs of Elder Jesse Mercer.* New York, 1844.

McCarthy, C. *The First Century of the First Baptist Church of Richmond, Virginia, 1780-1880.* Richmond, 1880.

McGlothlin, W. J. *Confessions of Faith.* Philadelphia, 1911.

Merriam, E. F. *A History of American Baptist Missions.* Philadelphia, 1900.

Morse, James King. *Jedidiah Morse.* New York, 1929.

Myers, John Brown. *The Centenary Volume of the Baptist Missionary Society, 1792-1892.* London, 1892.

Newell, Harriet. *The Life and Writings of Harriet Newell.* Ed., American Sunday School Union. Philadelphia, 1831.

Newman, A. H. *A History of the Baptist Churches of the United States.* New York, 1894.

Northboro Church Record. In possession of the Unitarian Church of Northborough, Massachusetts.

Northborough Historical Society. *History of the Northborough Free Library.* Northborough, 1908.

Nowlin, William Dudley. *Kentucky Baptist History, 1770-1922.* Louisville, 1922.

Parkman, Ebenezer. *The Story of the Rice Boys.* Westborough, 1906.

Pease, Charles Stanley, *Luther Rice, Missionary and Educational Pioneer.* Unpublished MSS in the American Baptist Historical Society, Rochester.

Perry, Arthur Latham, *Williamstown and Williams College* (Williamstown, 1904).

Pierce, Richard Donald. "A History of the Society of Inquiry in the Andover Theological Seminary, 1811-1920." Unpublished thesis in the library of Andover-Newton Seminary.

Pollard, Edward B. and Daniel Gurden Stevens. *Luther Rice.* Philadelphia, 1928.

Prime, E. D. G. *Forty Years in the Turkish Empire.* Boston, 1891.

Records of the Evangelical Church in Northborough. Attributed to Rev.

Samuel Austin Fay. Now in the Northborough Historical Society.

Rice, Charles Elmer. *By the Name of Rice*. Alliance, Ohio, 1911.

Rice, William W. *The Centenary of Leicester Academy*. Worcester, 1884.

Richards, Thomas C. *Missionary Pathfinder, Pioneer and Promoter*. Boston, 1907.

Robbins, Sarah Stuart. *Old Andover Days*. Cambridge, 1908.

Rowe, Henry K. *History of Andover Theological Seminary*. Newton, 1933.

Sprague, William B. *Annuals of the American Baptist Pulpit*. New York, 1860.

Spring, Leverett Wilson. *A History of Williams College*. Boston, 1917.

Stewart, W. S. *Early Baptist Missionaries and Pioneers*. Philadelphia, 1925.

Stockton, Charles Herbert. *Records of the Columbia Historical*. Vol. 19. Washington, 1916.

Strong, William E., *The Story of the American Board*. Boston, 1910.

Sweet, W. W., *The Story of Religions in America*. New York, 1930.

Taylor, G. V. *Life and Times of James B. Taylor*. Philadelphia, 1872.

Taylor, James Barnett. *Memoir of Rev. Luther Rice*. Baltimore, 1841.

Titterington, Sophie B. *A Century of Baptist Foreign Missions*. Philadelphia, 1891.

Torbet, Robert G. *A History of the Baptists*. Valley Forge, 1963.

Tracey, Joseph. *History of the American Board of Commissioners*. New York, 1842.

Tracy, E. C. *Memoir of the Life of Jeremiah Evarts, Esq*. Boston, 1845.

Vail, A. L. *The Morning Hour of American Missions*. Philadelphia, 1907.

Valentine, T. W. *A Historical Discourse delivered before the First Baptist Church of Northborough*. Brooklyn, 1877.

Ward, Andrew Henshaw. *A Genealogical History of the Rice Family*. Boston, 1858.

Wayland, Francis, and H. L. *A Memoir of the Life and Labors of Francis Wayland*. New York, 1868.

Wenger, E. S. *Missionary Biographies*. Vols. I, II.

Whitney, Peter. *The History of the County of Worcester*. Worcester, 1793.

Williams, W. R. *Lectures on Baptist History*. Philadelphia, 1877.

Willing, James C. *Brief Chronicles of the Columbian College*.

Winchole, Dorothy Clark, *The First Baptists in Washington, D. C.* Washington, D. C., 1952.

Woodbridge, Timothy. *The Autobiography of a Blind Minister*. Boston, 1856.

Woods, Leonard. *A Sermon Delivered at the Tabernacle in Salem, February 6, 1812, on the Occasion of the Ordination*. Boston, 1812.

Worcester, Samuel M. *The Life and Labors of Rev. Samuel Worcester*. Boston, 1852.

Index

Adams, Abigail Smith, 4
Adams, Ebenezer, 31, 42
Adams, John, 9, 10
Adams, John Quincy, 121, 173, 183, 191
Adele, the, 74, 76, 78
Africa, 89, 112
African Church, 147
African Missionary Society, 112
Allen, Samuel, 6
Allison, Burgiss, 103, 108, 111, 114, 117, 163
American Baptists, 81, 87, 88, 89, 95
American Baptist Home Mission Society, 194
American Baptist Magazine, 111, 169
"The American Board of Commissioners for Foreign Missions", 47, 84, 85
American Indian Mission Association, 105
Amherst, 34
Andover Academy, 41, 42, 43, 44, 45, 46, 49, 53, 54, 55, 57, 61, 64, 123
Anglican Church, 44, 68
Annual Report, 110, 111, 138, 139, 142
Annual Report, Second, 111
Arbuthnot, Captain, 78
Atwood, Harriet, 54, 59
Atwood, Widow, 54
Austin, Samuel, 26, 34, 42, 56

Babcock, Reuben, 39, 185
Bacheller, Jonathan, 177
"Backus", 175
Bagby, John, 145
Bagby, Luther Rice, 145
Bagby, Richard Hugh, 145
Baldwin, Thomas, 78, 85, 86, 93, 95, 96, 97, 98, 107, 115, 124, 152, 154, 165, 167, 169, 175, 181
Ball, Eli, 185, 186, 188
Ball, Jonas, 14
Ball, Dr. Stephen, 13, 14
Ball, Jr., Stephen, 31
Ball's Tavern, 10
Balls, the, 12, 63
Baptist Board of Foreign Mission for the United States, 98

Baptist, Rev. Edward, 144
Baptist General Tract Society, 172
Baptist Missionary Magazine, 175, 180
Barbour, James, 173
Bardstown Society, 164
Barnes, Daniel H., 187
Bartlett, William, 10
Battle, Dr. Cullen, 144, 151
Battles, the, 150
Battle of Bunker Hill, 5, 50, 145
Baxter, Richard, 23, 25
Benedict, David, 175, 183, 185
Benjamin Rush, the, 104
Bennet, Aunt, 23
Bennet, Elizabeth, 6
Bennets, the, 15
Bentley, Rev. William, 56
Berkshire Mountains, 34, 43
Berkshire Mountain Association, 41
Bibbs, Mr., 32
Big Harpeth Church, 143
Billings, Pliny, 17
Billings, William, 30
Birnam, Captain, 40
Board of Commissioners at Worcester, 133
Board of Foreign Missions, 157
Bogue, Dr., 52
Bolles, Rev. Lucius, 85, 91, 95, 103, 168, 171, 175, 176, 178, 182, 185
Bombay, 58, 69, 82
Boone, Squire, 116
Boston, Baptist Missionary Society, 85, 168
Boston, Sarah, 14
Boston, Siege of, 5
Boston Statehouse, 6
Boston Tea Party, 9
Botsford, Edmund, 90, 93, 94, 157
Boylston, 6, 15
Boylston Baptist Society, 63
Boylston Road, 22
Bradford, 47, 48, 53, 54, 55, 59
Bradford Academy, 47
Brainerd, 1, 71
Brantley, William T., 90, 182, 185, 187
Brethren, 38, 40-49, 50, 52, 53, 123

Brigham family, 15
Brigham, Lucinda, 17
Brigham, Thomas, 4
Broaddus, Rev. Andrew, 89, 145
Broaddus, William F., 202
Brook, Rev. Thomas, 95
Brooks, Ivison L., 200, 201, 202
Brown, Captain Michael, 55, 66, 73
Brown, Rev. Obadiah B., 88, 95, 112, 113, 114, 119, 166, 167, 168, 173, 176, 181, 183-193
Brown University, 44, 58, 97, 115, 126, 154, 203
Bruington Church, 89
Bryce, John, 95
Buchanan, Dr. Claudius, 44
Bunyan, John, 1
Burma, 44, 52, 68, 69, 74, 103, 108, 122, 126, 130, 131, 133, 137, 155
Burmans, 58
Bushnell, Mrs., 150

Calcutta, 44, 55, 68, 71, 72, 73, 75, 77, 78, 79, 85, 123, 131, 132, 133, 136, 156, 203
Caldwell, John, 98-99
Calhoun, John C., 163, 164, 173
Calvinist, 12, 13, 25, 42
Caraven, the, 55, 61, 65, 66, 67, 73
Campbell, Alexander, 64, 116, 159, 160, 161
Campbellites, 95
Carey, Felix, 74
Carey, Jabez, 74
Carey, William, 7, 44, 45, 66, 70, 71, 72, 76, 77, 78, 87
Carey, William Jr., 74
Cary, Lott, 112
Caswell, Alexis, 1, 181, 185, 188, 189, 203
Ceylon, 69, 80
Chapin, Stephen, 187, 189, 191, 192, 194, 197, 198, 201
Charlestown, 1, 39, 124
Charlestown Association, 89, 97, 115, 118
Chase, Professor Irah, 114, 117, 118, 121, 137, 156, 173, 183, 195
Christian Baptist, The, 160
Christian Index, 194
Chowan Association, 2, 139, 150
Clay, Henry, 120, 173, 189
Clinton, George, 87
Clopton, Abner, 185, 188, 194
Cold Harbor Brook, 8
Cold Harbor Meadow, 7
Coleman, Andrew Jackson, 199
Colgate, William, 165, 168, 169, 172
Colmans, the James, 127, 128, 129
Colonization Society, 112

Columbian College, 3, 113, 119, 135, 137, 143, 145, 148, 149, 150, 162, 170, 171, 174, 176, 177, 181, 182, 190, 193, 198, 202
Columbian College Missionary Museum, 136
Columbian Star, 167, 183, 184, 185, 187, 194
"Columbus," 148, 149
Commerce, the, 78, 79
Committee of Correspondence, 5
Compere, Lee, 162
Conant, John, 177, 181, 183, 185
Cone, Spencer, 119, 147, 151
Congregational Church, 12
Congregational (Church) of Charlestown, 57
Congregationalism, 62, 102
Congregationalist, 2, 42, 76
Connecticut Evangelical Magazine, 39
Cook, Tom, 14, 15
Cornelius, Samuel, 171
Cox, F. A., 197
Crane, William, 88
Creole, La Belle, 79, 80
Cummings, Asa, 57
Cushing, Colonel Job, 5

Dagg, 185
Daphne, the, 62
Davis, Deacon Isaac, 12
Davis, John, 11, 31
Davis, Rev. Noah, 171, 172
Devin, Brother, 158
Dodge, Pickering, 55
Dodge, Rev. Daniel, 152, 154
"Domestic Mission to the Missouri Territory", 104
Donna Maria, the, 83, 123
Dugarreau, Dr., 62
Dunning, Mary, 125, 143
Dwight, Edwin Wells, 40, 41, 85

Eames, Brother, 149
East Andover, Maine, 17, 23, 26, 33
East India Company, 35, 44, 47, 62, 68, 71
East Indies, 155, 156
Eaton, Betsey, 51
Eaton, Ebenezer, 50, 51
Eaton, Nancy, 51
Eaton, Rebecca (Rebekak), 51, 52, 53, 54, 55, 57, 59, 65, 80, 81, 82, 123, 124, 125, 127
Eaton, William, 36-37, 50, 51
Edwards, Jonathan, 21
Edwards, Justin, 34, 61
Eliot, 71
Emerson, Joseph, 39, 51, 55, 80, 81

Emersons, 124
English Baptists, 89
English Baptist Society, 62, 87
Episcopalians, 146
Evarts, Jeremiah, 46, 85
Exeter Academy, 42, 53, 54
Exeter, New Hampshire, 60, 61

Farrar, Squire, 57
Fay, Nahum, 11, 12
Fay, Paul, 23
Fay, (Aunt) Rebecca, 23
Fay, Warren, 11, 26, 34, 63
Fays the, 15, 63
Female Society, 100
First Baptist Church, Philadelphia, 87, 88
First Baptist Church, Providence, 142
First Baptist Church, Richmond, 112, 151
First Baptist Church, Washington City, 88
First Congregational Church, 26
Fisher, Abial, 177
Fisk, Ezra, 38, 39, 44
Fitch, Rev. Ebenezer, 36, 39, 42, 49
Fort Williams College, 44
Framingham, 37, 50, 51
Franklin, Benjamin, 10
Fuller, 45, 87
Furman, James. 152, 155, 156, 157, 165, 166, 176, 198
Furman, Dr. Richard, 87, 89, 92, 93, 95, 96, 97, 98, 107, 112, 115, 117, 118
Furmans, the, 144

Galusha, Elon, 182, 183, 185, 188
Gano, John, 120, 142
Gano, Gen. Jonathan, 142
Gano, Stephen, 95, 97, 142, 154, 155
Gazette, Salem, 55
Georgetown College, 194, 195
George Washington University, 202
Giger, Simon, 14
Gillespie, the, 81, 82
Goddard, Captain Luther, 63
Goddard, William, 31
Goddards, the, 10, 15
Going, Jonathan, 167, 176, 177, 183, 185, 194
Goodell, William, 57
"Gospel Shop", 63
Goss, John, 142, 184
Graves, Catherine (Aunt "Katy"), 6, 32
Graves, the, 10, 15, 20
Great Post Road, 6, 7, 10, 11, 29
Green, Byram, 35, 36
Green, General, 182, 188, 189, 193
Green, Miss, 62
Griffin, Dr. E. D., 39, 45, 46, 55, 57, 58
Grigg, Rev. Jacob, 88, 93, 112

Grout, Seth, 63, 64, 77

Hague, William, 84
Hale, Chief Justice, 37
Hale, Mr., 48
Half-way Covenanters, 20, 21
Hall, Gordon, 37, 38, 41, 44, 46, 53, 55, 58, 60, 61, 68, 69, 72, 73, 75, 76, 77, 82, 199
Hall, Col. Michael, 142
Hallow, 23
Hancock, 9, 10
Harmony, the, 55, 60, 61, 62, 65-69, 73
Harvard (University), 11, 16, 34, 42, 44, 51
Hascall, Daniel, 177
Hasseltine, Deacon John,
Hasseltine, Nancy (Ann), 51, 54, 55
Hasseltine, Rebecca, 51
Heard, Captain Augustine, 55
Hendricks, Bets, 14
Henshaw, Colonel William, 31
Hill, Henry, 83
Hobbs, Hansom, 105
Hoby, J., 197
Holcombe, Henry, 2, 87, 95, 98, 130, 152, 153, 154, 156, 157, 176
Home Guardian (The), 125
Hopkinsian theology, 26, 42
Hough, George, 103, 125, 126, 127, 129, 130, 131, 132
Hough, Phebe, 103, 131
Houghs, the, 153
Houghton, William, 15
Howe, Elias, 4
Howes, the, 10
Hudson, Ebenezer, 4

Illuminata, 38
India, 45, 52, 59, 71, 88, 89, 91, 99, 143
Indians, 2, 4, 6, 9, 46, 89, 102, 105, 108, 109, 110
  Fox, Osage, Kanses, 106
  Cherokees, 107
  Hassanamiscoes, 14
  Nipmuck, 14
Ivimey, Joseph, 100

Jackson, Andrew, 190
Jackson, Brother, 163
Jackson, Major Jonathan, 10
Jeter, Jeremiah, 201
Johns, Mrs., 67
Johns, Williams, 61, 62, 64, 65, 66, 67, 70, 71
Johnson, Colonel, 120
Johnson, Joseph, 108
Johnson, Richard Mentor, 108, 163, 166, 179, 189, 190

Johnson, William Bullein, 90, 93, 95, 96, 97, 115, 116, 197, 201
Jones, Horatio G., 88, 95, 111, 117, 168, 172
Judson, Abigail, 124
Judson, Adoniram, 2, 3, 44, 45-48, 51-54, 58, 69-71, 75, 76, 78, 79, 81, 83, 85-88, 91, 155, 198, 199, 202
Judson, Adoniram Sr., 124
Judson, Ann (Nancy), 59, 72, 80, 169, 170
Judson, Elnathan, 124, 136
Judsons, the, 99, 103, 122-137, 143, 144

Keeling, Henry, 2, 113, 139, 150, 202
Keep, Rev. John, 46
Kentucky Missionary Society, 108, 158
Kincaid, 200
King, Rufus, 120
Kingsford, Edward, 149
Knight, 45, 87
Knowles, J. D., 137, 167, 171, 172, 185, 195
Lafayette, General, 173
Lall Bazar Chapel, 75, 77
Lall Bazar Church, 70
Latter Day Luminary, 110, 111, 113, 142, 143, 167, 170, 171, 177, 178
Lawson, John, 62, 64, 65, 71, 133
Leicester, 27, 31, 33
Leicester Academy, 30
Leland, Old Father, 93
Lincoln, Elder Ensign, 86
Lincoln, Heman, 177
Litchfield County, Connecticut, 34
Literary Association, 119
Livermores, 12
Livingstone, John, 39
London Missionary Society, 39, 52, 53, 62
Long Run Association, 105
Loomis, Harvey, 35, 40, 44
Lopez, Aaron, 31
Luther, Martin, 1, 75, 161
Lyman, Orange, 40
Lynd, Samuel, 174

McConnico, Elder, 143
McCoy, Isaac, 2, 104-108, 114, 140, 157, 158, 159, 162-165, 194
McCoy, Christiana, 104, 105, 164
McLaughlin, 166
McLean, Judge, 185
McKenney, Thomas, 179, 190

Maclay, 183, 185
Madison, President, 143
Madison, General William, 143
Madras, 68

Malcom, Howard, 177
Manly, Basil Sr., 201
Marlborough, 4, 6, 7, 9, 10
Marshman, Joshua, 71, 72, 73, 76, 77, 82, 123
Marshman, Mrs., 72
Martin, Judge, 79
Massachusetts Baptist Magazine, 90
Massachusetts Baptist Missionary Magazine, 111
Massachusetts Gazette, 6
Massachusetts Missionary Society, 42, 165
Mather, Cotton, 23
Mauritius (Isle de France), 62, 68, 69, 74, 79-80, 83
Mays, R. G., 199, 201
Mays, Mrs., 200
May, Mr. and Mrs. Robert, 62
Meehan, John, 167, 171, 172
Mercer, Jesse, 90, 107, 144, 151, 166, 177, 185, 194, 202
Mercers, the, 150
Mercer University, 194
Merrill, Rev. Daniel, 121
Messer, President Asa, 126, 130, 154
Methodist (s), 68, 141, 146, 147
Mills, Elder, 41
Mills, Samuel J., Jr., 35, 36, 38-41, 44-47, 54, 161, 199
Milton, John, 1
Missionary Baptists, 143
Missionary Jubilee, 178, 203
Mississippi Missionary Society, 165
"Mr. Baptist", 90
Monroe, President, 114, 121, 173
"Mordington," 145, 187, 192
Moore, William G., 95
Moore, Rev. Zephaniah Swift, 34
Morse, Jedidiah, 35, 39, 42, 46, 55, 58, 85
Mussey, Dr. David D., 58

Nepean, Sir Evan, 78
New and Complete System of Arithmetic, 11
New Castle, 61
Newell, Harriet, 66, 70
Newell, Samuel, 44, 47, 48, 53, 54, 55, 59, 66, 69, 81, 82, 125, 199
New England Female Reform Society, 124-5
New England Primer, 11
Newman, Mark, 43
Newton, Sir Isaac, 37
Newton, John, 21, 22
New York Education Society, 103, 115, 117
"Nonesuch", 148
Norris, John, 52

Northampton, England, 7
Northborough, Massachusetts, 4, 5, 6, 7, 10, 13, 18, 22, 23, 30, 31, 32, 42, 60, 62, 63, 86, 194, 203
"North Carolina Society for Foreign Missions", 92
North Church of Newburyport, 57
North District Association, 138
Nott, Roxana Peck, 60, 61, 70
Nott, Samuel, 44, 47, 53, 54, 59, 61, 68, 69, 73, 75-77, 82

Obookiah, 40, 41, 44
Oliver Street Baptist Church, 84, 86, 176

Panoplist, 42, 46
Parker, Daniel, 158, 159, 160, 161
Park Street Church, 46
Paxton, 30
Peale, Anna, 195
Peale, Charles Wilson, 121
Pearce, 87
Pearson, Professor Eliphalet, 42
Pease, Levi, 6, 37, 139
Peck, John Mason, 2, 101, 102, 103, 104, 106, 107, 109, 116, 142, 158, 159, 161, 162, 165, 181, 194
Peck, Roxana, 54
Peckworth, John P., 95
Philadelphia Baptist Association, 86, 97, 115
Philadelphia Education Society, 117, 118
Philadelphia Society, 91
Phillips family, 42
Pike, Nicholas, 11
Pollards, the John, 145
Pomeroy, Rufus, 44
Porter, Dr. Leonard, 38, 44, 46, 57
Posey, Humphrey, 107, 162, 163
Posey, Gen. Thomas, 108
Post Road, 9, 14, 63, 139
Presbyterians, 141, 146
Primitive Baptist, 143
Probyn, Edward, 95
Proudfoot, Richard, 95
Psalter, 11
Prudential Committee, 53
Puffer, Rev. Reuben, 13

Ralston, Robert, 55, 61
Ranaldson, James A., 95, 106, 110, 162, 164, 165
Rathbone, 185
Ready, J. C., 199, 200, 201
Redd, Emily, 186
Redds, the Samuel, 144, 186
Religious Herald, 137
Revere, Paul, 9, 37, 42-43
Revolution, 4, 5, 22

Reynolds, the Rev. Mr., 46
Reynolds, Enoch, 119, 166, 184
Rice, Abigail, 4
Rice, Amos, Jr., 5, 6, 8, 12, 17, 23, 33
Rice, Anson, 203
Rice, Asaph, 5, 8, 12, 15, 17, 20, 33, 34, 36, 39, 40, 54, 56, 60, 63, 77, 86, 145, 194, 201, 203
Rice, Asher, 9
Rice, Curtis, 5, 8, 13, 19, 40
Rice, Edmund, 4, 16
Rice, Elizabeth, 5
Rice, Hannah, 7, 39
Rice, Grandfather Jacob, 7, 9, 13, 16, 17
Rice, Uncle Jacob, 16, 34
Rice, Jacob, 5, 6, 8, 17, 37, 40
Rice, John, 5, 8, 19, 26, 33, 40
Rice, Uncle Luther, 7
Rice, Mary, 4
Rice, Sally, 40
Rice, Sarah (daughter), 5, 7, 17, 19, 27
Rice, Sarah (mother), 5, 6, 20, 39, 194
Rice, Seth, 15
Rice, Tamagine, 4
Rice, Thomas, 9
Rice, Timothy, 9
Richards, James, 35, 38, 39, 47, 53
Richards, Rev. Lewis, 95
"Richmond Baptist Society, The," 89
Robbins, Rev. A. R., 34, 53
Robbins, Francis L., 44
Robinson, Rev. John, 25
Rogers, William, 88, 98, 152, 154, 155, 156, 157, 176
Rolt, Mr., 70, 72, 76, 129
Rolt, Mrs., 76
Roxburgh, Dr., 70
Ruggles, William, 181, 183, 185, 188, 189, 194
Russell, Dr., 76
Ryland, Dr. John, 7, 185

Sagamore Association, 161
Saints' Rest, 23
"Salem Bible and Foreign Mission Translation Society," 85
Salem Tabernacle Church, 57
Sanborn, Dr., 47
Sands, Brother, 202
Sandy Creek Association, 46
Sanford, Dr., 46
Sansom Street Baptist Church, 87, 99, 142, 156
Savannah Baptist Society for Foreign Missions, 90, 93
Schismatics, 147
Sears, Bro. John, 163
Second Presbyterian Church (North Huntingdon), 141

Semple, Rev. Robert Baylor, 8, 9, 93, 97, 114, 125, 176, 177, 182, 185-193
Separatists, 63
Serampore, 65, 68, 71, 72, 85, 86, 123, 125, 131, 132
Serampore Circular, 44
Serampore Periodical Accounts, The, 39
Sewall, Dr. Thomas, 121, 187, 188, 189
Seward, John, 39, 41
Sharp, Daniel, 86, 175, 185
Shay's Rebellion, 17
Shelton, Dr., 138, 147
Shepherd, Rev. Mr., 69
Sherwood, Adiel, 185, 198, 200, 202
Shrewsbury, 6, 8, 9, 11, 14, 15, 29, 30, 31, 63
Sloane's Meadow, 35
"Society of Inquiry on the Subject of Missions, The," 49
Southern Baptist Foreign Mission Board, 202
Southern Baptist Theological Seminary, 203
Spring, Dr. Samuel, 39, 43, 46, 47, 48, 55, 59, 61, 133
Staughton, Miss Eliza, 151
Staughton, James, 121, 162, 175, 185
Staughton, Dr. William, 76, 78, 87-89, 95, 96, 98-100, 103, 108, 110, 112, 114, 115, 117-19, 121, 125, 130, 132, 134, 136, 139, 141, 148, 152-54, 157, 162, 166, 168-71, 174, 175, 181, 185, 187, 189, 195, 198
Stokes, Bro., 169
Stone, Barton, 160
Stout, Dean Benjamin, 138, 142, 143
Stout, Mrs., 151
Stow, Baron S., 137, 167, 172, 183, 184, 185, 189, 195
Stuart, Moses, 42, 45, 46, 47, 57, 85
Sudbury, 4
Summer, Dr. Joseph, 13, 31
Swedenborg, Emmanuel, 132
Swedenborgianism, 131
Symes, Michael, 44

Tallmadge, Judge Matthias, 87, 92, 93, 95, 98, 110, 117, 125, 142, 154-57
Taylor, James Barnett, 202, 203
Taylor, John, 161
Teague, Collin, 112
Thayer, Dr. Nathaniel, 13, 20
Thomas, Archibald, 45, 150, 151
Thompson, Hon. Alexander, 182
Thompson, Edward, 104
Todds, the Charles, 145, 201
Torrington, 34, 35, 40
Translyvania College, 143
Triennial Convention, 165

First
    [1814], 98, 103, 110, 115, 123, 142
Second [1817], 117, 142, 147
Third
    [1820], 131
    [1823], 169, 172, 179
    [1826], 174-76, 181
    [1832], 194
    [1835], 196
Turpin, William H., 150, 151

Unitarian, 22
Unitarianism, 42
University of Virginia, 202

Wade, Colonel Nathaniel, 5
Waite, Samuel, 185, 194
Wake Forest College, 194
Wallis, Widow, 87
Ward, General Artemas, 4-5, 11, 29
Ward, Mrs., 72
Ward, Rev. William, 71, 72, 77
Warren Association, 97
Warrens, the, 63
Warwick, New York Association, 101
"Washington Baptist Society for Foreign Missions, The," 88
"Washington City," 161
Washington, President George, 3, 10, 118
Wayland, Francis, 2, 170, 174, 175, 177, 180, 194
Welch, James, 2, 104, 106, 107, 142, 162
Wheelock, Edward, 127, 128, 129
Wheelock, Eliza, 132
White, Mrs. Charlotte, 104, 125, 153
White, William, 97, 99, 130, 153
Whitney, Pastor Peter, 4, 6, 12, 13, 20, 22, 24, 32, 63, 86, 87
Williams College (Academy), 34, 35, 36, 37, 41, 42, 43, 44, 48, 49, 50, 58, 64
Williams, John, 86, 87, 95, 176
Williams, Roger, 2, 95
Williamstown, 34, 49
Willson, Luther, 32
Wood, Abraham, 17, 25
Wood, George, 171, 172, 193
Wood, Captain Samuel, 4
Woodbridge, Timothy, 44, 45
Woods, Professor Alva, 162, 168
Worcester, 23, 26, 30, 50, 53, 56
Worcester County, 9, 16
Worcester, Dr. Samuel, 39, 42, 46, 47, 48, 55, 59, 61, 77, 84, 132

Yale, 40, 44, 45, 46, 87
Young, Brigham, 4

Zayat, 129